HELPING STUDENTS WRITE WELL

A Guide for Teachers in All Disciplines

HELPING STUDENTS WRITE WELL

A Guide for Teachers in All Disciplines

Second Edition

BARBARA E. FASSLER WALVOORD

THE MODERN LANGUAGE ASSOCIATION OF AMERICA
NEW YORK   1986

Barbara Fassler Walvoord, Writing: Strategies for All Disciplines, © 1985, pp. 7, 10–11, 94–95, 141, 225–27. Reprinted by permission of Prentice-Hall, Inc., Englewood Cliffs, NJ.

Library of Congress Cataloging-in-Publication Data

Walvoord, Barbara E. Fassler, 1941–
  Helping students write well.

  Bibliography: p.
  Includes index.
  1. English language—Rhetoric—Study and teaching. 2. Interdisciplinary approach in education. I. Title. PE1404.W35   1986   808'.042'071173   86–12504

ISBN 0–87352–201–X (pbk.)

Fourth printing 1991

Published by The Modern Language Association of America
10 Astor Place, New York, NY 10003

TO JOHN ALLEN
1923–1980
my longtime colleague and friend

Contents

Acknowledgments   xi

PART ONE: COACHING THE WRITING PROCESS   1

Chapter One
Why Write?   3

Chapter Two
Considering Goals and Options for Writing in Your Course   6
  The Instructor as Manager   6
  Purposes for Writing in a Course   6
  Types of Writing   8
  Writing in Class   9
  Level of Polish   17
  Audience and Context for Writing   18
  Sequence and Difficulty of Writing Assignments   22

Chapter Three
Planning to Coach the Writing Process   29
  The Importance of Coaching   29
  The Writing Process   29
  Questions to Guide Your Coaching   32
  Helping Students Understand the Writing Process   33
  Helping Students Become Involved   34
  Helping Students Pace Their Work   35
  Helping Students Analyze the Assignment   36
  Helping Students Find Help   49
  Helping Students Assess Audience, Purpose, and Context   52
  Helping Students Generate Ideas and Focus the Topic   53
  Helping Students Gather and Integrate Library Information   68
  Helping Students with Interviews   76
  Helping Students with Observation and Experiment   78
  Helping Students with Reasoning, Evidence, and Organization   79
  Helping Students with Drafting and Revising   84
  Helping Students with Visual Aids   89
  Helping Students with Style and Mechanics   89
  Observing the Writing Process   105
  Summary   110

Chapter Four
Using Student Peer Groups   111

Response Groups   111
Task Groups   118

Chapter Five
Course Plans: Some Case Histories   **123**
A Core History Course: John R. Breihan   123
A Sophomore Core Literature Course: Barbara Walvoord   125
An Introductory Psychology Course: Susan Miller Robison   128
Introductory and Advanced Biology Courses: Virginia Johnson
   Gazzam   130
An Introductory Sociology Class and a Word about "Journals":
   Michael Burton   133
Task Groups in an Upper-Class–Graduate Course in Marketing
   Research: Larry S. Lowe   134
Task Groups in an Introductory History Course: James
   Van Hoeven   135
More Suggestions for Specific Disciplines   137

PART TWO: RESPONDING TO THE STUDENT WRITER   **139**

Chapter Six
Principles of Effective Response   **141**
Pen, Tape, or Conference?   141
Being a Transparent Reader   146
Suiting Response to Purpose   147
Setting Goals and Rewarding Achievement   148
Using Praise   149
Being Thorough and Specific   149
Naming and Summarizing   150
Grading Writing   151
Sample Teacher Responses to Student Writing   153
Responding to In-Class Writing   158
Responding to Journals   159
Responding to Planning Statements   161

Chapter Seven
Responding to Problems in Focus and Organization   **162**
Responding to Problems in Focus   162
First and Last Paragraphs   180
Responding to Problems in Organization   184

Chapter Eight
Responding to Problems in Style   **206**
Analyzing the Situation and Setting Goals   206
Responding to Tone and Voice   207
Responding to Incoherent or Confusing Prose   210
Responding to Problems of Emphasis   210

Responding to Problems in Indicating Relations 212
Encouraging Economy 224
Encouraging Precision, Concreteness, Vividness 230

Chapter Nine
Responding to Problems in Grammar, Punctuation, and Spelling 234
Analyzing the Situation and Setting Goals 234
Addressing Performance-Based Problems 235
Addressing Knowledge-Based Problems 237
Summary 240

Works Cited and Selected Bibliography 241

Index 246

Acknowledgments

I am indebted to a large number of persons from various disciplines who read, and offered suggestions on, various parts of the manuscript or who helped me collect writing samples:

From Central College in Pella, Iowa: Arthur Johnson, John Miller, Donald Butler, John Allen, Mildred Steele, John Bowles, Thomas Kopecek, James Van Hoeven, Kenneth Tuinstra, Dorothy Bosch, Joyce Huizer, William Julian, Donald Racheter, David Crichton, James Graham, Allen Moen, Judith Lauber, Robert Schanke, Donald Huffman, Barbara Dieleman, Thomas Iverson, William Paul, Chad Ray, and Ronald Byers.

From Loyola College in Maryland: Francis Xavier Trainor, Faith Gilroy, Frank Haig, SJ, Linda Spencer, F. Xavier Spiegel, John Jordan, Daniel Duffy, Jack Breihan, Nicholas Varga, Paula Scheye, Barbara Mallonee, Donald Wolfe, and Thomas J. Higgins, SJ.

From Towson State University in Towson, Maryland: Margaret Benner, Karen Toussaint, Deborah Shaller, Marion Hoffman, Gary Wood, Barbara Frankel, Anne Burley, Linda Mahin, Jim Kim, Filmore Dowling, Karl Larew, Frances Rothstein, Harvey Paul, and Dan Jones.

From West Chester University in West Chester, Pennsylvania: Patricia Grasty, Phyllis Goetz, Betty Hasson, George Reed, Robert Green, J. Bernard Haviland, Laureen Meiswinkel, Anne Sessa, Robert Weiss, Nona Chern, and Judith Ray.

From George Mason University in Fairfax, Virginia: a group of faculty members from various disciplines, among whom Robert Karlson, Emmett Holman, Gloria Fauth, and Linda Samuels offered especially helpful advice.

I also wish to thank Donald Gallo of Central Connecticut State College as well as W. R. Irwin and Richard Lloyd-Jones of the University of Iowa for their support and for their advice about the manuscript. Others who offered useful criticism are Richard Larson of the City University of New York, Christopher Thaiss of George Mason University, Virginia Steinhoff of the University of Maine at Orono, and Beverly Palmer of Pitzer College in Claremont, California.

I owe a debt of thanks to Reva Rydstrand and Evelyn Loynachan for typing the first complete manuscript.

Acknowledgements

The preparation of the manuscript was financially supported in part by Central College in Pella, Iowa; Towson State University in Towson, Maryland; and Loyola College in Maryland.

B.E.F.W.

Acknowledgments for the
Second Edition

The second edition reflects what I have learned from working with colleagues at Loyola College in Maryland, at Towson State University, and at other Baltimore-area institutions within the Maryland Writing Project and the Baltimore Area Consortium for Writing across the Curriculum. I am particularly indebted to those who appear as case studies. I have worked closely with all of them in research, workshops, or team teaching; they have contributed much more to the book than merely the written case studies. Other colleagues with whom I have collaborated in Loyola College's Writing-across-the-Curriculum Program, and from whom I have learned much about writing in the disciplines, include Daniel Singer of Loyola's management and marketing department, Harold Fletcher of the finance department, and A. Kimbrough Sherman of the economics and decision-sciences department.

Dixie Goswami, Lee Odell, and Linda Flower have helped to shape my research and thinking about writing in various disciplines.

I am certainly indebted to the following colleagues who offered incisive suggestions for this revision: Carole Edmonds, Toby E. Fulwiler, Andrea A. Lunsford, and Susan Miller.

My husband, Hoke L. Smith, has used his training in political science and his experience as a university administrator to become one of my most valuable critics.

Walter Achtert of the Modern Language Association has been the perfect editor, willing to let me abandon the pages of the first edition, encouraging me to "write the book that has to be written." Judy Goulding, managing editor of MLA publications, and R. Neil Beshers improved the book through their sensitive and careful editing.

Finally, my thanks to Loretta Bartolomeo, Genevieve Rafferty, Terry Anne Ciofalo, and my son Brian Fassler, who typed the revised manuscript.

Part One

Coaching the Writing Process

Chapter One

Why Write?

This handbook is for the community college, college, or graduate school instructor of economics, physical education, literature, biology, history or what have you. It is for the tutor or the teaching assistant in any discipline and for the teacher-to-be. In short, it is meant to help any faculty member who must coach and evaluate students' writing.

The cry of many such teachers is "I already have more than I can do to cover my subject in a semester; I don't have time to teach writing." This handbook tries to be realistic about the time constraints all of us face. Throughout, it delineates levels of effort; if you can do only a little, the chapters suggest where you might best place your energies.

You may hear students and others ask why it is necessary to worry that much about students' writing. Modern citizens don't need to do that much writing anyway. C. G. Enke, a Michigan State chemist, provides part of the answer for that one:

> It is difficult to overemphasize the importance of writing in the professional life of a scientist. The amount of time my colleagues and I spend writing is out of all proportion to the fraction of our training devoted to developing writing skills. "Publish or perish" is a cliché, but it carries the unmistakable implication that experimental work and elegant theories have no peer value until they have been put in manuscript form. I was shocked to find that the time and effort of writing was often equal to that of the research work being described. . . . The tasks of writing fall heavily on industrial scientists as well. (40)

Despite technological advances in communication, the ability to put words on paper or on the screen is still crucial to the work of the world—to research, to learning, to thought, to business relations, to management, to government, to every human enterprise. Not only academics but also people working in other areas are aware of the importance of writing in their lives. In one study, college graduates working in many fields were asked to rank seventeen college disciplines in order of importance to them as employed adults. The graduates put English right at the top, second only to business administration (Bisconti and Solomon 36–37).

"All right," we might say, "if people are so enthusiastic about English, they should *take* English. Why doesn't the English department teach them how to write?" The English department can't do the whole job. Writing is so complex an activity, so closely tied to a person's intellectual development, that it must be nurtured and practiced over all the years of a student's schooling and in every curricular area.

The composition class can give students some transferable skills: the concept that effective writing is focused and well organized, strategies for structuring forms like comparison or argument, principles of clear prose style, and conventions of grammar and punctuation. Like every class, however, the composition class is a community, with its own set of expectations, types of writing, and unique values. When asked, "What is the goal of your course?" faculty members usually give a discipline-specific answer—"To make my students think like economists," or "To teach my students the basic questions, methods, and values of psychology." Instructors in those fields must show students how to *apply* composition skills and how to carry on the common types of thinking and writing in the individual discipline.

An even more compelling reason not to decrease the amount of writing in college courses, no matter what the pressures, is that writing is a vital tool for learning. To look on writing as the "extra" that can be abandoned if one needs more time to cover the subject matter reveals a basic misunderstanding of learning and verbalization. Within the past few decades, Vygotsky, Langer, and others have clarified relations between thought and language. Sense data are translated into symbols, which themselves are our ideas (Langer 42). In order to think and learn, we manipulate symbols by talking to ourselves in what Vygotsky calls "inner speech"—the mediator between thought and language (149). "Thought is born through words," he says (153). Research in cognition supports this contention; a study by Gagne and Smith showed that people who verbalized were superior in problem solving to those who did not, especially as tasks grew more complex (389–90).

In a seminal study, Janet Emig proposed that writing is a uniquely effective tool for learning because the two are strikingly parallel: learning is multifaceted, as is writing, which uses eye, mind, and hand, right and left brain. Learning profits from self-provided feedback—the kind available in writing, where the product takes gradual shape before the writer's eyes and is then available for review and reflection. Learning serves an analytical and connective function, as does writing, which organizes individual facts, images, and symbols into sentences, paragraphs, and whole essays. Learning at its best is engaged, committed, and self-rhythmed, as is the best writing ("Writing").

Other studies indicate that when an object is shown to children and then removed, they can describe the absent object more accurately if, while it was present, they talked or wrote about it (Anglin; Bruner, Oliver, and Greenfield). Such findings lead us to view writing as "the presence of things not seen"—as a way of freeing students from enslavement to present physical reality and of allowing their minds to abstract and conceptualize.

Another image of writing skills is that of a climbing rope whereby students can hoist themselves to the next level of intellectual maturity. Andrea Lunsford suggests that writing assignments can be structured to help college students build and exercise the skills on the final rung of Piaget's ladder of intellectual development: the skills of abstracting, synthesizing, and forming coherent, logical relations.

We may never find the perfect paradigm for the complex relation of writing to learning, but many of us know that the connection is there. We believe that until our students can express an idea with some sort of clarity on the page, they do not in fact really understand that idea. Along with one science journal editor, we suspect that "Bad scientific writing involves more than stylistic inelegance; it is often the outward and visible form of an inward confusion of thought" (Woodford 745). Despite our rueful recognition of the time and effort needed to assign and respond to students' writing, we cannot escape a conviction that writing is the mother's milk of learning.

Like any other teaching technique, writing assignments can be handled with more or less skill, with better or poorer results, and with an efficient or a wasteful investment of time. In the following chapters I suggest how teachers in every discipline can make writing assignments meaningful, establish a wholesome and stimulating writing environment for their students, coach pupils in the writing process, respond accurately and specifically to student papers, communicate clearly with students about their writing successes and failures, and help students improve writing *as they learn* and *in order to learn* their sociology, biology, business, law, or engineering.

Chapter Two

Considering Goals and Options for Writing in Your Course

The Instructor as Manager

Every teacher is a manager, setting objectives and then figuring out what techniques will most effectively meet those objectives. Like managers, we have more work than we can possibly do; we make tough decisions among priorities, and we are quick to jettison activities that aren't meeting important goals or that don't make efficient use of our time. As we plan to integrate writing into our courses, we should consider the goals that writing can serve in a course, the ways writing can be handled, and the time needed to implement various options. Writing can be productively integrated with courses in every discipline, even those with large classes and heavy teaching loads, and can yield enormous gains for students. It's a matter of planning, of working "smarter, not longer."

Purposes for Writing in a Course

Chapter 1 argued that writing is crucial to what we do because graduates find it important to their success and advancement, because it is a part of communicating that must be taught to students in every discipline, and, most important, because it is an integral tool for thinking and learning. Building on those points, I list below twelve purposes that writing may serve in your courses. A single writing assignment, or the writing for a single course, may serve several of the purposes; some types of writing and some ways of responding to writing will be more or less effective for certain purposes; and, most important, not every writing assignment needs to serve all the purposes. Once we grasp these principles, we are free to assign various types of writing and to handle writing in various ways, with various investments of time, to meet differing goals.

The purposes fall roughly into three groups, emphasizing, respectively, writing as a tool for learning, feedback for the instructor, and producing finished written pieces. In practice, however, purposes will mingle, and all the types will promote learning and discovery for students.

- To give students a mode for self-expression, creative thought, and musing
- To force students to read an assignment by a certain date
- To make students active in their learning
- To help students apply what they have learned
- To help students push more deeply into a subject
- To help students organize or summarize ideas
- To help students store information
- To enhance students' understanding and recall of a subject
- To keep students in the habit of writing; to build fluency
- To train students in the basic skills of writing—focus, organization, evidence, reasoning, style
- To train students in the particular forms of writing they will use as professionals in their fields
- To teach students to polish for grammar, spelling, and punctuation
- To provide a basis for grading
- To identify students who need extra help
- To evaluate how much a class is learning, as a basis for teacher planning

Your decisions about which purposes have priority for a particular course or assignment will depend on your estimate of what your students need, what you can best teach, and, sometimes, the task apportioned to your course within a department's plan for its students. In some upper-class courses, for example, a primary goal may be to prepare students for the type of professional writing they will be asked for in the career world. One physics instructor has been asked by his department to use his course, which is part of the required sequence for majors, to ensure that students know how to write a laboratory or technical report. So he focuses heavily on guiding students through the process of writing such a report, emphasizing the format, conventions, and polish that will be expected of them. For a core literature course that enrolls primarily non-majors, another instructor gives minimal attention to the professional form—the essay of literary criticism—and concentrates instead on a large number of informal, ungraded writing exercises that help students engage with literature and analyze plot, character, setting, and theme. Later literature courses teach students how to put together coherent literary-critical essays. A department with a different philosophy may assign to the core literature course the task of teaching students the literary-critical essay, even if those first essays are shallow in content, so that in later courses students have already practiced the essay form. Many other goals and combinations of goals are possible in courses across the curriculum.

To meet such a wide variety of goals, the instructor can choose among a wide variety of types of writing; have students write in or out of class; specify levels of polish, audiences, and contexts; and assign tasks of various levels of difficulty. Finally, there are many ways of coaching students through the writing process. At the risk of creating a blizzard of options, we will discuss each of those areas. Then, in chapter 5, case studies of actual college teachers offer some guidelines for putting options together to serve the goals of a course, within the constraints of time and teaching style.

Types of Writing

Below is a list of types of writing that may be employed for various purposes in a course. Some types, such as the personal letter, the journal, and the freewrite, lend themselves to students' exploration of thoughts and feelings. Some, such as the outline, the annotated bibliography, and the review of literature, can be used to practice specific skills like summary and analysis, or they can serve as building blocks toward a larger finished piece. Some types are unique to the academic setting—the term paper and the case analysis; they build skills necessary in certain kinds of professional writing but are not precisely like any forms students will write after college. Other types, such as the business letter, the memo, the letter to the editor, and the scientific report, are professional modes students will use later. None of the types serves one goal only, and all can lead students to learning, clarification, and discovery.

Types of Writing in a Course

abstract
answer to a question
briefing paper or "white paper"
brochure, poster, advertisement
case analysis
character sketch
contemplative essay
definition
description
description of a process
dialogue
editorial
essay exam
instructional manual
"I-Search"
journal
laboratory or field notebook
letter to editor or open letter
list
materials and method plan
memo
microtheme
narrative

news story or feature story
newspaper "filler"
notes on reading or lecture
outline
personal letter
play
proposal
question or muse
response or rebuttal
résumé
review of book, play, work of art,
    performance
rough draft
script for film or slides
summary
survey of literature
technical or scientific report
term paper
thesis sentence
timed freewrite
web or diagram of ideas or planned
    paper
word problem

A few of the types may need some explanation. The journal is a forum for student thought and response, discussed in the case-study chapter later in this volume. The freewrite, the thesis, and the web appear in chapter 3. Briefly, the freewrite is a timed writing exercise in which the writer merely spills ideas without worrying about coherence or commas; the thesis is a one-sentence condensation of the writer's main idea; the web is a planning device shaped like a spider's web. The microtheme is a brief essay, written on a five-by-eight-inch notecard; the limited scope forces students to be direct and precise and limits what the instructor has to read.

The "I-Search" is a narrative, first-person account of the writer's process in researching a question or developing a paper. The "I-Search" encourages students to appropriate the topic as their own. It gives students an easy structure—the narrative—for their first writing about the research. Such writing also gives the instructor a window into the methods, questions, insights, and fumbles the student has made. The "I-Search" can serve as an end in itself, or it may be the first step in a process that ends with the writing of a formal report, article, or essay. The technique is explained in Ken Macrorie's *Searching Writing* (53–198).

James Britton and his colleagues (*Development*) have classified writing according to its functions: expressive, transactional, and poetic. Expressive writing is closest to speech with intimates, closest to the writer's immediate flow of thought; it may be its own end, as in a journal, or it may later be shaped more deliberately for communication to an audience. Transactional writing is the writing that gets work done in the real world; its purpose is to communicate usable information to a reader. Poetic writing fashions the writing itself as a work of art, as in poetry and fiction. Britton and others, in a large study of British schools, found that 63% of all school writing was transactional writing. They and many other writing specialists suggest that instructors, even at the college level, have students do more expressive writing, where they avoid premature pragmatism and closure and can speculate, manipulate what they have learned, apply it, experiment with it, figure out what it means to them. As we select the types of writing to assign our students, we will want to keep in mind the value of expressive writing and to check our customary tendency to assign only transactional writing. Ways of assigning and integrating expressive writing will be treated in the coming chapters.

Writing in Class

Students may write an entire piece in class, not to be further revised (the informal in-class exercise or the essay test). Alternatively, they may write part of an assignment in class, as when the instructor gives them 20 minutes to brainstorm or free write about a topic, just to get them started, or has them bring in their papers midway in the writing process, for an in-class work session. The decision to use one or both of these modes, or to have students complete an assignment entirely outside of class, should be based on clear goals and an understanding of what in-class writing can and cannot do.

In-Class Writing as Test: The Essay Exam

The essay exam is a unique genre, with its own demands and constraints. If it is to function well as a test of students' knowledge, a way for them to pull together what they have learned, and a healthy exercise of writing abilities, students must learn to meet its demands.

Write the answers to one of your own essay tests. Try to be conscious of the particular skills you are exercising, the difficulties you face, the strategies you use. Just after an exam, ask your students, "What was most difficult? How did you go about writing the exam? What do you wish you'd done differently? How did you study for the exam?" Your goal is to learn as much as possible about the specific skills and strategies your exam demands and to pass that information on to your students. John Miller, at Central College in Pella, Iowa, offers direct classroom guidance in essay exams for his students. He follows a chronological plan, beginning with students' note taking. He advises them to find out, early in the course, what the professor is emphasizing, what sorts of questions will appear on essay tests, and then to organize their class and reading notes toward those issues from the start. He encourages them to guess the instructor's essay questions and shares with them a teacher's secret: "If you've ever composed essay exam questions, you know that the possibilities for good questions, based on what you've emphasized in the course, are really quite limited. Students ought to be able to guess what the instructor will ask." Students can compose, and write answers to, trial questions as part of their preparation for the exam.

John also pays careful attention to students' notions of their audience for the essay exam—an aspect he believes is crucial to their success. He asks them to define their instructor as reader and to anticipate what that instructor will be looking for. Trouble comes, he finds, when students write to their instructor as a person for whom basic principles need not be explained or illustrated, whereas the instructor is often looking for the students to demonstrate just such knowledge. Sometimes the student is best advised to write as though for a classmate, who needs definitions, examples, and proof.

Finally, John moves into strategies for taking the exam itself. He, Bill Julian, and I developed the following handout for students at Central College. You may use or adapt it for your own students.

Taking Essay Examinations
A Student's Guide

Essay exams are a matter not of quantity but of quality. The race goes not to the swiftest writers but to those who best organize and present what they know. The problem facing the student who must take an essay test is simple: how can that quality be achieved?

I. General principles

    A. Organize around a clear focus.

        You must have some point of view to help you organize and select the facts you wish to include. Choose a focus that is limited enough to cover in the time allotted and that allows you to include all the material the teacher will expect to find. Write a thesis that clearly states your focus or main point and that indicates the main sections of your answer. For most types of essay, the thesis sentence should state a conclusion, not merely announce the sections. For example, sentence A below merely announces the sections of the paper. It is certainly better than no thesis at all, but in most cases it is not as helpful to your reader as a thesis that embodies your conclusion, as in B.

        Q. Discuss the concept of love in D. H. Lawrence's novel *Women in Love*.

        Thesis sentence A: This essay will discuss bisexual, homosexual, and familial love in Lawrence's *Women in Love*.

        Thesis sentence B: An examination of bisexual, homosexual, and familial love in *Women in Love* reveals the hatred and the isolation that are present even in the closest love relationships.

    B. Outline your answer.

        Do not begin writing your answer without first making an outline. Write down the three or four main points you want to make. They should all help to develop, explain, or prove your thesis sentence.

    C. Come right to the point.

        Don't waste time with a general introduction or any sort of beating around the bush. It is usually a good idea to state the main point (thesis) of your answer at the beginning.

    D. Stick to your subject.

        Everything you say should relate directly to the subject you have announced in your thesis sentence. Do not try to tell everything you know. Essay tests measure the excellence of your ability to select, organize, and analyze the details you have mastered.

    E. Be thorough within your limits.

        Make your answer complete. If a question asks about a subject discussed in class or in your reading, the teacher probably expects you to deal with all the main points made there. In addition, after you have written your outline, ask yourself, "Have I left out anything important to the defense of my thesis sentence?"

    F. Support generalities with specific and relevant evidence.

        Evidence is crucial. The teacher is testing your detailed knowledge of a body of material, not just your ability to make or repeat generalizations. Show that you know the specific information. Do not merely state *what* you believe; explain *why* you believe it.

II. Some common essay topics

A. Discuss, describe, or analyze.
The challenge in such questions lies in the student's ability to impose organization on a broad subject. First you must decide: How shall I limit X? How shall I divide X into sensible, manageable segments? Let us say the direction is "Discuss political elites." The very phrasing seems to entice you to blurt out everything and anything you happen to recall about elites and their societies. Resist temptation. Take time to write an outline and make efforts to limit your approach to an angle of the problem that will most favorably display your knowledge and understanding.

Sometimes you can better deal with a discuss-or-analyze topic if you turn it into one or more questions. Answers to these questions will give you suggestions for a thesis sentence and an outline. For example:

1. *Direction:* The Reformation was caused by economic factors. Discuss.
Ask yourself: Was the Reformation caused solely by economic factors? Which noneconomic factors should I mention?

2. *Direction:* Analyze the theme of social class in nineteenth-century novels.
Ask yourself: What do the authors of nineteenth-century novels think about social class? What do the novels' characters think? What social classes are illustrated in the novels?

B. Compare and/or contrast.
If you are instructed to compare and/or contrast, you are still confronted with the basic problem of selecting a focus, organizing your facts, and indicating to the instructor what your approach will be. Don't automatically give every fact you know about X and then every fact about Y. Instead, outline the major similarities and/or differences. Under each similarity or difference discuss both X and Y, making specific and concrete comparisons.

C. Identify or define.
Follow two rules: (1) put each item into a major category, and (2) separate it from all other items in this category.

D. Agree or disagree.
Usually it is possible to write an A exam whether you agree or disagree; the instructor is interested in whether you can marshal evi-

dence to support your position. Often it helps to keep in mind the major arguments on the other side and try to refute them in your essay.

III. Study hints
   A. In looking over your notes, try to see relations between parts, comparisons, and contrasts. Try to guess what might be some typical questions and outline answers to them.
   B. Then study the outlines as well as your class notes.

IV. The exam
   A. Read the directions thoroughly. In particular, see if a question has more than one part, and answer all parts.
   B. Outline your answer before you begin writing. The outlines you prepared in studying should help a great deal here.
   C. Bring a watch and budget time.
   D. If you run out of time, outline main points and examples, and write "out of time" to tell your professor what happened.
   E. Proofread your answer, if possible, to catch careless errors.
   F. Write precisely what you mean. Always choose the most specific and accurate word.
   G. Make every word do a job. Don't eliminate necessary examples and evidence, but do present them without wasted words.

In addition to offering advice about taking the essay exam, give your students a chance to practice. You might make the first exam short, so students have more planning and revising time, or have students revise their first essay exam, so they learn specifically how it could be improved. You might give them a trial run—followed by class distribution of the best essays, class discussion of successful students' strategies, conferences or small groups to discuss the exam—then administer a real exam, either on the same questions, so students have a chance to apply directly what they learned from the trial, or on different questions, to test students' ability to apply to a new essay what they learned from the old.

You can also build essay exam skills through short, informal in-class writings that also help students learn the material. For example, if you frequently ask students to compare and contrast on essay exams, try having them write some 10-minute compare-and-contrast pieces in class, to be shared with peers or used as the basis of class discussion.

In-Class Writing and Plagiarism

Many instructors have told me they dislike some aspects of in-class writing, but they use it because they believe it to be the only method that guarantees students have not plagiarized. In-class writing is one way to guard against plagiarism, but not the only way. Here is one simple technique that combines both in- and out-of-class writing and also helps to prevent plagiarism: at a certain point in their planning and research for an outside paper, students have 10 minutes in class to write, from memory, their paper's main ideas, or, if they're not that far, to explain two interesting pieces of information they've found, or to specify how they intend to fulfill their purpose for their audience. This exercise is a good check against plagiarism, without binding the instructor solely to in-class writing. It also frequently helps students discover or clarify their ideas and questions and improves the quality of their final work.

Another way to make plagiarism more difficult is to ask students to hand in, along with their final paper, an early draft and/or a log that tells how they wrote it. More broadly, instructors who follow the guidelines in chapter 3 find that because the instructor is looking at notes and drafts, or because peers must talk to one another about their plans and ideas, students cannot plagiarize. It's one thing to phone a term-paper service and pay for a finished paper; quite another to ask the service also for a set of notes, an outline, a couple of successive drafts, and a script for what to say about the paper in a peer group or in a conference with the professor.

In-Class Writing to Learn

Short, carefully planned in-class writing exercises can dramatically increase students' mastery of the subject matter and of analytical skills and make students more active participants in their own learning. Further, these activities need take little or no instructor time outside of class. The time they take in class does cut down on the number of minutes the instructor can spend lecturing or demonstrating; however, sometimes learning is better served by fewer lecture minutes and more time for students to process and articulate what they are learning. Again, instructors must judge what activities best serve the goals of the course and the needs of their students. If you're imparting priceless wisdom in lecture but tests show that students aren't absorbing as much of it as you wish or that they can't manipulate or apply the concepts you're explaining, then the integration of some short in-class writing exercises may significantly improve student learning. Below are some suggestions:

- Before beginning a lecture, announce your topic and ask students to write for five minutes about what they expect you will say or to jot down at least three questions they would like to have answered about the topic. At the end of the lecture, ask whether their questions were all answered or how the lecture differed from their expectations; you may get lively class discussion.
- At the end of the class period, take five minutes for everyone to write a summary of what was covered or to write down the most useful or surprising thing in the lecture, demonstration, or film.

- When the third pair of eyes closes in slumber, stop the lecture and ask everyone to write for five minutes. You can have them summarize, ask further questions, anticipate where they think the lecture will go from here, or muse about how the material they are being taught makes them feel, questions it raises for them, ways it may be applied in their lives or professions.
- A discussion period that begins, "Are there any questions on the reading?" sometimes results in deadly silence. Help students be ready to speak by giving them five minutes to write down two questions. Then, when the discussion begins, even the normally quiet students are likely to volunteer.
- When an argument has been presented in class, stop for five minutes and ask students to write down all the counterarguments or counterevidence they can think of.
- When a new technique has been introduced, ask students to write for five minutes, describing the technique to someone who was absent from class.
- When you've used a new teaching strategy, ask students to tell you, in five minutes on paper, how they responded to it. You're likely to pick up good tips on how to use it more effectively next time.
- Pose any question, definition, or comparison you want your students to master, and have them write the answer.

Once the class has written such a short exercise, there are several ways to handle it:

- Simply go on. You trust that the writing has served its purpose.
- Give students a chance to ask questions or to clear up confusions they discovered while writing. You might have each turn to a neighbor and, in pairs, share their answers. Most students can learn something from someone else's answer, and some inaccuracies can be cleared up by peers.
- Begin a class discussion or blackboard list of, say, all the counterarguments to a certain position, so that individual writers can complete or revise their lists.
- Collect the papers. You can read them for your own information, or you can grade them. One instructor awards three points for each exercise; students build points toward the final course grade. Another has students keep their writing until the semester's end, then hand in their five best for grading.

Note Taking

A type of in-class writing that goes on all the time but that instructors rarely guide is students' class notes. You can help improve the quality of your students' note taking. You may rely solely on exposure to a variety of other students' notes to help instruct those whose notes are inadequate. Each day, ask one or two students, on a rotating basis, to hand in their notes at the end of class, then duplicate copies for all class members. Every student has a chance to compare his or her notes with the duplicated notes of other students. If you want to enforce careful reading and comparison of the distributed notes, ask students to write, in or out of class, a short piece on the differences and similarities between their notes and the duplicated notes or to say what they've learned from the duplicated notes.

Alternatively, you can ask all the students to hand in their notes on a given day, yourself choose the best two, and duplicate them for distribution, accompanying the distribution, if you wish, with a short discussion of what makes them good. To give your students some clues about how good notes are produced, ask the students who have written the best notes to explain how they go about it. Such requests sometimes flop because some students are not aware of their own note-taking strategies, but some students are capable of articulating useful advice to their peers.

In-Class Writing as Preparation for Outside Papers

Another use for in-class writing is as a yeast for out-of-class writing. Have students keep all their in-class exercises and polish three each semester to hand in as one-page papers. Or plan in-class exercises that will help students with the papers they are writing outside of class. For example, you might have them summarize a part of the lecture you know most of them will be using as background for their papers.

In-Class Writing as Training for Time Pressures

In-class writing can be used to help students learn to work under time demands. Some excellent writers produce first drafts that are extremely rough, fragmented, and full of errors. These writers normally save editing tasks for later drafts. In some courses or professions, producing completely smooth or grammatically correct first drafts is not important or necessary, so such writers may be left alone. For in-class writing the instructor cares only about the student's ability to explain a point in a readable and reasonably clear way or to capture the needed information on paper. (At the same time, the course may require students to turn out polished final papers when they have time for editing at home.)

In some disciplines, however, it is important that students be able to produce first-draft writing that has a clear focus and organization, sentences that read smoothly, and conventional grammar, punctuation, and spelling. If so, the instructor should work deliberately on those first-draft skills. Such guidance might include giving students a longer time for in-class essay answers at first and only gradually increasing the time pressure. You might allow students to take their first drafts home for a revision, in the hope that, by amending first drafts at leisure, they will learn to perform those emendations as they write in class. After an exercise, have the students read their writing aloud to a peer, pick out the smoothest sentence for praise, and revise the most awkward sentence.

You may also want to recommend work in a learning center or with self-paced learning tools, to help students internalize aspects of organization, grammar, and style that they now achieve only through painstaking revision.

Finally, give the students some strategies for improving their first drafts. Books or parts of books on taking essay tests contain good suggestions: using the first five minutes of the in-class period to jot an outline; using the last five minutes to edit; or leaving a half page at the beginning of one's essay so that later a first paragraph may be inserted that accurately introduces the entire essay the writer has completed. Make a list of these for your students, or put some advice books on reserve and guide students in practicing the advice.

Level of Polish

In both in-class and out-of-class writing, the instructor can demand various levels of polish. Sometimes a piece of writing may serve its goal without being neatly typed or edited for style, grammar, spelling, and punctuation. In some cases, even rougher drafts, not yet completely clear in focus or logic, may serve worthy ends and be given full credit without further work.

To produce writing that is sent to its readers in various states of polish is common in the career world: an in-house memo to one's peers will not be worked over with the same intensity as a letter to a prospective customer or a formal proposal to the board. Sound pedagogy may reflect such situational variety in the classroom. It is important, however, to clarify for students the reasons for expectations about polish. If you are accepting a low level of polish on a project, explain the reasons and make clear that your policy on this paper in no way indicates that you consider polish unimportant in finished public writing. Emphasize the career damage that may be done when a person sends an insufficiently polished piece of writing in a situation where high polish is expected.

Some instructors ask students to write a number of outlines or drafts of papers and then to choose their best one or two for high polish. Such a technique gives students the experience of achieving high polish but takes less time for both students and instructor than polishing all the papers.

To identify those students who will have trouble producing polished work, try a diagnostic exercise early in the course, where students are asked to give high polish to a short piece of their writing. Students in need can then be referred to a learning center or given extra practice or instruction, so that by the end of the semester they are more ready to produce the required polish.

Audience and Context for Writing

Researchers have found that expert writers plan and execute their writing with a keen sense of their audience (Odell and Goswami, "Writing"; Flower and Hayes). In effective writing, knowledge of one's audience is the basis for many crucial decisions such as one's approach to the topic, the amount of time one spends on an argument, one's choice of authorities, the amount of explanation needed for certain procedures, the inclusion or omission of sensitive material, and so on. In most writing texts today, considerable space is devoted to teaching students how to analyze the audience, how to address multiple readers, and how to meet readers' needs in the organization, content, and tone of their writing. It's a bit embarrassing, then, when the history or chemistry professor, assigning a paper, spends lots of time on topic, length, and deadline but never mentions the audience for the paper. Such practice probably contributes to the tendency of novice college student writers to spend less time considering their audience than skilled adult writers do (Flower and Hayes).

Having you as their audience, standing in front of them, doesn't eliminate student confusion about audience. In a survey of college students, Walter Cannon heard statements that reflect students' confusion about their instructor as an audience:

> STUDENT 1: I kinda think that I don't explain things really in detail because the teacher already knows what these things are about. . . .
>
> STUDENT 2: I didn't know how to write it. I wasn't sure if we were supposed to write it like he had never read the material or not. And so I think basically I wrote it like he had never read it. . . .   (4)

The issues of audience and context are much more complex than they might appear on the surface. Once you peel off the easy generality, "Picture your readers and write for them," other layers appear. Is there just one reader? Is there a typical reader? If the writer addresses a typical reader, is that reader not at least partly a fiction? To what extent do format, genre, and a host of other conventions shape reader expectation for a given piece of writing? Does the writer, or the text, change the reader in the course of reading?

The impact of a fuzzy conception of audience and context on student writing is reflected in the following situation: A chemistry instructor wants her students to learn how to write instructions for laboratory procedures. She has asked them to describe on paper how to transfer a precipitate from a beaker to a filter. So far the teacher has spelled out her purpose in giving the assignment and the subject on which the students are to write, but she has not designated the audience to whom the explanation should be addressed, and unless she does, her students face a difficult task. They know that their teacher, who will read their papers, does not herself need to be told how to transfer a precipitate. But what *does* she need or want to know? To whom is the process to be explained? Which procedures should be spelled out and which taken for granted? What is the proper tone? How much technical language can be used? The problems are amply illustrated by the papers students actually wrote for this assignment. One writer begins, "Set up the filtration apparatus," assuming the reader already knows how to do that. Another paper spends the whole first page explaining how to set up the filtration apparatus. The real disasters are the papers that have no clear sense of audience. They explain some simple procedures and take others for granted; they at one time instruct an ignoramus and at another time coach a somewhat knowledgeable peer. By neglecting to define the characteristics of the audience, an instructor encourages students to think of writing as the production of an artifact rather than as a means of communication intended to serve the needs of a specific audience. To prepare students to do a better job a teacher might take time to ponder the kinds of audiences for student writing: the "real" audience, the hypothetical audience, and the instuctor as audience.

The "Real" Audience

One of your options is to find an audience composed of real persons other than the teacher—those who will actually read the paper—for example, classmates, tourists, the editors of the school newspaper. You can help the student prepare the most effective message for the intended readers, but the readers themselves will prove the writer's effectiveness—by indicating that they understand the writer's ideas or expressing praise, by buying and using the tour guide, or by publishing the letter to the editor. For some audiences the writer may have to broadcast the seed with no way to measure the harvest. But even then an audience that will read the student's written message is known to exist. With such an audience the teacher's role is to emphasize the importance of writing with that audience in mind, meeting its expectations, deflecting its prejudices, and answering the questions it is likely to have. The teacher acts as coach, helping the writer prepare an address for the intended readers. The advantage of the real audience is that students often become more interested and engaged, since the situation seems genuine.

The Hypothetical Audience

If no real audience is present you can establish a hypothetical one. You might, for example, ask students to write reports for the governor of the state or proposals for a company's managing board. If you do establish a hypothetical audience, you will want to define it thoroughly so that students can shape their writing to suit their imaginary readers' tastes and needs.

I have talked to many instructors who, with the best intentions, have only increased confusion by introducing a hypothetical audience. Unless the hypothetical situation is clear and manageable for the students and unless the instructor is absolutely consistent in having the students write exactly as they would for the hypothetical audience, the students will write partly for the hypothetical audience and partly for the instructor as audience. In a business class, for example, students had been writing case analyses, directed to the instructor, though the instructor had never discussed himself as reader. When, in a writing-across-the-curriculum seminar, he correctly saw that some problems he complained about in students' writing were directly traceable to their confusion about addressing him as reader, he decided to remedy the problem by constructing a hypothetical audience. So he told his students to write their case analyses in the form of a report by a consultant to the board of directors of the firm. However, he gave them no instruction in the format such a report would follow or in the rhetorical stance a consultant would have to take. In one case, for example, the company's central problem was that the elderly founder, Brogan, who chaired the board, resisted new technologies and refused to give up power. A consultant writing a report to the board would have to handle the issue with extreme tact and circumlocution and might in fact choose to make recommendations to certain board members in person or over the telephone rather than in a written report. But the instructor wanted the students' unequivocal and simple statement—Brogan is not sufficiently informed about, or open to, new methods and is not promoting promising young executives; he must be persuaded or forced to give up power, if the firm is to survive. Students were afraid that if they did not say this directly enough, the instructor would think they didn't know its importance. So most of them wrote their case analyses in the old way, addressed to the instructor. They followed case-analysis format, not report format. Yet their papers contained occasional nods to the board-report fiction that weakened their consistency and coherence. The instructor had made the rhetorical situation more rather than less confusing.

If this instructor had taken the time to instruct his students in report format, had discussed with them the rhetorical stance a consultant could have to take in a report to the board involving Brogan, and had made it clear they would be graded on their ability to handle the report tactfully, he could have given them valuable practice in a set of real-life decisions. The moral is that hypothetical situations can offer useful practice but must be planned carefully and handled consistently.

The Instructor as Audience

The business instructor could have decided to remain the audience for the students' analysis but to clarify his role as audience. We find it easy to assume that our students know how to write for the instructor who is standing before them, giving them the topic, length, and due dates. Yet if you think back over the familiar ways in which student papers written for your eyes go wrong, you will probably recall, as I do, that many papers are poor because students assume our knowledge of things that they should have explained or because they spell out details that we would have taken for granted or because they adopt a tone we find too familiar or too stuffy or too affected. These errors all reflect misjudgments about what the audience—the teacher—needs or likes. We could help our students greatly by being more specific about ourselves as audience.

Think for a moment about yourself as audience and about the dilemmas students face when asked to write papers for which you are the assumed reader. When you read most student writing, you are not totally you; there are likely to be hypothetical audiences mixed in with the "you" students write for. Let's say, for example, that you ask for an informative report about the nesting habits of red-tailed hawks. If the real you knows all there is to know about that subject, you're certainly not going to read this informative report to get informed. You may in fact be asking the student to write as though informing someone not knowledgeable about the subject. So there *is* a hypothetical audience, and you are the judge who decides how well the student has addressed this imaginary reader. If this is the case, define for the student who the pretended audience is, what the audience knows about hawks, how familiar it is with biological terms, and how it will want to use the information the report provides. Describe what you, as judge, will be looking for.

On the other hand, if you do not know all there is to know about hawks, the student may have explored the subject in more depth than you ever have. If so, perhaps the essay will function primarily to transfer information from an inexperienced student who has thoroughly explored an area to a reader who is more highly trained but who nevertheless has something to learn from the report and will enjoy this accession of knowledge. In these circumstances the student can freely use technical terms and can merely refer to, without explaining in depth, information the teacher already possesses. The student's tone will be that of pupil to teacher but also that of one colleague to another, sharing information about a subject of joint interest.

A third possibility is that the student will share with the teacher the learning and musing process. The teacher will learn not about red-tailed hawks but about the student. Such an essay will be more personal and reflective in tone. It is likely to record not only the information the writer gathered about the nesting of red-tailed hawks but also the process of developing the topic, the importance attached to this intellectual task, or the questions that remain about the subject or the research procedure.

Finally, the paper might be written primarily so that the teacher can judge whether the student has read the material about hawks, mastered the information, or learned the procedures for investigating nesting behavior. In the same way a person might repeat the directions you've just given for driving to your house at the seashore. The student writes so that the teacher can tell for sure that the student sees the connections, knows the information, or can apply the principles. The student tries to illustrate competence. The teacher evaluates competence.

You could think of other possibilities the hawk topic suggests. Britton delineates four categories of student writing addressed to the teacher:

Child (or adolescent) to trusted adult
Pupil to teacher—general (teacher-learner dialogue)

Pupil to teacher—particular relationship (based on a shared interest in a curriculum subject)
Pupil to examiner.   ("Composing" 15)

You may not totally comprehend either these categories or mine; in fact, you may be mentally fashioning a set of terms you like better. But the point is that it is wrong to assume that when students know you will be the reader you need say nothing more about the audience for their papers. You can make their assignments more fair and their writing processes more successful if you carefully define for them the role you will play as reader and the expectations you will hold.

Sequence and Difficulty of Writing Assignments

A crucial part of planning the writing assignments for a course is to select tasks that will challenge and build skills yet will not be impossibly difficult for your students. Since writing is such a complex task, and so influenced by its context, no universal taxonomy arranges types of writing according to their difficulty for inexperienced writers. We do observe that easier types of writing have a narrative or chronological structure, or follow the structure of a written source from which the student draws. Writing seems easier when it treats a subject the student knows thoroughly.

Benjamin Bloom's taxonomy is a guide to the ascending difficulty of intellectual tasks, but Bloom makes no attempt to classify writing tasks per se, so his taxonomy is of questionable application for writing assignments. Malcolm Kiniry and Ellen Strenski suggest a sequence of difficulty for a composition class, but their sequence can be usefully adapted in any discipline. Your best clues about the relative difficulty of writing assignments may come from observing your students. Midway through their work on an assignment, ask them to write for five minutes on the aspects they find most difficult. Or have them keep a daily writing log, to be handed in with the papers, in which they discuss their work on the paper, especially the problems they face and questions they have.

Another way to analyze the difficulty of writing assignments is to examine finished writing students have handed in, identifying the qualities of successful papers. To do this, you can adapt a procedure called "Primary Trait Scoring," which was developed to assess the essays of thousands of students at several age levels, in the National Assessment of Educational Progress (Lloyd-Jones).

The purpose of Primary Trait Scoring is to isolate the traits essential to effective completion of a given writing task. The first step is to read a group of papers written for a particular assignment to discover the central characteristics of successful papers; in other words, you learn precisely what students had to do to produce good papers for this assignment. You can then use that information to refine the assignment next time you make it and to give more help-ful guidance to students.

To illustrate this kind of analysis, let's take the example of a college class in marketing. The instructor gave the forty-five students a case history of Toni Rocco's attempt to ensure the success of his new restaurant. The instructor wanted the students to analyze Toni's marketing policies, identify his mistakes, and suggest alternative procedures. The students were to write their essays dur-ing a fifty-minute class period.

Obviously it was crucial that students be sufficiently skilled in analysis of marketing techniques to decide which of Toni's actions were unwise. An anal-ysis of the forty-five student papers written for this assignment shows, how-ever, that some students who came to valid conclusions about Toni's marketing errors were nevertheless unable to write successful papers. So it is clear that the students had to have, in addition to the required knowledge, the ability to ar-rive quickly at a summary statement or statements about Toni's mistakes and to use that summary as a key to organizing the essay. Quotations from several papers will illustrate. This student's first paragraph immediately presented a basic interpretation of Toni's errors:

```
Though it appeared in reading this case that Rocco had some definite plans

before opening his restaurant, his plans were strictly product oriented,

rather than market oriented.
```

The student goes on to describe each of Toni's mistakes in terms of his over-emphasis on product. Another student, after presenting some background in-formation about Toni's Restaurant—background information that revealed the student's confusion about how much the audience could be expected to know about Toni—finally gets to that saving summary. She says that Toni "did not find a target market nor did he adequately provide a satisfactory marketing mix, especially in the area of promotion." The paper goes on to discuss Toni's mis-takes under those two headings.

In contrast to these two rather successful papers, the following student's essay—although it contains the same insights as the other two—fails because it is not organized around those insights. As a result, the essay is a random list of Toni's mistakes: it does not cohere as an essay:

```
Poorly timed radio commercials change possibly to morning and early afternoon.

He should have advertised more initially instead of later.

He was product oriented, thinking that if he offered a good place to eat

people would come to him.  Reputation comes after having been in business for

awhile.

He didn't really have a target market.  Didn't think about catering to his
```

Italian neighbors, nor of extending his services beyond full-course dinner. When he located his restaurant he was thinking of the heavy traffic area, not about whether he actually could serve them as customers. He didn't research enough before opening a restaurant, what his market is. He didn't use facts such as the income, nationality, or location for deciding what his market is. He might have considered serving breakfast and lunch, by varying the size as well as kind of meals offered.

[The final paragraph suggests offering family-style meals and guesses that initially Toni was hiring more help than he needed. There is no sense of summary or conclusion.]

This student's paper is typical of a number of the less successful essays in the class; several were similarly disjointed. Instruction in the class had obviously been effective, however: this student and most others did express some sound ideas about what Toni did wrong and how he could have done better. The crucial element in writing successfully about Toni's experience was the student's ability to establish some overall view of Toni's mistakes to use as an organizing center for the paper. Some students may have been capable of achieving such an organization but incapable of doing so before the fifty minutes ran out. This student's paper may be one such effort. The highly elliptical and tentative first paragraph is like a windup. As the student begins to find her stride, the language gets smoother. Given the chance to rework this rough draft, she might have built her essay around two or three of the more significant insights—such as her statement that Toni did not sufficiently research his market and her assertion that he was too product-oriented.

Let's take a somewhat different assignment—this time from the field of biology—and analyze the particular skills students will need for success. Here an instructor asked a class to read articles from professional scientific journals—any articles that caught their interest. Then each student was to summarize the article in a single page and give a personal response. Here are three representative papers.

Student Summary and Response to Biology Article

Raymond J. Hock, "The Physiology of High Altitude," <u>Scientific American</u> 22 (1970): 52-62.

This article was very interesting. It told about the effects of high altitude has on a person. It mentioned how the breathing rate increases, heart rate increases, red blood cell production increases.

Something the article mentioned which is of great interest to me is the effect high altitude has on exercise. It pointed out how at 18,000 feet, the ability to bring in oxygen is only 50%.

The article went into the subject of how people who are living in high altitudes develop certain characteristics. One such thing is an increase in chest size.

There were studies done on rats and deer mouse. The deer mouse had increased size with increased altitude. This was true only up to a certain point. They also studied such things as adjustment to hypoxic environment, exercise, and metabolism. It was found in the study of mice, the higher altitude mice were less efficient in their use of oxygen during exercise. This was compared to the low altitude mice. There were actually little treadmills made to test the mice on during exercise.

The article had graphs to demonstrate different rates in metabolism, endurance, cell count, etc.

Student Summary and Response to Biology Article

Ron L. Snyder, "Some Prey Preference Factors for a Red-Tailed Hawk," *Auk* July 1975: 547-52.

The purpose of this study was to examine the role of activity in prey selection. The first of three experiments reported herein examined the role of prey activity when a Red-Tailed Hawk (Buteo jamaicensis) was offered a choice between two live prey animals. The second experiment examined changes in prey activity preferences when the hawk was offered two comparatively large prey animals. In the third experiment the hawk was offered two prey of different weights to determine if this would affect the selection against more active prey.

In the first experiment the hawk preferred the more active of the two prey animals when no other differences were apparent between them.

The second experiment varied in its results. If one of the large prey was relatively inactive, the hawk went for it. Over many trials, however, the preference for the less active animal was often replaced by a high-activity preference if the hawk was successful in subduing the larger animals.

Experiment three showed a clear preference for heavier, less active prey. Comparing the data in experiment one, showing a strong preference for the more active prey, with the third where the larger prey was less active and still preferred, may have demonstrated a tendency in the hawk to choose the apparantly more profitable prey item in terms of relative biomass.

Student Summary and Response to Biology Article

W. A. Calder, "The Timing of Maternal Behavior of the Broad-tailed Hummingbird Preceding Nest Failure," <u>Wilson Bulletin</u> 85 (1974): 283-90.

The article dealt with an experiment done concerning the temporal behavior of female broad-tailed hummingbirds for the period preceding natural abandonment of the nests.

There were two classes of nesting failure to be considered: early and late failures. The early failures were due to infertile eggs and the death of a check. Attentiveness persisted four days beyond normal incubation period and at least one day after the chick was dead. In the latter nest, abandonment was preceded by a lengthening of the recess periods.

Of the late failures, three hens abandoned suddenly, while the other two exhibited a series of lengthened recesses. One of the latter two became hypothermic for a portion of the two nights preceding abandonment. The lengthened recesses are thought to be related to the declining food supply. Two chicks remained in both of those and one of the suddenly abandoned nests.

Overall, I thought the article was quite interesting. I found especially interesting the persistence of those hens with early nesting failures. It's as if the hen didn't want to believe her eggs were infertile or her chick had died, just as humans don't like to believe their babies are dead when it happens. I also never realized hens would abandon nests with live chicks in them. It makes me wonder about their reasons for their abandonment, especially in light of the persistence of some of the other hens.

The first trait of the summaries that successfully fulfilled the assignment is a clear explanation of the steps of an experiment. The altitude paper and the hawk paper are confusing; the hummingbird paper is less so, but perhaps only because that article involved an observation less complicated to explain. Reading comprehension and knowledge of experimental method, as well as familiarity with the format and purpose of science research reports, all play a role here. To simplify those aspects of the assignment, preselect journals or articles at a certain reading level and show students how to read an article for summarizing. Study-skills books and some freshman composition texts have chapters on summarizing from which you can draw.

Another key to success seems to be an early sentence that tells the reader the purpose and the broad outline of the experiment, so that the rest of the steps are placed in a context.

A third quality of the good papers is attention to the structure of sentences, so that they accurately indicate relations between ideas. The next-to-last paragraph of the altitude paper, for example, uses three sentences where one well-constructed sentence would have done a much better job: "Mice at high altitudes were less efficient than mice at low altitudes in their use of oxygen during exercise on treadmills." Some students may not possess the sophistication to construct such a sentence, but in giving instructions about this sort of paper you can ask them to give particular attention to sentence structure.

A fourth quality of the good papers is an orderly presentation of the information and the student's reaction. The altitude study makes a major mistake in what it includes in the last paragraph. The hummingbird article, though much better organized, does not successfully order the material in the two middle paragraphs: for example, the information on lengthened recesses in paragraph 3 is cut in two by the sentence about hypothermia.

A final quality of excellence is some originality in the student's response to the article. The altitude study has a clue (the writer is most interested in the effect of altitude on exercise), but the summary does not focus on exercise in the way that paragraph 2 would lead the reader to expect. The hawk paper pretends that no response was asked for. The hummingbird paper does the best job, despite the writer's reliance on the word *interesting* (also found in the altitude paper and in I'd like you to guess how many others in this batch). In the hummingbird summary, the writer's genuine involvement shows through, and the reader is treated to a bit of musing that is most effective.

Once you get a clear idea of the ability of your students and of the skills needed for a particular assignment, you can make appropriate adjustments: change to a simpler assignment, give more time, plan one or more preparatory exercises that build necessary skills, guide students more carefully through the writing process (more on that in the next chapter).

In summary, the teacher-manager, in the light of appropriate goals, tries to create the most intelligent combination of types of writing, in-class and out-of-class writing, levels of polish, audiences, and levels of difficulty.

The effectiveness of the planned writing assignments, however, as well as the amount of time they will take from you and your students, depends heavily on how you guide the writing process of the students. The next chapter, on coaching the process of writing, is therefore a crucial ingredient in an instructor's plans for writing. Following is a chapter on student response groups, and then some case studies of instructors who effectively integrate writing with learning in courses.

Chapter Three

Planning to Coach the Writing Process

The Importance of Coaching

At the age of ten my son mixed, baked, and elaborately decorated a birthday cake, using a pastry tube to fashion painstaking roses, prim borders, and perfect lettering. Not until we had admired, lighted, sung, blown, wished, sliced, and tasted did we realize that the cake was so heavy we could hardly swallow it. If only I had monitored his progress in the early stages, I could have saved him all the work of polishing a fundamentally unsound product and taught him something about the care with which good cooks measure ingredients.

Students sometimes have only a fuzzy idea of how good writers produce their work. For example, one misconception is that divine inspiration plays a major role in the writing process. Only reluctantly do students come to believe that most good writers arduously generate and develop their ideas and that behind a fine essay probably lie several incubation periods and scores of revisions. If you are to help students write better, you must teach them how to behave when they are trying to produce effective pieces of writing.

In fact, some recent research shows that while little or no improvement in students' writing results from increasing the amount of writing assigned, the number of teacher markings, or the study of traditional or new grammar, there is demonstrable improvement when the teacher coaches students in the *process* of writing instead of merely judging the papers they turn in (Haynes 87; Singer and Walvoord).

Coaching may seem too time-consuming, or too contrary to your own teaching style, but in the light of evidence of its importance, it seems worthwhile to do whatever is possible. This book, throughout, will suggest ways in which you might do some coaching despite constraints of time and style.

The Writing Process

Take a moment to think about what good writing behavior is. Immediately you'll ask, "What sort of writing?" Your behavior is different for a memo, a committee report, or an article for a professional journal, and people in your field who are not teachers may engage in other types of writing as well. Furthermore, good writers differ in their writing behavior. For example, Janet Emig's study of the composing practices of sixteen professional and academic writers revealed that, for expository writing, some professionals made detailed outlines, some made rough outlines, and some made no written outlines at all. Student writers exhibit the same variety of methods. In Emig's investigation of 109 themes written by 25 eleventh-grade English honors students, only 8.3% of the essays were preceded by a formal written outline and only 36.7% by some sort of written plan. The hardest pill for us pedagogues to swallow is that Emig found no difference in quality between the work of those who made outlines and that of writers who didn't. (*Composing*; for a case study of an engineer who depends heavily on outlining, see Selzer.)

Another revelation about outlining: professional writers, Emig found, do not restrict outlining to the planning stages but may use it toward the end of the writing process as a way of checking organizational tightness or as a guideline to reworking the piece, perhaps after it has lain fallow (26).

All this leads to the conclusion that your attempt to help students develop more effective writing behavior should not consist merely of seeing to it that every student makes an outline at a certain stage of the writing process, though you will want to stress outlining as one good way to plan writing, and you may want to force the uninitiated to try it, just as I force my young son to try my spinach soufflé.

Well, then, what *is* effective writing behavior, and how can teachers help students develop it? First, choose a type of writing similar to the writing that students do in your class. Begin by making a list of the steps that you or other successful practitioners in your field follow in this type of writing. (Your list will be more accurate if you keep it as a log, while you are actually writing a paper.) Include information about what motivates you to begin, how you plan your writing, how and when you begin to put ideas down on paper, and what function is served for you by rules such as "every paragraph should have a topic sentence" or "scientific papers of this sort should begin with an introduction, followed by a review of the literature, followed by. . . . " Also, tell how you achieve good focus and organization, at what points you set aside a piece of writing for a while, how long these incubation periods last, what suggestions you seek from colleagues or friends, how many revisions you make, how much time you need for revising, how you achieve accuracy in punctuation and grammar, and how you decide when the piece is finished. Your record is a clue to some of the procedures that distinguish the behavior of successful writers from that of unsuccessful writers.

We have much to learn about the sorts of writing behavior that work best for different people in various situations. Nevertheless, from what we do know we can infer a general pattern of effective writing behavior that resembles your own best processes or those of articulate colleagues.

Ideally the writing process begins when one becomes aware of the need to synthesize, clarify, or record facts or ideas, either for oneself or for another audience. A writer may use a number of techniques to get the writing started: mulling silently; talking to the wall or to friends; dictating on tape; making notes from memory or observation; jotting down ideas in random fashion, just to get them on paper; reading either to find ideas or to verify and support ideas; writing notes and summaries based on reading; making lists of points; outlining; or systematically answering some questions such as the journalist's five W's. Research indicates that one fruitful activity good writers share is an active and extensive attempt to determine who their audience will be, what they want to do with that audience, and what stance or tone they should assume. In other words, they view the writing challenge more broadly than novice writers do (Flower and Hayes; Odell and Goswami, "Writing").

The gathering of information may begin at any time and may be more or less crucial to the ideas and structure of the piece. The writer may observe, experiment, interview, consult memory, or read. Gathered information is evaluated, sorted, arranged. The writer may alter the original ideas radically as new facts emerge.

Some combination of these methods—plus some subconscious germination, about which little is known—enables the person to produce a first draft. In the process of writing and revising this first copy, the author may well discover new ideas. Writing, typing, or dictating this draft, the writer may stop, hesitate, look back over the work, say thoughts aloud, or skip ahead, leaving a section for later. In revising the first draft the writer may stumble on a structure or may sharpen or even radically alter the focus; in other words, the writing may serve as a means of clarification or discovery. Major forays into the field or library may add significant new information. Thus changes in the drafts may produce almost a whole new piece, based on something that appeared only tangentially in the first attempts. Some authors cut and paste, switching sections for a more effective progression of ideas. A writer may bring new material from the sidelines into the limelight or reduce stars to second billing, either by giving them less space or by positioning them in dimmer parts of the paper or the paragraph. (For one analysis of the parts of the revising process, see Flower et al.)

Ideally, consideration for the needs of the intended audience shapes the planning and writing from the beginning, but as the revision process goes on, concern for the needs of the reader takes a different form: the writer makes transitions explicit, provides definitions and explanations, corrects spelling and punctuation, and casts ideas into forms that will be clear to readers. In Linda Flower's now widely used phrase, the writer moves from "writer-based" to "reader-based" prose ("Writer-Based").

Along the way, good writers often seek help from "test" readers. They present their colleagues, spouses, or lovers with a draft and ask for responses and suggestions. A writer may also ask someone to correct spelling, punctuation, and grammar.

Throughout the process there are times of discouragement when, in Virginia Woolf's poignant image, "[the] mind, turned by anxiety, or other cause, from its scrutiny of blank paper, is like a lost child—wandering the house, sitting on the bottom steps to cry" (21). Writers discover their own best ways to get out of these sloughs—they may jog, sleep, push doggedly on, talk ideas through with a friend, turn to another task, or fix a hero sandwich.

Having analyzed your writing behavior and that of others, and having read the model just presented, you might list the steps you think most students follow when they do similar writing for your class. Researchers have found that poorer students often produce only two drafts, both written the night before the paper is due. The first draft is not a means of discovering meaning or achieving focus but, rather, a dogged, sentence-by-sentence production of words, generated by a basic idea and following a standard organizational pattern. The second draft is often merely a prettied-up version of the first: the student types the work neatly and removes mechanical errors for the benefit of the teacher, who is viewed as a hunter for errors. Though we know that good writers often change their focus, or discover it, while revising their drafts, these students do not go back and recast a paper in the light of their writing discoveries (Sommers, "Revision" 382–83).

Clearly the behavior of good professional writers differs markedly from that of many student writers, but better student writers come closer to following ideal procedures. One study found that more successful students spent more time in the planning stages, as well as in the writing process, and did significantly more revising (Stallard 211, 217).

So there are two important groups of studies: those that show the characteristics of student writing behavior and those that indicate that helping students with the writing process actually pays off.

Questions to Guide Your Coaching

Different teachers, exercising their ingenuity within their own disciplines and depending on their class loads, will find different ways to help students develop effective writing practices. It is important, however, to avoid imposing a rigid method on students, such as requiring outlines at a certain point in the writing process. Instead, teachers should try to make students conscious of their writing behavior and help them find their own best writing techniques. The following list of questions serves as a guide to the suggestions that form the rest of this chapter.

How can I help students

- understand the writing process?
- feel the involvement and interest that will make the writing process seem important to them?

- start early to allow time for effective planning, incubation, and revision?
- understand assignments and analyze what is expected?
- seek constructive help during the writing process? know the difference between the legitimate and the illegitimate use of helpers? acknowledge their helpers?
- assess, and write for, their audience, purpose, and context?
- generate rich ideas and focus their papers appropriately?
- gather appropriate information from library sources, interview, experiment, or observation; evaluate its worth; select what is useful; and integrate the information into their writing?
- reason, use evidence, and organize their thoughts?
- understand that revision is more than merely editing for mechanical and grammatical mistakes? see what needs revision in their drafts?
- compose and integrate effective visual aids?
- control style and mechanics?

Helping Students Understand the Writing Process

1. *Present in class several models of the writing process.* Show students outlines, free writing, and rough drafts done by you or other professionals. The chapter "The Student Rewrites" in Don Murray's *A Writer Teaches Writing* contains some good examples of professional revising.

2. *Pair students off in a buddy system.* Each buddy keeps in touch with the writing process of the other, recording progress and making suggestions. As the final papers come in, each student also turns in a report on the writing processes followed by the buddy. You can merely make sure that these are handed in, or if time permits you can read or scan them, respond to or summarize them in a discussion with the class, analyze a few in class, put them in some spot where all students can read them, or have a committee of students read them all and summarize them in a twenty-minute report to the class.

3. *Ask successful former students to come to your class* and describe how they handled your assignments.

4. *Present case studies* of student and professional writers. Some recent freshman composition readers include, along with some of the readings, the writer's accounts of how they were written. For example, Maimon and her colleagues have an extensive reproduction of the drafts of the Declaration of Independence (*Readings* 6–30) and a short letter from Elizabeth Janeway about how she wrote *Man's World, Woman's Place* (226–27). Journals also present case studies (e.g., Selzer). You can find other case studies by conducting a search of ERIC, a computerized or paper data base; use the search terms "Cognitive Processes," "Writing Processes," "Writing Research," and "Case Studies."

5. *Invite writers to your class.* A psychologist, for example, might describe to your class the entire process of writing a diagnostic evaluation or an article for a psychology journal.

Computer Programs That Guide the Writing Process

If your assignment lends itself to a series of well-defined steps, if most or all of your students have access to computers, and if you have programming skills, you can compose a program that leads your students through the steps necessary to produce the paper. Some such programs (you can probably locate them through your computer center staff) are already available for use in composition classes where students write essays.

It is important not to let a prescriptive set of steps limit your students' thinking and exploration or make them believe that writing can be done by strict adherence to formula. Computer programs or handout sheets that delineate steps to the writing process are tools to be used gingerly, and only with certain types of writing. Observe your students carefully, to discover whether the programmed steps inhibit free investigation or result in writing that is too stiff and mechanical for its situation or for your pedagogical purposes.

Helping Students Become Involved

Involvement and interest may be the most important keys to students' writing success. Over and over, in talks with students about their writing for a variety of courses, I hear them say, "That was my best paper because I was interested in it." We know for ourselves that our most engaged and committed writing is often our most effective. Below are some suggestions to help students capture and hold the curiosity, engagement, and commitment that will enhance the quality of their learning and writing.

1. *Make clear your own interest in the subject.*

2. *Ask your students informally*, in hallways and before class, "What are you doing your paper on?"

3. *Get peer support on your side.* Ask students to prepare to talk in small groups about their subjects. Each group member should say what interests him or her about the idea and then should offer one question or observation that invites the writer to go further. Such talk helps the writer to feel that the group is waiting to see how the ideas develop. In-class group conversation also encourages supportive exchange of ideas among students out of class.

4. *Refer to papers, whenever possible, by some specific genre name*: "your reviews" or "your essays," not "your papers." This practice helps students see their writing as a recognized form of real writing, not just as a "paper"—a genre known only to schools, whose very name omits reference to words and ideas. (I am indebted to Lucille McCarthy for this suggestion; it was a difference she noted between two instructors in her study.)

5. *Create genuine writing situations*, in which your students will communicate with real audiences that have a genuine need for the information writers will convey.

6. *Provide some type of "publication"* for at least the most successful

writings. Papers may be posted on a bulletin board or on your office door, put on library reserve, duplicated for class distribution, even published in a booklet. At the end of the school year, some departments ask all instructors to submit the two best papers they have received, for publication in a department booklet, to be distributed to majors, or to the next semester's classes, as models. Some departments present a small stipend or a book and/or hold an awards ceremony for the best papers written in a given year.

7. *Never let students overhear you complaining about grading papers,* even in joke. Everything they hear and overhear from you should communicate your interest in their learning and ideas.

8. *Communicate clearly your reasons for every assignment:* what you expect students to learn and gain.

9. *Emphasize to your students the importance of selecting an angle that genuinely interests them.* Suggest ways to keep that interest going: asking questions about one's topic, breaking down a task into manageable goals, explaining the topic to a friend, and so on.

10. *Bring in writers* who can enthusiastically describe the importance of writing in their professional or personal lives and can explain how writing and thinking are carried out in the profession.

Helping Students Pace Their Work

Both students' interest and the quality of their writing may be trampled in the frantic rush to meet a deadline too long ignored. As part of an experiment I carried out with Daniel Singer (Singer and Walvoord) I undertook, with no business training, to respond to drafts of case analyses by upper-class business majors. In their end-of-semester evaluations, some of the students noted my lack of business acumen and doubted my ability to help them with business analysis, but unanimously they acknowledged that my forcing them to have a draft ready for their appointment with me—one week before the final paper was due—had been crucial to the success of their analyses. Even if you only glance at prospectuses or topic statements, or even if peers give unsophisticated responses to early plans and drafts, at least you will have helped students pace their work.

Some of your coaching, in fact, may have pacing as its only or main goal and need take little or no time from you. For example, ask students to bring to class their topic, hypothesis, or thesis and give five to ten minutes of class time for them to describe the topic for a buddy. A student who is not prepared must at least tell someone else why and may get inspiring help from the peer; most students will prepare something, just to avoid embarrassment. The exercise will help many students, even if you never see or hear the planned topics—though of course you may want to participate directly, in ways discussed later in this section.

Your attitude toward the intermediate deadlines for a project will significantly influence the seriousness with which the students meet those deadlines. The loosest way is to announce in class that you are happy to see any student's plan or to look over a draft during your office hours. This method, which will bring in only a few students, hardly constitutes coaching for the class or for those students who probably need it most. To coach any significant number of students, you will need a schedule, with deadlines by which students must have something particular to bring to class, hand in, or share with peers. In setting these deadlines, some instructors are comfortable with a flexible schedule, and plans and drafts swirl around them in a merry confusion of excuses and missed deadlines, consonant with the lives of students who work, take other classes, interact with family, and get caught in traffic. Within such a method, one must be willing to tolerate a number of students who will not hand in any plans.

A tighter weir will bring more fish into your net. You can use any of the methods below:

1. *Operate by a system of points,* where a certain number of total points are needed for an A, somewhat fewer for a B, and so on. Then you award some points for drafts and plans submitted on time and some points for various aspects of the completed paper. You might rig the points so that the final paper, even if excellent, doesn't carry enough points to get an A, unless accompanied by some points for drafts or plans.

2. *Grade the intermediate plans* (you may use a scale such as ok, ok+ ok-). Like those for any other assignment, these grades are averaged into the course grade. (Some pros and cons of grading plans and drafts are discussed in chapter 6 in the section on grading.)

3. *Require the student to submit the plan, on time, as a condition for acceptance of the final paper.* If the plan is not in on time, the grade for the entire paper is F.

Helping Students Analyze the Assignment

The essential elements of the assignment should be communicated in writing. Many writing tutors, when a student comes for help on a paper, begin by asking, "What was the assignment?" because they know that students are often confused on this most basic point.

When you communicate your assignment to students, orally and in writing, they need, as writers, certain information to guide their decisions:

- *Audience.* To whom are they to write? Is this audience knowledgeable about the subject? familiar with specialized vocabulary? What are its present opinions and biases? its expectations in this situation?
- *Purpose.* What use will the reader make of the piece of writing? What is the writer's purpose in writing the piece? What is your purpose, as an instructor, for giving this assignment?

- *Topic.* Are you giving them a broad topic area they must narrow and define? Are they expected to organize around a thesis?
- *Length.* How flexible are you on length? Do you want them to reach your expected length at all costs?
- *Expectations.* What do you expect from the papers? What qualities in a finished paper please you? What standards will students be graded on?
- *Mechanics.* Standard format, required margins, form of the title page, form for citations, and so on.
- *Level of polish.* How important is the final polishing in grammar, spelling, and punctuation?
- *Process strategies.* What steps or strategies might be useful to the students in developing the paper?

Probably all the above information should be included in the written assignment. Some of it, such as purpose and expectations, may be summarized in the written assignment and elaborated orally.

My textbook for student writers teaches students four steps for interpreting an instructor's assignment (*Writing* 73–83). Below, I have adapted the steps as a guide to help you shape written assignments that convey your precise intentions to students.

Checking Your Assignment

1. Analyze the parts of the assignment. Will it be clear to students what they are being given: a required sequence of parts? a suggested sequence of parts that they may change if they wish? a complete list of the material to be covered in the paper, with the sequence left to the student? a partial list of questions or ideas, merely to get students started? hints for planning, researching, and developing the paper? You may want to add some of these guides to your assignment.

2. Underline words that tell the topic of the final paper. Circle the one word that is most central to the paper's subject. Will students be able to tell what they should focus on?

3. Circle verbs that tell the student what to do. Predict the pattern of organization implied by the verb(s). Are you saying "describe" when "analyze" would be more precise? Will your students know from your verb choices what to do?

4. What thesis or topic and what pattern of organization for the final paper are implied by the wording of your assignment? Will students correctly infer what you want?

When you analyze the tasks and potential difficulties within an assignment, you can specifically warn and guide your students. For example, the instructor who came to understand the crucial role that early determination of a central idea played in his assignment to analyze Toni's Restaurant (p. 23) might have opened the in-class essay period by saying:

This exercise will test your ability to pick out the mistakes Toni made and suggest how he could have done better. Just listing mistakes in random order, however, will seem to the reader to be too hard to remember or follow. So you will need to find a way to organize Toni's mistakes into subgroups and to arrange them in an effective order. You might decide, for example, that Toni's main errors were all due to one or two misguided notions. That should be your opening statement, and then you can treat the details as aspects of those main problems. Alternatively, some students have gone through the four *P*'s of marketing (place, promotion, product, price) and discussed Toni's mistakes or successes in each area.

You might begin by listing Toni's mistakes in random order. Then look over your list and try to group some mistakes together or decide which ones are aspects of the same larger problem. Then write out your ideas following that organization. If, after you have thought for a while, you find yourself running out of time and sense that your ideas are still in random order, just begin writing—things may fall into place as you write. If you are out of time and have begun to pull the essay together, take the last few minutes to jot down an outline of how you would organize the next draft of your paper, so that I can see that you have an idea of what good organization is and that you were making progress toward it in this essay when you ran out of time.

An explanation such as this identifies for students the primary traits of successful papers, warns of the pitfalls that can trap inexperienced writers working on this particular assignment, and suggests several techniques for achieving effective communication. Note that standards should be expressed not as absolute rules but as ways of meeting the needs of the reader. For example, ideas should be grouped and organized so that the reader can easily understand and remember them.

Below are three written assignment sheets that illustrate the principle discussed so far. The first was handed to students in Michael Burton's sociology course, as part of their syllabus, at the start of the semester. Burton augments the written sheets during class with suggestions for journal topics. Notice that he discusses purpose, audience, and expectations.

Keeping a Sociological Journal
A Student's Guide

(Developed by Michael Burton for students in sociology at Loyola College in Maryland.)

You are to keep a sociological journal throughout the semester. It is to contain short essays and exercises—a total of at least 24 entries. I will assign topics and guidelines for a little over half the entries, and you will choose topics for the rest. When you choose a topic, it should be sociologically relevant, and it should demonstrate deep thought and a serious effort to make sense of the world around you. In others words, it should be very different from the typical diary entry. Below are some specific points:

1. The *purposes* of this assignment are to give you opportunities to practice viewing the world from a sociological perspective and to develop your writing skills.
2. Unless otherwise indicated, I am to be the *audience* for your entries.
3. In grading the journal, I will be concerned with (a) your grasp of sociological concepts, ideas, theories, and facts; (b) creativity and imagination, as shown by your ability to take an idea, concept, or fact and do something interesting and meaningful with it; (c) the quality of your writing—it should be clear and coherent and free of major mechanical errors.
4. I will collect the journals twice during the semester for grading. Some assignments will also be collected on the day for which they are assigned.
5. Write all entries on standard-size (8½" × 11") lined paper. Be sure your handwriting is legible—if I can't read it easily, your grade is likely to suffer. Keep your entries in a letter-size manila folder. All entries should be dated.

The following guide for writing physics lab reports emphasizes the reader's needs and the rationale behind the recommended sequence. It also does a good job of warning students against some common errors or misconceptions, and it wisely suggests that, in preparing the report for submission, the writer seek suggestions from peers.

Directions for Writing a Lab Report
A Student's Guide

(Developed by Xavier Spiegel for students in physics and engineering at Loyola College in Maryland.)

Introduction

The "scientific method" is a phrase used to describe procedures followed by most successful experimentalists: stating the problem, searching the literature for relevant information, observing and collecting data, forming hypotheses, testing and modifying these hypotheses, and publishing results. We notice in this methodology that the beginning and the end of all experimental work involve the communication of experimental results. This serves to underscore the importance of communication in scientific experimentation. The communication of experimental results is accomplished by various means, such as the laboratory report, the technical report or paper, and the research paper.

The laboratory report, technical paper, and scientific article have one thing in common: they are written documents composed to communicate information and ideas. The laboratory report is generally written for an instructor or a fellow student. A technical paper is usually an in-house document of an organization and has limited circulation, whereas a scientific article is published for a larger audience in a scientific or professional journal. In the context of this course we will use the term "laboratory report" interchangeably with "technical paper" and "scientific article." Just as there are conventions for writing a letter, there are conventions for writing a laboratory report. We can draw comparisons between a letter and a laboratory report to explain the way in which the scientific community shares its experiences, develops new laws, and generally broadens our knowledge of nature.

The Laboratory Report in General

A letter has seven essential parts:

Address of author
Date
Greeting
Introduction
Body
Closing remarks
Signature

The purpose of each of these should be obvious, but to ensure that we agree, let us examine briefly the reason for such a structured document. The name and address of the author are given so that a reader who wishes to answer the letter can reply quickly and efficiently. The date is included to give the letter a reference in time—to date the information. The introduction tells the reader why the letter is being written, and the body of the letter transmits the information. The closing remarks generally draw conclusions, ask for advice, or reiterate important parts of the body, and the signature tells the reader who is writing the letter.

A laboratory report has 15 essential parts:

Name of author
Date
Address
Abstract
Title
Object
Theory
Procedure
Apparatus
Data
Sample calculations

Results
Conclusions
Discussion
References

The purpose of the date and the name and address of the author are the same as for the letter. In a lab report, they also serve as documentation for scientific credit for any new discovery or theory. The title and abstract are similar to the greeting in a letter.

The writer would like the report to reach the appropriate audience. The first step is to select a journal that publishes articles on the subject. But those who buy a particular journal seldom read all the articles, and the title of the report is meant to allow selection by those interested in the author's special area. The title, however, is not sufficient indication of the exact subject, and the abstract, which is a short summary of the report, further narrows the audience to those who are interested in this specialized approach or experiment.

The object of a laboratory report corresponds to the introduction of a letter. The procedure, apparatus, data, sample calculations, results, and conclusions correspond to the body. The discussion section corresponds to the closing remarks of a letter. The reference section documents information that the author supplies to the reader.

The Laboratory Report in Particular: The Object, Theory, Procedure, Apparatus, Data, Sample Calculations, Results, and Conclusions

The object-of-the-experiment section states, usually in only a sentence or two, exactly what the writer will do in the report.

The theory section explains the guiding principles or laws that govern the phenomenon being investigated. The author can assume that the reader is generally knowledgeable in the subject area and knows as much about the theory as the author did before starting to work on this experiment. This means that the writer should not bore the reader with the obvious. It also means that the author should try not to lose the reader by assuming too much or supplying only sketchy details. The theory section will generally include a mathematical derivation of the equations governing the phenomenon under investigation. Since these are seldom original and can usually be found in textbooks or other articles, they should be documented, as is often true of the whole theory section. The most popular reference system in use today in scientific journals relies on numbered superscripts. Equations should be clearly labeled (e.g., Eq. 1) so that they can be referred to later. Since the theory does not depend on either the procedure or the apparatus, it should be general and include any boundary conditions or limitations that apply.

The procedure section describes the particular measurements taken and the number of times each was taken. The writer should not lead the reader by the hand, as in a cookbook or instruction manual, but should give the general approach to the measurements. Often authors are tempted to write in the imperative, ordering the reader to take this measurement or that measurement and to be certain of this or that, but such a tone should be avoided. The author can assume that the reader is familiar with the general laboratory equipment and procedures. The reader will assume that the author would not perform the experiment without knowing the proper use and care of the equipment or without checking for faulty equipment. Procedure sections generally vary between one paragraph and three, depending on the complexity of the experiment.

The apparatus section can be simply a list of the apparatus used, but it usually includes a line drawing or picture to illustrate the equipment better. Each drawing or picture should have a name and a title. A name (e.g., Fig. 1) helps the reader refer to it easily, and a title (Apparatus for Simple Pendulum Experiment) aids the reader who just skims the report looking at figures and pictures to get an idea of what it includes. The author should not include a drawing or picture of apparatus that is in general use. For example, most laboratories have various types of thermometers, so that a drawing of a therometer would be unnecessary; a statement of the thermometer's range and its smallest division, however, would be useful.

The data section of the report is a display of the measurements. This can be handled in various ways, but the most popular forms are tabular and graphic. A table should have a name and a title and should list the variables measured, the units of measurement, and the accuracy of the measuring device. A graph also has a name and title, and the abscissa and ordinate are clearly labeled as to variable, dimension, and scale divisions. Graphs should be drawn on graph paper in such a way that the data points and the error flags show clearly and the curve extends across two-thirds of the paper. This is all that should appear on the graph; calculations, equations, and comments should be left to the text of the paper.

The sample calculation, although not always necessary, is meant to lead the reader to a thorough understanding of any complex or difficult calculation necessary for the complete understanding of the report. If a sample calculation is necessary the author should define the variables used and explain where the values for the variables were obtained and exactly how the calculation proceeds. A good guideline here is a basic text in the particular subject area concerned.

The results section can be a simple statement of the final result of the calculations or a few sentences summing up the scientific facts discovered.

The conclusions are the author's interpretation of the results and the experiment as a whole. They tell the reader what the particular results mean in terms of the object and theory presented earlier in the report.

The discussion section of the report presents the author's personal speculations or views on what further experimentation would be necessary to complete a new concept or theory. This is also the author's chance to determine the state of the art and the value of such an experiment or to suggest modifications that others might make in future experiments.

The references, as mentioned previously, support the information that the author used in the report. They are used in place of or in addition to footnotes. The author supplies this information to enlighten the reader about details not included in the report, to document confirming or controversial theory and data, and to inform the reader of any other materials that would help in understanding the report.

After Completing the First Draft of a Laboratory Report

Since *communication* is the goal of the laboratory report, it is often helpful to have a colleague read the report and judge whether it is indeed clear, concise, and comprehensible. It is best to choose someone who has the necessary background to grasp your experimental work and to evaluate the report but who has not been involved in writing the report and can thus discern whether the report does indeed say what the author intended to say. In addition, it is useful for the author to reread the report to check for common mistakes:

1. Are the correct person and tense used throughout the report?
2. Are spelling, punctuation, grammar, and syntax correct?
3. Are quotations properly footnoted, and is credit given for ideas taken from others and used with only minor modifications?
4. Are all graphs and figures labeled with descriptive titles and referred to in the text of the report?
5. Are graphs plotted correctly? Is the scale of reasonable size? Are the experimental points plotted with error flags? Is the curve *smooth*?
6. Are equations numbered, particularly those used or referred to in other sections of the report?
7. Are all symbols in the equations adequately defined?
8. Are numerical data and results presented with the appropriate number of significant digits and/or a statement of precision?

The next handout nicely integrates examples with its instruction about format and content for the paper.

Writing a Diagnostic Evaluation
A Student's Guide

(Developed by Linda Spencer, Speech and Hearing Center, Loyola College in Maryland.)

	Diagnostic Evaluation
Name:	Date of Evaluation:
Address:	Date of Birth:
	Phone:

Parents' Names: Age:
Referral Source: Sex:
Reports Sent to:

Identification

Name, age, sex, parents, sibling order, school. For example:

> Jimmy is a four-year-old white male, the oldest of three children. Parents
> are separated, and Jimmy lives with his mother. He is enrolled at Happy
> Acres Nursery School and attends every morning.

History

Summarize all the data on the client's history that you have obtained from
such sources as the case history, a physician's or psychologist's report, informants (parent, foster parent, counselor, or anyone else who accompanies the
client), or the client, in the case of an adult.

Use separate paragraphs for each type of information, beginning with
prenatal history and birth, including anything significant from the neonatal
period, then motor development up to the present, then general health, and finally speech and language development. History extends up to the parents' or
adult client's present concerns and description of the problem. (In previous report styles this contemporary information was entered under a section enti-
tled "Chief Complaint.")

Behavioral Observations

Describe the child's or adult's behavior or appearance when you first met
him or her, and then describe how he or she acted in the room, that is, the degree of cooperation (separated easily and attended well throughout an hour of
testing; cried loudly and asked that his mother return to the room; answered
all questions readily and in detail, suggesting eagerness to receive assistance
with this problem). Also, describe play behavior and other indicants of cognitive level, such as knowledge of colors and body parts. Indicate how valid
you feel your observations are.

Test Results

Receptive Skills: Separate into paragraphs each bit of test information,
with hearing test results appearing in the first paragraph. Then devote a separate paragraph to each receptive test you administered (discrimination, recep-
tion). For example:

> Joey's responses to pure-tone screening indicated normal hearing bilater-
> ally. The Northwestern Syntax Screening Test (NSST), receptive portion,
> was administered to assess Joey's understanding of English syntax and
> morphology. (Or, this test uses a picture-pointing response to assess a
> child's understanding of English syntax and morphology.) Joey responded
> correctly to ____ out of 40 possible items, placing his performance in the
> ____ percentile (don't abbreviate percentile) for normal children age 4–10

to 4–11. Incorrect responses were noted for the following syntactic elements: regular past tense, *who* versus *what*, etc.

Expressive Skills: Here enter, in this order, results of oral peripheral examination; articulation test results, including your own perception of intelligibility in conversation; expressive syntax test; voice quality; fluency and rate; an overall indication of expressive ability or characteristics. Regardless of the presenting problem, assess all areas of communication and describe your findings here. Some examples:

> An oral peripheral examination indicated normal structure and function. *Not*: The oral peripheral examination was normal (the child's mouth was normal, not the examination).
> *Or*: Although oral structures appeared normal, movement was slow, as indicated by the following oral diadochokinetic rates: /pʌ/—5 in 5 seconds; /tʌ/—4 in 5 seconds; /kʌ/—2 in 5 seconds. The three syllable utterance /pʌtʌkʌ/ was not produced in order, suggesting poor (or inadequate) oral sequencing skills. These voiceless stop plosives were produced with inadequate intraoral pressure, as well, suggesting reduced strength in the oral structures.
> The Goldman-Fristoe Test of Articulation was administered to assess single-word articulation ability. The following phoneme errors were noted:

Initial	Medial	Final
n/g	d/g	-/g

An indication of distinctive feature errors is then in order. For example,
> Articulation errors were characterized, in general, by the use of stops for fricatives and reduction of all phoneme blends that incorporated /s/, /l/, and /r/.

Then say something like this:
> Despite the large number of phoneme errors noted on this test, intelligibility in conversation was fair, even when the topic was not known to the clinician.

If the presenting problem is fluency, present the fluency rate for each context in which you obtained speech samples. For example:

Context	Fluency
Counting	90%
Reciting	75%

Then, describe the dysfluency pattern, noting whole- or part-word repetitions, interjections, blocks on initial phonemes, and so on, and secondary symptoms, such as foot tapping and eye blinking.

Psycholinguistic Skills: Interpret your ITPA results here, in terms of significant deviations from mean or median scale scores, noting apparent areas of strength and weakness.

Summary and Recommendations

The first paragraph is a summary of all pertinent information obtained during the evaluation. Start out like this:

> Joey is a three-year-old boy who is the oldest son of May and Ralph Smith. The family brought him to this center because of their concern with the unintelligibility of his speech. Test results and observations indicate that receptive language skills and expressive syntax are at age level. Articulation skills are poor, however, resulting in poor intelligibility. Joey is quite stimulable, though, for most error phonemes and attended well in the therapy setting.

> *Or:* Joey's speech is characterized by multiple consonant substitutions and vowel distortions rendering conversational speech nearly unintelligible.

> It is recommended that Joey receive articulation therapy for two half hours weekly. Prognosis for improvement is good, since Joey's other language skills are at age level, and he can produce several phonemes with stimulation at this time.

> The single long-range therapy goal for this child is the attainment of age-appropriate phonological skills. Specific short-term therapy goals will be established after probe procedures have been completed.

Linda E. Spencer, PhD, or
Carolyn Martin, MS or
Libby Kumin, PhD
Clinical Supervisor

Mary A. Jones, BA
Graduate Student Clinician

Some general notes:

1. Your first draft should be as complete as possible and in legible form.
2. Avoid colloquial phrases, such as *lots of*, for *several*, *going to*, for *will*, *sounds*, for *phonemes*, and so on.
3. The word *presently* means "in a short time." Don't use it to mean "now" or "at the present time."
4. Do not include in the summary any information that did not appear in the body of the report.
5. Behavioral descriptions should appear in your report; often these are more important than test scores.
6. Check the spellings of words you are unfamiliar with.
7. Use the past tense in describing test results and behavior unless you are mentioning a behavior that is ongoing or typical. For example, you may say that Joey "goes to the store by himself" but switch to past tense to say that "he misarticulated a number of phonemes."
8. Avoid the use of such words as *could*, *could not*, or *not able to*. These

terms suggest that you have complete knowledge of the client's capabilities, when this rarely is the case. Instead, say what the client did or did
not do, and indicate that this suggests or indicates a particular condition
with which you may be familiar.

9. If you administer a test battery, such as the Detroit or the ITPA, that yields
a variety of scores, enter this information in the form of a table on a separate page. For the ITPA, include subtest names, raw scores, age scores,
scaled scores, and deviations from mean or median scores. Enter only
your interpretations of the test results in the body of this report.

A variation on the assignment sheet that describes and instructs is the
list of expectations for the paper, phrased as questions. The instructor or peers
then use that same sheet as a checklist for responding to the paper. Anthropologist Mark P. Curchack at Beaver College in Pennsylvania uses the following sheet to guide students' writing and to structure peer response to papers.
The sheet particularizes the criteria for the paper in an exceptionally clear and
specific way.

Peer Evaluation of First Draft of Term Paper
A Student's Guide

(Developed by Mark P. Curchack for sociology students at Beaver College.)

Author of Draft _____ *Name of Reviewer* _____

Title of Draft _____

Directions: By answering the following questions thoughtfully and clearly, be
as helpful as possible to the author of this draft. Use complete sentences and
specific examples to ensure clarity in your advice. You will be evaluated on the
thoughtfulness and helpfulness of your responses.

1. *Overall situation*: How near to completion is this draft? What steps should
   the author take to complete this term paper? Be both specific and helpful in listing the three most important steps below:
   a.
   b.
   c.

2. *Organization*: Is this draft organized in a standard pattern: an introductory section; the body of the paper, presenting the information in a reasonable sequence; and a summary and analysis of the situation? If there

is an alternative organization, say what it is and whether it is effective.

3. *Introductory section*: The first few paragraphs should prepare the reader (another student in the course) for the research that has been done on the topic.

   a. Does the introduction explain the topic and why it is important? Briefly state why you think it is important.

   b. After reading the paper, say whether you think the introduction introduces what you've read. Does it? How?

4. *Body of the paper*: The major portion of the paper should present the collected information in an orderly and clear fashion.

   a. In the space below, outline in some detail the major points established in the body of the paper and the evidence used to support the points.

   b. Is the style of the writing appropriate to the intended audience, you and the others in the class?

   c. Compared with that of the textbook, is the style more or less formal? How?

   d. Has the author thoroughly paraphrased the information from the references so that the writing style is consistent? Remember that inadequate paraphrasing is a common student problem and may even approach plagiarism.

   e . Has the writer organized the information in the most effective way?

      1. If not, suggest improvements.

      2. How would you characterize the organization? Is it a list of equal points, an arrangement of topics and subtopics, a chronological sequence, an argument with two or more opposing viewpoints, or what?

   f. How has the writer handled citations?

      1. Are they in an acceptable style, used consistently?

      2. Is the number of citations adequate to the information taken from sources?

      3. How has the information from sources been organized?

         a. One source per paragraph (give an example)

         b. Multiple sources for each paragraph (give an example)

   g. Are the tables and/or figures used in the paper

      1. clear and easy to understand?

      2. referred to in the text?

      3. labeled with a title or legend?

      4. cited (at the end of the title or legend)?

5. *Conclusions*: A conclusion can take several forms: a restatement of the overall argument of the paper, a summary of the key points, a combination of several points to make a final point, an analysis of the data, and so on.

   a. What form has the writer used to conclude the paper?

   b. Does the conclusion seem to be supported by the evidence? How or how not?

6. *Features of the writing*:
   a. Are there any problems in the grammar, spelling, punctuation, para-graph structure, sentence structure, transitions? Which one(s) in par-ticular? Do these problems interfere with the meaning the writer is trying to express?
   b. Has the writer acknowledged the help of others?
7. *General evaluation*: In the space remaining, give your general impression of the paper. Did you like it and why? What did you learn from it? What else do you wish you had learned from it? Give any other ideas that you think might help.

Helping Students Find Help

Teachers who begin to get involved in their students' writing processes and researchers who study students' writing behavior become quickly aware that many students operate within a network of classmates, friends, parents, and spouses who provide various sorts of help with the writing process. Most of us, as writers, operate the same way. We ask a colleague in the next office to respond to an article draft; we talk over a research project with the depart-ment head; we work as part of a task force or research team where plans and drafts are mutually authored; we have a spouse or secretary review a draft for style and mechanics. We also have appropriate ways to acknowledge another person's help, and we know the difference between legitimate and illegitimate help. Our students need guidance in learning how to use their networks effec-tively, how to identify legitimate kinds of help, and how to acknowledge help.

A formal source of help is your college's tutoring or writing center. Whether any of your students go there depends greatly on you. Find out where the center is, how its help is structured, and whether it offers drop-in help on specific courses or papers. Do the tutors work on focus and organization or only on style and mechanics? Are there tutors familiar with your discipline? Can you guide your students to specific tutors you think are good? Can you recommend some students you know to be hired as tutors? Once you have knowledge about, and confidence in, your center, try to work out effective ways of getting your students to go. Talk about the center in class. Have the director or a tutor visit your class. Emphasize that the center is not just for poor stu-dents but for any *smart* student who knows that good writers seek interim responses to their work.

You can reinforce your recommendations with carrots and clubs. Offer extra points to students who visit the lab for writing help. If the student is other-wise competent but has problems with grammar, spelling, and punctuation, some instructors work out an arrangement with the lab whereby the student is rewarded for hard work in the lab. One professor I know gives a grade of Incomplete if by the course's end mastery of content is adequate but grasp of grammar and punctuation is not. The grade merited by content mastery is given only after the student has completed a certain number of additional sessions in the lab to review problems in grammar, spelling, and punctuation. The lab director lets the professor know when the required sessions have been completed satisfactorily. If you use this method, work hard to present the required sessions as help, not punishment. Writing as punishment is a phenomenon your students have probably met in grade school and high school, and it has not enhanced their love of writing or their image of themselves as writers.

Another method, discussed in chapter 4, is to structure peer networks by organizing response groups.

You can also help your students as they seek guidance from friends, classmates, and relatives outside class. More of this common activity would be useful if the student knew how to structure the helper's aid. Many helpers focus too quickly on fixing the grammar and punctuation, or they appropriate the paper and do it over their own way. Suggest to your students how they can get better help. Teach them what constitutes legitimate help and how to acknowledge the help they get, in the ways that are appropriate in your field or type of writing. Below is a guide you may duplicate for your students.

Using and Acknowledging Your Writer's Network
A Student's Guide

Most writers interact with others during the writing process. They may work in groups on a company report or research project; they check drafts with supervisors; they ask friends to look over an outline; they talk over their project with a colleague who makes several suggestions for organization of the writing; they have a secretary or friend check the paper for grammar, spelling, and punctuation. Such help is not wrong. It's the way writers work.

When you get such help, you should acknowledge it. You can do that with an acknowledgments section. In a formal report, use a separate page at the beginning of your paper, after the title page and before the table of contents. If the paper is short, just use a note at the bottom of page 1. The acknowledgment may be phrased in any of several ways; you can get a feel for wording by reading acknowledgments in your textbook, library books, and articles. One good all-purpose pattern is, "I am indebted to Myrna Washington for help with the organization of the paper." One kind of help is unethical: to let someone else write your paper or any part of it. To be safe, keep the pen in your own hand, and write your paper in your own words. (A friend or tutor may suggest occasional phrases or may condense a sample paragraph to show you how to tighten your language.)

Two kinds of help are often used in the outside world but may not be acceptable in classes (check with your instructor):

- to have someone else do part of your research or observation or to gather data for you.

- to have someone else correct spelling, punctuation, and grammar. Many instructors want you to use school as a place to learn how to edit your own grammar and punctuation, so they want you to make your own corrections. Your helpers may tell you the grammar rules and help you spot problems but should not just take the paper away and fix it for you.

When a person gives you *information* or *ideas*, as opposed to suggestions about organization or focus or research tactics for your paper, treat the information as you would any information from an interview, and cite the person in a footnote or parenthetical citation, using the form acceptable in your discipline for citing interviews. Any help you get from a printed source, whether you quote it directly or phrase it in your own words, should of course be acknowledged by a citation, using the form acceptable in your discipline.

Because writers have so many issues to consider as they prepare a final piece, they tend to focus their attention selectively. In early plans and drafts, most writers concentrate on the content, focus, organization, line of reasoning, and evidence or support for their points. In later drafts, they may, as time permits, still be open to suggestions for major changes in focus or organization or major additions of new material, but they focus more and more on clarity of language and on grammar, punctuation, and spelling. Your helpers, however, may focus too early on grammar and spelling and may not help you appropriately with organization and lines of reasoning in your early drafts. You may have to ask them specifically to reply in ways that will help you. Below is one good technique for finding out from a helper whether your main point is clear and your organization logical. Instead of asking your friend, "How is this paper?" ask, "Would you do some specific things to help me with this paper?" Then ask the friend to follow the steps below:

1. Read the first paragraph, and tell me what you think the paper's main point is and how you arrived at that impression.
2. Read the rest of the paper, and make a list of its main points as you discover them. Tell me where you felt confused about the organization. Do you have suggestions for better organization? for additional points? for deletion?
3. If you were someone who didn't agree with my findings or arguments, what criticism or counterarguments would you raise? Do you think my paper answers these as strongly as it could?
4. (Add other questions about content and structure, depending on the requirements of your assignment.)

In later drafts, you may want your readers to point out matters of style, grammar, punctuation, and spelling. If possible, get this kind of help only after you've already done your best to edit the paper yourself. Then your helper catches what you missed and explains rules or reasons for changes. Try to emerge from that helping session knowing more about style, grammar, and punctuation than you did before. Your goal is to increase your ability to edit your own writing.

Helping Students Assess Audience, Purpose, and Context

In chapter 2 we discussed the kind of audiences instructors could establish—the "real" audience, the hypothetical audience, the instructor as audience. We discussed various roles for the instructor as audience. When you help your students address their audience appropriately, one task is constantly to remind them of their audience; another is to help them analyze that audience.

When you speak with students about assignments, try to refer frequently to audience, purpose, and context. When a student asks a question like "How much should be put in about X?" say, "What do you think the audience would find most useful?" When giving instructions, you could say, "Your abstract should be no more than 50 words," but you can pound audience awareness in a bit deeper by saying, "An abstract is usually limited to 50 words so readers can quickly identify the main point and decide whether they need to read the entire report."

To help students analyze their audience, suggest that they ask two types of questions: questions that help students imagine the actual persons who will read their report and questions that help them understand the conventions of presentation that an audience will expect in a certain context—for example, one person may read articles in both *Psychology Today* and the *American Journal of Orthopsychiatry*, but this reader will not expect the same presentation from each periodical. Arthur Walzer calls for helping students not only with discourse that depends primarily on "the immediate needs and particular backgrounds of actual readers" but also with discourse "in which rhetorical choice is dictated more by the point of view a community of readers chooses to take on a subject" (156).

Imagine yourself writing your students' assignment. What qualities of your audience, purpose, and context would shape the writing? Frame questions that help students find those qualities. Some questions might be:

1. Who is my reader? Who are secondary readers? Who must approve or have input? What is their age? educational level? range of interests? familiarity with my subject?
2. What is my purpose with each reader? To inform? persuade to a point of view? goad to action? allow the reader to perform a task?
3. How do I want these readers to view me? As an expert in the field? a novice investigator? a business executive especially attentive to customer complaints? a person who sticks to my principles?
4. What is the organization's or instructor's purpose in causing this piece to be written? Does the instructor want to know how I'm learning? to know

that I read the chapter? to push me deeper into the subject? to assess my competence for a grade? The organization wants to make a sale? inform employees of a new rule?

5. What conventions guide this type of writing? What format is expected? what stance toward my subject? what style of language? What purposes guide the writing?

You can make these questions the object of class or small-group discussion and/or have students write out the answers. Give students actual examples of the type of writing you expect, and have them analyze the conventions, assumptions, and roles for reader and writer. If you are the audience, hand out a sheet of qualities you look for. (For more guidance, see Nancy Roundy, who explains in detail how she leads her students through an audience analysis that informs a business writing project.)

As you help your students define their audience, purpose, and context, you will find the issue more complex than it may seem on the surface. Students will disagree about qualities of the audience. It will become clear that the audience is partly a fiction, created by each student. You may have to fight students' tendency to stereotype audiences. Questions about the ethics of writers who adapt what they say to their intended audience will surely arise. The literature on these issues is summarized in Lisa Ede's "Audience: An Introduction to Research." The May 1984 issue of *College Composition and Communication*, in which Ede's article appears, contains several other provocative articles about audience analysis.

Helping Students Generate Ideas and Focus the Topic

Many assignments, in one way or another, ask students to select the ideas about which they will write or to limit and focus within an assigned topic. When limited topic areas are assigned, both instructor and students sometimes overlook the need to focus. Even a topic like "Discuss the history and influence of the Warren Court" will require students to omit some facts they know and to select others, since they can't possibly tell everything about the history and influence of the Warren Court.

When you assign any topic, ask yourself whether, in the allotted time or length, students can say everything they know or might find out about your topic. If not, you are forcing them to choose. Their easiest choice is to select items randomly, giving you a hodgepodge of facts, or to follow the choices of one or two of their sources, giving you a barely disguised paraphrase. To steer them away from these two solutions and enforce some basic principles about the need for focus in writing, make clear that you expect them, within the broad area you have delineated, to carve out a manageable territory for themselves, to survey the land from a single watchtower, or to find a single vehicle in which to explore it. Otherwise many writers will try to cover the whole plain, and their work will lack both specificity and focus.

For example, a history teacher, during the study of modern Japan, asked students to read a novel that reflects that culture and then to "hand in a book report." He did not define the audience or the purpose, and he did not enlarge on the need for students to treat a limited aspect of the book. This is one of the papers he received:

Student Book Report on Junichiro Tanizaki's Diary of a Mad Old Man

The novel, <u>Diary of a Mad Old Man</u>, by Junichiro Tanizaki, is a portrait of an old man who does not have much longer to live. Tanizaki utilizes the diary form very effectively, telling a story that could have taken place anywhere. In the story, Tanizaki mixes not only humor, but also a certain amount of sadness.

Utsugi Tokusuke, who relates the story, is an old man in his mid-seventies. Tokusuke's body is beginning to fail; he has suffered a heart attack which has caused problems in his arms and feet. Despite his physical impairments, his mind is still capable of functioning normally.

[The paragraph continues with more plot summary. Then come three long paragaphs of continued plot summary, each centered on one of the novel's main characters. Next appear three short paragraphs: one on death in the novel, one on sexual attitudes in the novel, and one on Japanese medical practices as reflected in the novel. The concluding paragraph reads:]

In the novel Tanizaki has given a rather subtle picture of Tokyo and of a modern Japanese family. The combinations of new with old and western with Japanese makes the book insightful as well as interesting. However, the novel retains a universal flavor that is difficult to miss in reading.

The paper is a grab bag. The student has not decided whether his audience knows the plot of the book, and he has not sufficiently narrowed his topic. The first and last paragraphs reflect the paper's lack of focus; they are conglomerations of statements about the novel, none of which gives a proper clue to the paper's main theme. If the teacher, at the time of the assignment, had given more specific guidance, the student might have written a stronger paper. For example, you might define the audience for this assignment in either of these two ways:

You are writing this book report for someone who has read the novel and knows the plot but who needs help interpreting a particular aspect.

You are writing this book report for a fellow student who has not read the book and who wants to know whether it is worth reading to get insights into some aspects of modern Japanese culture.

In addition to defining the audience, you could help the student narrow the topic by saying not merely that students should "hand in a book report" but that the book report should have a specific focus. Then you should give some examples:

In three pages you can't possibly put down everything there is to say about this novel. So don't try! Nor should you write down a series of random observations about the book in an attempt to cover as much as possible and thereby convince me that you've read the book. Instead, you should pick one aspect of modern Japanese society and explain to me in depth how the novel reflects it. Assume that I have read the book but that I want to hear your interpretation of and insights into that one aspect. You might choose death in modern Japan or family relationships or old age or Western technology or religion or medical practices or any other area that interests you.

If you want a somewhat broader treatment you could say, or better yet write, to the students:

In the book report you should summarize the novelist's view of life in modern Japan. You will need to organize your summary around three or four main ideas. Don't summarize the plot, don't tell how interesting the book is, and don't include anything except your main topics, plus examples or explanations that support each main idea.

To make the point even clearer, you might hand out or put on the screen an unfocused book report like the one in the example. Then you can show the class how much mere plot summary there is, how the plot summary fails to direct itself toward any particular point, how the writer mentions many different topics in a series of skinny paragraphs, and how in the opening and closing paragraphs he tosses in still other topics that are completely unrelated to anything else developed in the paper—topics like the use of the diary form, the mixture of humor and sadness, or the "universal flavor" of the novel. You will probably have to tell and show your students that they must narrow and focus within a broad topic. For many, you'll also have to guide these processes throughout the planning and drafting stages.

A crucial task is to define, for yourself and for your students, how much focusing you expect. Does the instructor who composed the Warren Court question above expect a thorough history of the Warren Court or only selected facts? If the latter, which facts? Should the history section be unified with the influences? Should the influences be more prominent in the essay? Which influences does the instructor want covered? Will students do better by mentioning every influence they can think of or by selecting a few of the most important and developing them?

For the instructor, the answer to these questions depends on the goals of the assignment. If you want students to prove that they know all the influences, then make clear to them that comprehensive coverage is the most important value and that composing a tightly coherent argument of the most important influences is not to be their predominant concern. Rather, they should focus on constructing a set of subpoints for the essay that gives as much coherence as possible to their list of influences. You might help students by showing them how to group and order items for greatest coherence: proceeding from broad to narrow, most important to least important, or (the loosest organizational plan) simply telling the reader, "The first influence is. . . . The second influence is. . . ."

The following procedures may help your students generate ideas and focus their topics. Suggest these exercises as outside activities or structure them into your class time, your deadline list, or group activities.

Generating Topics from Reading

Students often do not know how to cross the bridge from what they read to a manageable topic. You can help by showing them how papers written in our field arise from what is already in print. Below is an all-purpose list that I used in my freshman composition text (*Writing* 55–57). You can compose one for your own situation.

Developing a Topic through Reading
A Student's Guide

Select a general topic area—the colonization of Algeria, for example— and just begin reading about it. As you read, look for unanswered questions, for positions you can take about some controversial aspect, for general statements you can apply to specific situations, and for techniques you can use to investigate a related topic. Below are some questions that may spur you and some suggestions for papers that may arise from the questions.

Question*	Possible Paper Ideas
What is being assumed (taken for granted) in this passage? Does your experience or the other material you have read lead you to accept or to question the assumptions? Why?	Question the writer's argument by pointing out unjustified assumptions. Analyze the assumptions underlying a particular argument, telling what they are and upon what basis they rest.

---

*Adapted from questions proposed by Richard L. Larson (*Writing* 8). Used by permission of the author. The publication was supported in part by the US Department of Education Grant Number G008001687 under Title III Strengthening Developing Institutions Program.

Question	Possible Paper Ideas
If what the passage says is true, what follows from the statements in the passage? Are you satisfied and comfortable with those implications? Why or why not? If not, does your judgment affect your evaluation of the passage?	Apply a general rule, theory, or principle to a particular individual or situation.
Does the passage assert a causal connection or a relationship between events and conditions? Is the asserted connection sound in its reasoning and evidence? (Common sense will often help.)	Question or support the causal connection or the relationship.
Does the passage contain terms that different people might define differently? Does the author define terms? Are the author's definitions compatible with your experience? With definitions of other writers on the same subject? If not, why not?	Define terms. Analyze the different ways terms are defined by various people in the field.
Does the passage assert a value judgment concerning an idea/object/incident? Are the criteria for such a judgment made clear? Are they fairly applied?	Question a value judgment. Assert and defend a value judgment. Analyze the various possible judgments.
What would you need in order to prove or confirm the statements made in the passage?	Question the proof and evidence for a statement. Collect and present proof or additional proof for a statement made or implied in the passage.
Does the passage assert a generalization (conclusion based upon evidence about individual instances)?	Question the evidence behind the generalization. Gather additional evidence to support a generalization.
In what sense does the passage or incident present a problem requiring or inviting someone to do something? How might you move toward solving it?	Analyze what causes the problem. Suggest solutions to the problem. Compare various solutions.
Does the passage place a person/object/event into a category or class? Is this classification acceptable to you? Why or why not? What follows from the classification? What is affected by it?	Suggest a new classification. Discuss the ways in which different people have classified this person/object/event.

Question	Possible Paper Ideas
Does the incident or passage call to mind any similar incidents or passages or assertions in your experience? How are these items similar? Different? What, if anything, do you learn from examining these similarities and differences?	Compare incidents or passages. Explore what you learned from examining similarities and differences.

Below are some examples of how students developed papers using the questions above.

A student reading arguments about raising the drinking age in his state realized that the arguers were assuming that making drinking illegal for young people actually prevented them from drinking. His own experience was that underage people easily and frequently acquire alcoholic beverages. The legal age laws merely change where and how they drink. He tracked down some studies about the impact of drinking-age laws on alcoholic consumption. His paper began by summarizing the arguments made by those who wanted to raise the drinking age. Then he pointed out the unwarranted assumption and presented the studies that call the assumption into question. He might have gone on to suggest a different course of action for reducing teenage alcoholism and drunk driving, or he could simply have let his paper question the assumption.

A student read a magazine article that showed that wage earners with incomes between $50,000 and $100,000 do not feel wealthy. They feel strapped for money and say they have difficulty meeting their bills. The student decided to investigate whether the same was true of college students. Using a version of the same questionnaire the magazine had used, he tested differences between college students who had more than $50 per week spending money (after room, board, tuition, and books) and those who had less.

A student read the words of an alcohol treatment center director who suggested a definition for measuring whether his program had been "successful." The article briefly mentioned that there were other ways of defining the "success" of alcohol treatment programs. The student decided to research various definitions of "success" currently used in the field of alcohol treatment.

In addition to giving students such a list, you can ask for written exercises that help them use information to focus a topic. For example, assign a particular reading and ask them to find one procedure they can apply to a question of their own. Or have them read the article, lay it aside, then free write for 20 minutes. Have them bring those writings to class, and take a few minutes to have them share ideas with a neighbor, or ask three students to volunteer a topic idea from their reading, and discuss its appropriateness. In such discussions of emerging topics, be careful not to reject the topic *area* when you only mean to say that the present version of the topic is not yet narrow enough or is otherwise flawed. The chosen topic may already have garnered some of the student's interest; if the topic area is at all promising, your goal is to have the student leave the class, not feeling that the idea was stupid, but more committed and interested and ready to do the work needed to get the topic into shape. The feeling that one's ideas are stupid is a common form of writer's block, and you don't want to contribute to it unwittingly.

Talking

A good way for students to clarify a thesis is to talk through an idea with friends, with a small discussion group that meets during the class hour or outside class, with you, or with a tutor. Sometimes you may want to schedule such talking; at others times you may simply want to encourage your students to arrange it on their own. A helpful source for them is the last half of Peter Elbow's *Writing without Teachers*, which gives suggestions to students about making teacherless discussion groups work for them as writers. Talking can sometimes be a solitary activity: many writers talk out their ideas to a wall or to the sky.

Free Writing

It is often helpful to a writer to blurt out ideas about a general topic. One can do this on tape and then listen to the tape or read a transcription of it. Or one can sit down with pen or typewriter and just write for a specific period, say, 45 minutes. The key to this exercise is to keep writing, suspend editorial judgment, forget spelling and punctuation, forget even the attempt to find the right word, and just let the ideas spill out as freely as possible. Naturally, most of what emerges will be rough, irrelevant, mushy, vague, sloppy, and inept. Within such a spurt of ideas, however, the writer tries to find the "center of gravity," the idea that is trying to come through. The writer asks, What am I really saying? One way to handle the spurt of free writing is to circle the three best ideas or underline the most interesting or the most worthwhile sentence. Sometimes that sentence or phrase is the long-sought thesis, or at least the basis for it. Sometimes the student may want to write freely again around one of the ideas that emerged in the original pages or tape. The advantage of free writing is that it gets ideas flowing and sometimes unlocks for the writer a wealth of images, ideas, or insights that might never have emerged in a more constricted planning form such as the list or the outline. Again, Elbow's book—the first half this time—is a good guide to free-writing techniques, as is his more recent *Writing with Power*.

Students may use free writing for research-based topics, not just personal topics. Midway in their research, have them write for 20 minutes about their topic, without looking at any notes. Frequently, a useful approach, clarification of meaning, or revelation about what they don't yet understand will emerge.

Finding Relations

Many kinds of thinking and writing, especially in the sciences and so-cial sciences, establish a relation between two items or phenomena. Faith Gil-roy, a psychologist at Loyola College in Maryland, offers this suggestion: Ask your students to select one thing that interests them, such as anorexia. Then, from their own observation or a bit of general reading, they select something else they think is related to the first—say, social class. Now they have a hypothe-sis that may serve as the basis for original research or for library reading. Mak-ing students write such a hypothesis before they go to the library reduces the "paraphrase one article I happen to find" approach students sometimes use for their library research. Having asked their own question, they are better able to integrate the articles that address it or to judge whether a particular study has answered their question precisely.

Using Lists

One useful guide to developing ideas is a list of the classical topoi, or ways of developing ideas, used by rhetoricians from Aristotle to the present. One ver-sion lists the means of developing ideas as description, narration, classifica-tion, comparison, contrast, analogy, cause-effect, partition, and enumeration. The writer can mentally review these possibilities, asking, "Can I develop my idea by analogy? By narration? By contrast?"

To see how such a list might work, let us imagine the student who has decided to write a paper against the use of marijuana. The paper is to be ad-dressed to college students. The writer, pondering how to develop the paper, goes mentally down the list:

DESCRIPTION: Maybe I could describe society as it would be if everyone used marijuana. Or I can describe some people who have messed themselves up by smoking pot.

NARRATION: I could tell the story of marijuana use in the United States or in other countries, or the story of the drug's effects on a specific town, school, or person.

CLASSIFICATION: I could classify marijuana as a mind-altering drug and appeal to people's feelings against having their minds tampered with.

COMPARISON: I could compare marijuana with alcohol, as many people do to justify it, but my comparison could show how many of the horrors that result from alcohol use also happen with marijuana.

CONTRAST: I could contrast the characteristics of users and nonusers in my school to show how marijuana causes students to drop out or lose con-trol of their lives. Or maybe I could contrast the life of one or more per-sons before and after they began heavy marijuana use.

ANALOGY: I might draw an analogy between the story of Snow White and the use of pot: in both cases a young person is "put to sleep" and withdraws from the normal process of maturing, falling in love, and taking a place in the adult world. Or maybe Peter Pan—the age-old fear of assuming adult responsibilities and the desire to live in a fantasy land of the senses.

CAUSE-EFFECT: I could analyze the causes, as far as they are known, for pot use among Americans today. I could also describe the effects of heavy use on social relationships, schoolwork, and other responsibilities and on a person's health (genetic damage, etc.).

PARTITION: I could divide marijuana users into groups or marijuana use into its various aspects.

ENUMERATION: I could describe for the reader several persons I've known who have been harmed by marijuana.

The above list is based on rhetorical modes; students can also mentally review other kinds of lists. Ponder the various perspectives on an issue that guide exploration in your discipline and see whether you can formulate from them a useful idea-generating device for students. One formulation makes use of the various ways in which an investigator can view an object or a system. Drawing on these perspectives and on a seminal heuristic by Young, Becker, and Pike (126–29), W. Ross Winterowd has developed a simple list of five aspects for students to consider as they develop ideas about a topic (*Contemporary Writer* 98–101). For example, in planning a paper on seventeenth-century American witchcraft, the writer can view it in any of these ways:

1. *As an isolated, static entity.* Who were the people involved? What happened? What features characterized the phenomenon?
2. *As one among many of a class.* How does it differ from, or resemble, witchcraft in other cultures or eras? How is it different from or similar to other contemporary social movements?
3. *As part of a larger system.* How does it fit seventeenth-century American culture?
4. *As a process rather than as a static entity.* How did it come into being? How has it changed? What are its modern forms?
5. *As a system rather than as an entity.* What were the various dynamics and influences operating in the witch trials?

You or your students can compose such a list of perspectives, based either on patterns of thought in your discipline or on approaches relevant to the assignment you've given. Asking students to write a review of literature, for example, you could give them a list of the three most common patterns such reviews follow in the sciences and social sciences:

1. Knowledge about this topic has built incrementally: Jones found A, Smith added to our knowledge by the discovery of B, and so on.
2. The prevailing view is A, but objections or counterarguments are B, C, and D.
3. We used to believe A, but new knowledge has revealed B.

Instruct students, as they read the literature, to ask whether any of these patterns, or variations of them, fits the case.

Posing Questions

In addition to the list of perspectives, there can be a list of questions. A well-known example is the journalist's five *W*'s—who? what? where? when? why? These questions are helpful in many kinds of writing besides newspaper stories, and you might want to suggest that your students use the five *W*'s, or some variation of them, as an idea starter.

It is possible to compose a list of pertinent questions for any assignment in any discipline, and you may want to hand one out or have your students, in small groups, compile one. Here, for example, is a list of questions to prod the thoughts of a person who is reviewing or analyzing fiction. I have adapted it from a similar list compiled from a number of sources and distributed by the library of Towson State University in Towson, Maryland.

How to Write a Book Review (Fiction)
A Student's Guide

The major purpose of a book review may be simply to create interest in the book, but for most academic assignments its purpose is to report on the nature and quality of the content.

It is important to know very clearly who the audience is for your book review and what your purpose is in writing for that audience. Some questions to ask yourself are: Who is my reader? How much, if anything, does the reader already know about the book, or the topic the book deals with? Since I cannot tell everything about the book, what are the key ideas I want to get across? Do I want my reader to be persuaded that the book has some major strengths or weaknesses? Do I want my reader to understand better some aspects of the book—its structure, its literary devices, its approach to the problem, its underlying assumptions?

Once your audience and purpose are clear, the list of questions below will help you analyze most works. A good review usually focuses on one of these questions or a coherent group of them.

I. Questions about characters
    A. Has the author indicated the personality of the main character by what he or she says (and thinks)? By what the character does? By what other characters say about him or her? By what the author says about him or her, speaking as either the storyteller or an observer of the action?
    B. Describe a major character (attitudes, behavior) at the beginning of the book. What happens to the character and why? How does the ex-

perience affect the character? What new attitudes and behavior does he or she show at the end? What has the author shown about his or her own values by showing this change of character?

C. What two major characters are contrasted? What roles do they play in the story?

D. What two major characters or groups are in conflict? Why? How does each respond? Does the outcome of the conflict seem true to your own sense of human experience, or is the outcome merely exciting and surprising?

E. Which characters seem believable and which seem unbelievable?

II. Questions about plot

A. Is the plot fresh or commonplace or stereotyped?

B. How does the author complicate the plot and add suspense? By adding surprising incidents? By withholding information? By depending on characters to create incidents? Give examples. What are the means by which the author works out and solves the complications of plot?

III. Questions about idea content

A. What is the view of life (the message or the moral experience)? How does the methodology illustrate or support this view? How convincing is the author? Is the message important, bad, helpful, dangerous, or what?

B. How does the idea affect the style and structure of the work?

C. What facts or ideas specially informed you? How are the facts or ideas presented? Why does the new knowledge impress you? Does it change any ideas you previously had? Is the knowledge useful?

IV. Questions for comparing the book with another

A. How are the two books similar?

B. Give details and examples of the similarities in plot, characters, and outcome.

C. Which of the two books seems more successful in handling the matters on which the two are similar?

V. Questions for collections of short stories

A. What is similar in the contents of the stories? (Stories by the same author are likely to have similar characters or situations. Stories by different authors are usually collected by editors around a particular subject—for example, baseball stories.)

B. Discuss two or more stories that best demonstrate the similarity.

C. What does the similarity show about the author's view of people or life or about his or her way of entertaining readers?

Considering Patterns of Thought

In addition to lists of rhetorical techniques or perspectives and lists of questions, the prescribed modes of thought in a discipline or situation can act as a list, to help produce ideas. Richard Larson, for example, suggests that writers, to generate material for a paper, go through the steps of problem solving used by management. The writer begins by stating the topic as a problem, to find the focus of the paper. Below is an indication of how the question "What is the problem?" can lead the student toward a specific focus.

SITUATION: The student wants to write about abortion but does not know how to formulate a thesis sentence or find a focus.

TEACHER SUGGESTION: *"Try to formulate a problem, either as a question or as a statement."*

RESULT: Student formulates several statements of the problem, any of which could serve as a basis for a paper.
Problem: We need to avoid murder while at the same time preventing the abuse and neglect of unwanted babies.
Problem: Should we pass a constitutional amendment prohibiting abortion?
Problem: At what point is a fetus a human being whom society must protect from being killed?

Having defined the problem, the student follows these steps:

1. Define the problem: formulate a sentence that exactly states the problem to be attacked.
2. Determine why the problem is indeed a problem.
3. Enumerate the goals that must be served by whatever action is taken.
4. Where possible, determine which goals have the highest priority.
5. Find the procedure that might attain the stated goals.
6. Predict the consequences of each possible action.
7. Weigh the consequences: which are likely to best achieve the stated goals?
8. Evaluate the choice that seems superior, and plan how to reduce its negative consequences. (Larson, "Problem Solving")

Just as management's problem-solving methods can help to generate matter and sequence for a paper, so too can the methods used in other disciplines. One could also explore the steps used in developing a drawing, writing a piece of music, diagnosing illness, locating the cause of mechanical breakdown, or establishing legal guilt or innocence. Perhaps such procedures could serve in some situations as heuristics—idea starters. There is much to be done in integrating the methodology of various disciplines with the writing process, and you may be able to do some of it in your own discipline and your own classroom.

Using Watchwords

Watchwords or mottoes can serve the student as periscopes to sight the wealth of ways to develop an idea. Some useful watchwords:

1. *Trace your path*. You have arrived at a certain conclusion (the train was noisy; the plan won't work). You can't expect readers to join you on that mountaintop of certainty unless you lead them up the slope by the same path you took. How did you conclude that the train was noisy? You heard the clack of the wheels, the rattle of trays, the hubbub of conversation, the cries of the porters, the wailing of a baby. Let the reader hear them, too, in vivid detail.

Or, how did you come to the conclusion that the plan won't work? Trace for the reader, step by step, the evidence you observed or read and the line of reasoning you followed.

2. *Show, don't tell*. Don't just tell me that Americans waste water; draw me a word picture so that I can see and experience it. Show me the teenager standing at the sink, letting the faucet run full force while he leisurely brushes his teeth. Compare the number of buckets the American family's daily water supply would fill with the number used daily by Iranians or Tanzanians.

Taking Only Part of a Topic

Sometimes students can successfully limit a topic by extracting one subtopic or statement from a draft or plan and making that the whole paper. For example, the student writing the book report could have been encouraged to select just one of the many aspects of the novel he mentions. The advice to cut one beast from your herd can be applied on a classwide basis. Ask the students to arrive one day, with an outline of their planned papers. Have peers read the outlines, circle two subpoints or statements they think could be the basis for the entire paper, and write three questions they would like to see answered as the writer delves into the newly limited topic. Many writers will rightly decide to stay with their original topic, but some will be helped by at least considering the narrower options.

Resolving a Contradiction

Taking only a part of a topic may prematurely close off investigation, as Richard M. Coe convincingly argues. He suggests that in some situations it is better for the writer to keep the broader topic but to look for a contradiction in it. The contradiction should not be a traditional debating topic such as "University Education—For the Many or for the Few?" Rather, the student should look for an apparent contradiction between two statements. For example, a particular story of Hemingway's seems inconsistent, yet Hemingway is a skilled and experienced writer. The thesis comes when the writer resolves the apparent contradiction—in this case, by discovering that the story makes sense if read as an imagist poem.

Coe sets contradictory statements next to each other in boxes; suggest that your students, as they observe, read about, and think about their topic, find pairs of seemingly contradictory assumptions or statements, place them in boxes next to each other, then seek to resolve the contradiction. Here is Coe's example:

Late-20th-century industrial societies demand higher levels of literacy from workers, citizens, and consumers than were demanded at any previous times in human history.	Extremely large numbers of 19th-century English artisans and mechanics read scientific and political texts which would cause difficulties for many of today's college graduates.

An apparent contradiction between two statements may be dissolved by disproving one of the statements: perhaps . . . late-20th-century industrial societies do not demand such high levels of literacy as is ordinarily believed. A genuine contradiction is resolved by generating a statement which combines the two originals and demonstrates the extent or sense in which each contains some truth. It is this sort of contradiction which constitutes the sort of "problem" which can focus a piece of writing. (275)

Writing a Prospectus

To help students achieve clear focus, have them prepare a planning tool such as a prospectus, hypothesis, or thesis sentence (perhaps with an accompanying outline or a list of subtopics) that you or an assistant or a group of classmates will check. On the facing page, for example, is a prospectus form developed by Mildred Steele of Central College in Iowa.

Any format that asks students to state the topic they will cover, the thesis they will develop, or the questions they will answer can be a useful prospectus. You can also use the prospectus assignment sheet, as Steele does, to set deadlines that enforce early starts and to give additional advice and warnings about the writing task ahead. You can return the prospectuses with written suggestions, use them as the basis for a student-teacher conference, or ask students to share them with classmates and to respond, make suggestions, and support one another's efforts.

Stating a Thesis

A thesis sentence often starts as a list of random thoughts about a subject, gathered from pondering, reading, talking, or observing. Many students need to be encouraged to list ideas more fully and stay longer at the listing stage in order to generate a greater wealth of possible focuses for the paper. With a

Prospectus for a Research Paper

Your name _____

(Please bring two copies of this prospectus, filled out, to our conference to be held _____.)

The topic I propose for my research paper is: _____

Five questions that I hope my paper can answer are:	Subject headings to check:
1.	_____
2.	_____
3.	_____
4.	_____
5.	

I have examined each of the five sources listed below, and I have found that they contain material that may help me with this topic. At least one of them has been published in the past year and one-half. I have listed them in bibliographic form, following Lester, *WRP*, ch. 6.

1.
2.
3.
4.
5.

I have written a research paper: ____ many times ____ seldom ____ never.

SOME GENERAL SUGGESTIONS:

The above topic, after we have talked it over, is still somewhat tentative, in that you are free to narrow it further or shift its emphasis on the basis of your findings. I will, however, discourage you from changing to a completely different topic, but if you come up against some kind of roadblock, come in and talk it over with me. Otherwise I will assume that you are progressing in your background reading, notetaking, and writing on this topic. Consult Lester, *Writing Research Papers*, as your guide.

As mentioned above, some of your sources must be recent, even if you base much of your work on a fine older source. Many new developments and findings take place each year, and a paper based on outdated information is usually a waste of time for all concerned.

The source material you discover in your search, carefully weighed in terms of its validity and usefulness to you in developing your topic, forms the foundation for your paper. As you write, you must give credit for all material that is not your own, unless it is general information. This includes not only direct quotations, but the ideas, facts, and statistics from other persons. I should not be in doubt, anywhere in your paper, as to which ideas are your own and which are from others. In most cases this means that you need to introduce your documented material to your reader, showing its significance and alerting your reader to the key point of the passage. Envision your audience as interested persons in our class.

Give your research paper the time and attention it deserves. It may grow into an absorbing interest for you, perhaps leading to publication eventually. You may add something to the world's knowledge.

list in hand, the student begins to ask, Which ideas might make a good thesis for the paper? Which concepts can I combine? Which items are irrelevant to the topic? Which ideas are subsidiary to other points? Suggest that the student write ideas, evidence, reading notes, or questions on cards; arrange the cards in piles; then ask which of the piles can form the basis for a paper, or what central statement will cover several or all of the piles, or what the student would now say, after two hours of sorting the cards, if someone walked into the room and asked, "What do you want to say about all that material?"

If you require students to hand in thesis sentences, you will probably want to offer some guidelines such as these:

The thesis sentence is not necessarily the first sentence in the paper. The student asked to submit a thesis sentence sometimes pictures it as beginning the paper and produces a sentence that is arresting as an introduction but not adequate as a focal point for the paper. Emphasize that the thesis sentence is a planning tool and may not appear in the paper. Its function is to guide the writer's work.

The thesis sentence should be a complete sentence. A single word or a phrase or a question is not wrong; it is simply an earlier, incomplete stage. The student must try to write a complete sentence that precisely summarizes what the paper will say.

The thesis sentence should have a workhorse verb. Urge students not to begin thesis sentences with comments like "this paper will discuss." Rather, the subject of the sentence should be the subject of the paper, and the verb should reflect what the writer will say about that subject. Urge also that writers avoid predicates like "is very interesting" or "is controversial" (unless the existence of controversy is the true point of the paper) or "has many results." Such phrases often occur in the working stages, but the writer should search for verbs that more precisely summarize the points of interest, the content of the controversy, or the particular results. (These guidelines are discussed for students in my *Writing* 59–67.)

Other planning devices are the hypothesis, the conclusion, and the statement of a problem. Some will be more appropriate than others to your particular discipline or to the individual assignment you are giving.

Helping Students Gather and Integrate Library Information

Locating Sources of Information

When students must depend on library research for their writing, decide whether you want to teach library search method or whether you are only concerned with the students' ability to evaluate and use information. If the latter, you can put relevant books and articles on reserve or hand students a select bibliography from which they may work.

Your teaching of search skills will vary, depending on whether you are content to have students rely on the *Reader's Guide to Periodical Literature* and a random selection of books listed in the card catalog or whether you want them to use other types of sources. If the former, find out, by a show of hands, how many of your students know how to use the *Reader's Guide*. For those who don't, you or your librarian can arrange an instruction session.

A student may know how to use the *Reader's Guide* and card catalog but not understand their place in the larger body of indexing guides. Quiz your students on the following:

1. The card catalog does not list periodical articles.
2. The *Reader's Guide* lists only popular magazines; many other similar indexes cover professional journals.
3. The *Reader's Guide* is organized by year. Searchers need to cover all the relevant annual volumes.
4. On-line computerized indexes allow rapid searches under multiple headings.
5. Most articles in popular magazines draw on more technical sources such as government statistics, professional journals, and books. These, too, are in the library and are indexed. Some searches necessitate working back to these primary sources.

Another skill students often don't possess is identifying appropriate headings—a complex activity that we too frequently take for granted. You can help by devoting a few minutes in class. Have one student announce a paper topic. Then ask the class to brainstorm a blackboard list of possible headings. Make sure they know the following:

1. How to go up to more abstract or down to more particular headings.
2. How to find subheadings under larger headings.
3. How to identify headings in all appropriate categories—not only subject headings but author, citation, agency, and so on—as relevant for their task.
4. What to do if one heading yields no sources, or fewer sources than one would expect. The material is probably filed under another heading. One can:
   a. brainstorm other headings and try them until one stumbles on the right one;
   b. consult tracings: find one good source, locate its author card in the card catalog, consult the tracings at the bottom of that card for other headings where that source is filed, and use the headings to find other sources;
   c. use a list of headings.

This last resource, the list of headings, requires fuller treatment. For the card catalog, use the *Library of Congress Subject Headings*, which most libraries keep near the card catalog. That source will likely contain the words the student is thinking of and tell the student where to look in the card cata-

log. For example, a student looking under "film" will find out that the card catalog files most film material under "motion picture." Even without knowing what
the "x" and "sa" marks mean, students can gain from the *LC Subject Headings*
a list of words, some of which they will find in the card catalog.

For journals, the list of headings may appear within one volume of an
index, or as a separate "thesaurus" to the index, or there may be no guide to
headings (the *Reader's Guide* has no guide to headings). Heavy cross-referencing
in the index itself, as with the *Reader's Guide*, may be an adequate substitute
for a thesaurus. Your library may have a staff member who is skilled and experienced at teaching students how to use periodical indexes and a thesaurus.
If not, you can develop a presentation yourself. In years of experimentation
with Robin Martin at the Central College Library in Pella, Iowa, and Geraldine Gray of the Loyola–Notre Dame Library in Baltimore, I have found the
following sequence useful for a lesson on using an index to professional peri-
odicals and a thesaurus.

1. *Gather students in the library*, if possible.

2. *Brainstorm*. Pose a paper topic, with audience and purpose. Define
questions and goals for the information search. Ask students to brainstorm
headings they might use to locate the information. Write these on the board.

3. *Use the thesaurus*. Hand out volumes of the thesaurus, and ask students to identify which of the brainstormed headings are actual headings in the
index.

4. *Use the periodical index*. Hand out volumes of the periodical index,
and ask students to look up relevant headings. Teach them how to interpret the
citations and how to find the list of full names of the journals indexed.

5. *Use the abstracts*. Hand out volumes that contain abstracts, or show
students how to find key words or an abstract of the article they have located.

6. *Use the periodical holdings list*. Show students one page of the library's
list of periodical holdings, and be sure they know how to find out whether the
library carries the periodical issue they need and where to find the periodical
on the shelves.

7. *Compile bibliography, notes, and log*. As homework, have students
define a topic or question and use the index to compile a set of three notecards,
each carrying the name of one relevant article (you can ask for proper citation
form if you wish) and a sentence or two summarizing that article, taken from
the abstract or the key words. Students should indicate how they think that
article will help them in the paper. Have them locate one of the articles and bring
in a photocopy of its title page. Have them keep a log, telling how they searched.

8. *Demonstrate a computer search*. Once the students have done a paper
search, you can demonstrate a computer search. Geraldine Gray, librarian at
the Loyola–Notre Dame library in Baltimore, sets up a TV monitor that all students can see, then gets on the computer and does the search, talking her way
through the decisions and trials and allowing students to see how the wise investigator guides the librarian who is doing the search. (John Lawrence's *Electronic Scholar* contains a fine discussion of how to guide a librarian's search

[92–109].) Finally, make a computer printout of the 10 to 20 mo~~~
sources and photocopy that printout for each student, so studer~
brary with the results of the search.

The steps above incorporate our long, hard experienc~~~ ~~~ students have *hands-on* experience with reference mater~~~ ~~~u say will
be lost. We have also found that teaching compu~~~ ~~~ques works
best after the students have done a paper search, so~~~ ~~~understand the
work that the computer performs.

Library search may be taught as a separate unit, e~~~ding when each student submits an annotated bibliography of the sources he or she thinks would
be the strongest. Grade these bibliographies, photocopy them, and put them
on reserve as a master list, so that as the actual reading begins, students start
from the same list of sources, even if their own search was ineffective. By this
method, mistakes in initial library search result in one poor grade but do not
ripple out to the final paper, though, of course, in most good papers, some
sources will be located during the later stages, so the adequacy of the student's
later search strategies will influence the final work.

Citing Sources

You'll probably have to explain to students both what they should cite
and what form they should use.

It is sometimes wise to give the whole class, orally or in writing, all your
advice on citation. Here, for example, is a first-day handout adapted from one
developed by John Breihan for his Loyola College history students. Feel free to
copy or adapt it for your own students.

Using and Citing Sources
A Student's Guide

1. Whenever you use another writer's exact words, or state another
author's idea in your own words, or use facts from a source (unless these facts
are so common as to be part of the generally accepted store of knowledge in
the field), you must give credit to that other author and tell the reader where
the information or idea came from. Note that I said you must give credit even
when you use your own words. This may be contrary to some habits you've
developed in high school, but it is very important, because not to do so is plagiarism, which has serious consequences. It is a kind of stealing—stealing someone's idea or the data someone has collected, without giving that person credit.

2. In the humanities, the basic forms used to give credit to another author and to tell the reader where the information came from are parenthetical
references in the text and a reference list or list of works cited at the end. (In
the other disciplines somewhat different forms are used, so check with your
instructor.)

3. It is easy to get "captured" by another author's words or organization and to end up using too much quoted material, or too many ideas from other authors, in a paper. To avoid this problem, you must establish your own purpose, your own plan or outline, and your own point of view. You must also be sure about who your audience is. Then search for the facts or ideas you need to support your own goals. That way, material from sources will *fit into* your own plan, not *be* your plan. If you need more help doing initial reading and establishing a plan for your paper, consult Barbara Walvoord, *Writing: Strategies for All Disciplines*, which is available in the college bookstore. It's used in freshman composition at this school, so you may be able to borrow a copy from another student. It's also on reserve at the library.

4. When sources contradict one another, or when there are several places from which to get information or ideas, you must evaluate the worth of the sources and use the most reliable. Consider such factors as the date of the material, the reliability of the person or journal or newspaper reporting it, the likelihood of a person's being knowledgeable about, or present at, a reported event, and so on. The least reliable sources are encyclopedias, secondary compilations of documents, quotations of quotations, prefaces, introductory surveys, or chapters in broad, general texts. More reliable, as a rule, are original documents, firsthand accounts, the work of original researchers or thinkers or compilers who first printed an idea or a research report or a statistical table, and people who are experts in a specialized field, not writers of some compilation such as an introductory textbook or a popular magazine account. Common sense will often help you decide which sources to use (whom would you call as witness in a trial—the person who saw the accident or the person who only heard about it?). If you need help evaluating the worth of a book, check the *Book Review Digest* to see how others have viewed it. If you need help selecting from several possible sources, see whether there is a recently published selected bibliography. The word "selected" tells you that someone who knows the field more or less well has selected from many possible books and articles the ones he or she considers best for a certain purpose (make sure you know what that purpose was; if it was different from yours, that person's choice may not be useful to you). If you are unsure how to evalute the worth of a written source, ask for help at the desk of the reference librarian. That desk is near the reference section; it has a sign saying "Please disturb." The librarians mean it: don't be afraid to ask for help.

5. Many students quote too much. The guide is this: use a direct quotation only when the precise words of the author are needed to justify your interpretation, or when those words are too exquisite to be missed. Avoid long, dull quotations. Consider paraphrasing (saying in your own words) most of a long passage, even if you do want to quote some of it.

6. When you use material from a source, whether you quote it directly or not, you must use a citation. If you need help with form, consult Walvoord's book, cited above. Walvoord covers both MLA and APA forms. For this course, use MLA.

7. When you quote material directly, you have an additional responsibility besides the citation. If the quotation is shorter than four lines, use quotation marks and just include it right in your paragraph, making sure that it fits in smoothly. Remember to include both sets of quotation marks, at the beginning and at the end of the quote. If it is longer than four lines, then use no quotation marks. Instead, indent the whole thing 10 spaces (but double-space). The indentation serves instead of quotation marks to tell the reader that the passage is quoted and to make it easier for the reader to identify and read long quotations. If you need more help with this aspect, consult Walvoord.

Some students need practice in recognizing differences among direct quotation, indirect quotation, and paraphrase. Here are some common patterns (a citation would be required with each of these sentences):

- He said, "My investigations have revealed that the bureau is a thicket of deceit."
- He said that his investigations had revealed the bureau to be "a thicket of deceit."
- He said that his investigations had revealed widespread dishonesty in the bureau.
- There is widespread dishonesty in the bureau, reports Maxwell.

Many texts, including my *Writing* (398–407), give explanation and drill in punctuating all kinds of quotation and paraphrase. Or you can give students a short passage from a research source, as well as the sentences above to serve as models, and you can ask them to compose sentences quoting and paraphrasing the passage in different ways.

To help students learn to apply the guidelines for quotation and citation, hand them a short article from a professional journal or a student paper from a previous semester, with the quotation marks and citation marks removed. Ask them to put in the quotation marks and to indicate with an *x* where a citation (footnote number or parenthical reference) should be placed. You can correct these exercises quickly by yourself or have student peers correct them during class time.

Your students may have been exposed to at least one documenting system before they came to you. Since in many high schools and colleges English teachers are charged with teaching documentation, they teach the system of their discipline—the Modern Language Association (MLA) style. In 1984, the MLA changed significantly, moving from a system of documentation in notes to a parenthetical mode of citation that uses author and sometimes title or page numbers in the text and an alphabetized list of works cited at the end:

OLD: . . . all in one."[3]
NEW: . . . all in one" (Brown 45–46). [Brown's title would be cited only if other works by Brown were included in the works cited list.]

Since the change is so recent, your students may have been exposed to the old or the new MLA style. They're likely to believe that whatever form they have been taught is the only form and to have little notion about how or why citation styles develop. Thus when you teach students the form of citation used in your discipline, explain to them what citations are for, how there came to be various forms of citation, and what elements are common to all forms (abbreviated information in the text so as not to interrupt the flow of reading, plus a final list that gives author, title, and publication information, so readers can locate the source). My own text (*Writing* 407–09) contains such an explanation; so do some (not all) other composition texts and handbooks.

When you refer students to a citation manual, you may need to do two things: impress on them the importance of following the manual exactly and teach them how to use it. Punctuation marks within a citation seem both small and dizzying; students are apt to think that a reasonable approximation to the form is good enough. The organization of citation manuals, too, can seem impenetrable to the uninitiated.

You can build citation skills by giving students copies of several title pages and copyright pages and having them use the manual to put the information into correct citations. You may find that students need help finding the right information on title pages and copyright pages. For example, a copyright page often contains separate dates for various printings and editions—which should the student use as the date of publication? Students can bring their citations to class for checking in pairs or for collection by you. You could also have students bring their copies of the manual to class and take 20 minutes to do a citation—that way, you'll know that everyone is working independently, and you, or knowledgeable classmates, can help those who have trouble.

You can present, in lecture form or through a printed text, the guidelines used in your field to evaluate sources and information. To help students learn those judgments, give them a quick exercise either in five minutes of class time or at home, modeled on the exercise below but using appropriate sources for your assignment. Then take 10 minutes in class to have students explain their choices. (This and similar exercises appear in my *Writing* 94–95.)

Evaluating Information
An Exercise for Students

For the situation below, discuss the strengths and weaknesses of each of the sources. For each topic, list the three other types of sources you would most like to have: for example, "a textbook chapter published since 1984" or "a popular news magazine's summary of research, published since 1984."

Situation	Sources
For a science term paper you explore the evidence that links dietary cholesterol to heart disease.	Chapter of a 1979 textbook 1983 *Newsweek* article 1980 scientific journal reporting a research study on rats 1985 scientific journal article reporting a scientific research study on how cholesterol works in the body 1985 article in *Good Housekeeping,* summarizing research on the topic 1985 *Reader's Digest* summary of the *Good Housekeeping* article

---

Preventing Plagiarism

Written and oral warnings about plagiarism ought to be presented to every class—especially to freshman, who often don't understand what constitutes plagiarism and may have been taught in high school that copying or paraphrasing information from the encyclopedia without acknowledgment was accepted practice. But rather than limit yourself to warnings about copying, teach students how to build a paper that has its own focus and audience—then they won't need to rely on someone else's words or organization. Have a student state a thesis, then list information from three sources that will support that thesis. I think this practice works better than simply telling them they must use three sources in their paper—an injunction that often leads students to paste together plagiarized material from three books.

You can catch overreliance on sources in the draft stage by having someone (yourself, a classmate, or the writer) read the student's first paragraph and the first sentence of each succeeding paragraph and then try to state the paper's thesis and subpoints. Comment on whether they seem coherent and appropriate to this situation and audience. Next, the reader should turn to the reference list or endnote page to see whether varied references are interspersed. Those two activities are common to instructors or scholars first reading a paper; when students see their paper being read that way, they learn to write for that reader and to check those aspects for themselves.

Taking Notes

Perhaps the first question about notes is whether the student will take any. I like to treat the "no note" paper as a deliberate choice on the writer's part. In fact, students may competently handle some short papers, with few sources, by spreading the books and articles out on the floor around the typewriter and writing the paper directly from them. There are significant disadvantages in such a method, however, especially for longer or more complex papers. In a short writing exercise, you could ask your students to discuss the disadvantages.

To guide the use of notes, introduce the concept of the "middle ground": notes, field notebooks, lab notebooks, tapes of interviews, graphs, tables— any mode of recording information between its original source and its integration into the paper. Ask your students what the middle ground does— organizes, stores, makes accessible, selects. What sorts of middle ground are appropriate for your assignment? Explain how you or other experienced writers would organize the middle ground for this assignment—note cards? notebook? If so, what format? What headings? On a given day, take five class minutes and ask students to share with a partner the ways they've found to organize their middle ground.

Some instructors ask to see notes or other records during the writing process. If you collect notes and take them home, you can judge some aspects of the student's work, but the task is time-consuming, and the handwriting may be difficult. Further, since each student's mode of note taking and organizing information is legitimately individual, you never know whether you're interfering with an effective personal method in favor of your own. If you have students bring their notes to a conference with you, even a five-to-ten-minute conference, you can engage the student in planning and discussion rather than put yourself in the difficult position of "correcting" notes.

An alternative way to help students with note-taking skills is to give them one or two reading selections, together with a hypothetical topic, audience, and purpose. Have them write the notes they would take from that reading for that topic. Since they've all faced the same task, you can teach through discussion and comparison. Take just a few minutes in class to have students compare and discuss their notes, or collect all the notes and selected representative approaches to discuss in class.

Helping Students with Interviews

Part of helping students search productively for information is to remind them about interviewing as an option. Many papers constricted to library research would benefit from the up-to-date, practical information provided by an interview; many student searches could be more efficient and more productive if the student interviewed someone who could help guide the search.

In the planning stages of a paper, ask students to think of someone they know or have learned about who might provide useful information. What information could this person best contribute? When should the person be approached? What, specifically, should be the request? If students write such plans as part of their early reports to you, they are more likely to follow through on interviews.

To encourage students, remind them that most people love to talk about what they know or can do. Researcher Lee Odell, who studies the writing processes of people in agencies and businesses, might have one of the hardest interviewing jobs—he needs interviews of considerable length, over a period of time; he needs to watch what people do; and he needs both samples of, and information about, that most sensitive of artifacts, a person's writing. Yet he says that nearly all the people he approaches feel gratified by his interest in them and gladly cooperate. You can tell your students his story or a similar one.

One useful guide to give your students is to differentiate between the exploratory and the in-depth interview and encourage students to set appropriate goals and procedures for each. The exploratory interview might be the phone call to the state police to ask whether they have statistics concerning seat-belt-related accidents in the state, or the discussion with a local historian to ask guidance in locating informaton about early railroad lines. The in-depth interview probes a person's knowledge more extensively and in greater detail.

My text, *Writing*, gives students strategies for both types of interview (122–27). It includes suggestions for preparing interview questions and conducting and recording the interview. Its guide to preparing interview questions is included below. You may use or adapt it for your own students.

Preparing Interview Questions
A Student's Guide

1. Be sure the questions are clearly phrased. Ask someone else to read them as a check.

2. Avoid questions to which the respondent can merely answer "yes" or "no."

3. Phrase questions so that the respondent is genuinely free to answer in his or her own way. For example, avoid questions that begin, "Don't you think. . . ."

4. Avoid questions that are so vague the person may not know how to respond, or may respond in terms too vague for you to use. For example, when you are interviewing a mountain climber, the question, "Was it difficult?" is a poor one because the person could answer simply, "Yes." You could ask, "What were the difficulties?" That would probably bring a list of problems, perhaps in random order. If you wanted to ferret out the most important difficulties, you could ask, "What were the three most difficult aspects of the climb?" Ask questions in such a way that your respondent is making the judgments and evaluations you need for your writing.

5. Don't ask things you can find out for yourself. Do some homework. Don't waste the time of an official of the E.E.O.C., for example, by asking what those letters stand for. You can easily find that out from your library, as well as other background facts about the agency. Interview time should be used for other questions. When you arrange the interview, ask whether the person wants to suggest some things for you to read ahead of time. (*Writing* 123–24)

Depending on how mature and reliable your students are, you may want to remind them of appropriate behavior, so they do not embarrass themselves, you, or the college. Hand them a check sheet about setting up interviews, introducing themselves and their goals, dressing in a businesslike way, being on time, staying within the designated hour, asking permission to record, letting the interviewee do most of the talking, and writing a note of thanks.

You may want to conduct a model interview, with a volunteer visitor, before the entire class, or have students role-play interviews with you or each other.

Some students will have to be told that interviews must be cited, just as books must, and that citation forms are included in your discipline's style manual.

Helping Students with Observation and Experiment

When all or part of the student's writing depends on observation or experiment rather than on library research or interviews, students need additional information-gathering skills. These skills are the very stuff of your discipline, and often you spend the whole semester teaching them—how to formulate a hypothesis, set up an experiment, take water samples from a river, use an electron microscope, gather primary historical sources, analyze the architecture of a building, and so on.

Since such procedures vary greatly by discipline and since most instructors and texts give students a great deal of information about discipline-specific research procedures, this discussion merely states two general guidelines that may be helpful: guide the process, and use writing to shape the investigation.

Guiding the process of research uses the same basic methods as, and is closely integrated with, guiding other aspects of the writing process. The case studies in chapter 5 show instructors in a number of disciplines guiding their students' observation and experiment. Particularly, see the studies on Susan Robison and Virginia Johnson Gazzam.

Writing can help the student experimenter or observer clarify observations, plan further procedures, and shape meaning. As you teach procedures, have students write for five minutes in class about how they responded to the learning experience or how your demonstration might better help them. Or have them write instructions to a peer who missed class. Use writing to help students understand the larger context: for example, after explaining the use of a piece of equipment, zoom them back out to the larger view by having them write about what the instrument's main purpose is and how it can be used to advance knowledge in your field.

As students carry on research for a paper, have them report to each other or to you on their procedures; have them summarize in a paragraph where they are and, in another paragraph, plan their next steps. In addition to the factual elements of a lab or field notebook, encourage them to speculate more broadly about what they're discovering, to record feelings, and to write down "how I would have done the experiment if I'd known what I know now." Such speculations increase student involvement, encourage the broader view, give rise to new writing ideas, and deepen the discussion of the research in written reports.

Helping Students with Reasoning, Evidence, and Organization

In addition to coaching on any single paper, you can promote learning activities that increase student's organizing and reasoning skills. Below are several suggestions.

1. *Present lecture information as though it were a paper.* For example, in a literature class discussion of *King Lear*, the instructor wants students to understand the richness of sight and blindness imagery. The instructor might say, "This could be a good paper topic, couldn't it?" Then write the topic on the board, "Images of Sight and Blindness in *King Lear*," and ask students to contribute to a blackboard list of the points that might compose a paper on the topic. From the random list, students could discuss possible sequences for the points and evidence for each. At the end, remind them that any explications of literature can be developed in that same way—a random list of points and evidence, then decisions about selection and arrangement.

2. *Have students write plans.* When you want students to cover a topic by outside reading, have them write a planning form. For example, a business professor who has no time to cover the unit on production wants students to read the material on their own and to write about it as a way of learning it more thoroughly. One type of written assignment that fulfills these purposes, as well as helping students with the strategies they need in developing papers, is the planning form—a list of five paper topics from their reading, or one paper topic with a list of its supporting points, or a formal outline of a paper. (To help students select an appropriate topic, give them parameters for the topic, an audience, and a situation.)

3. *Scramble a reading.* You can use ordinary assigned readings to help students attend to organization. When you assign a well-organized article or book chapter, cut it up and rearrange its sections or paragraphs, then photocopy the rearranged version and hand it out as the assigned reading. Students must restore its sequence and justify their choices. To make discussion easier, number the paragraphs in your rearranged version. Then a student can say, "I'd arrange this as paragraph 2, 5, 3, etc." You can do the same with a list of subheadings from a chapter or article.

A simpler version of the above exercise is to assign a reading, give numbers to its paragraphs or sections, then ask students to write a paragraph explaining whether they would accept putting section 3 before section 2, and why. Or ask them whether a certain piece of evidence could be deleted.

In addition to providing exercises that help students with general reasoning and organizing skills, you can help them with their written assignments, using the suggestions below.

4. *Have students keep a log.* In it they list their activities as they develop the paper (i.e., "March 13: went to the library, looked in the card catalog under X, Y, Z, found five sources I think might be useful"). To get complete logs, give students a list of questions they should answer in the logs (i.e., "Name sources you used. How useful was each? What questions or conclusions guided you?"). You can ask students to bring their logs with them each day. Then every few days, call on a different student to read from the log, then let other class members compare their own procedures or offer suggestions to the writer.

5. *Free write.* Tell students that by a given day, they must have read at least five sources on their chosen topic and must bring you an annotated bibliography of those sources. Then give them 10 minutes in class to free write on their chosen topics, exploring their thoughts based on that reading. The freewrite may help them clarify their ideas and achieve some perspective on their readings. You can let the freewrite serve its purpose without response, you can take a few class minutes for peer sharing, or you can collect the freewrites and respond to them. If topics need narrowing, go through the freewrite, underlining possible paper topics. If shaping arguments is the task at hand, mark the freewrites with comments such as "The main problem with this argument is X" or "Here you have three commonly cited arguments for position Y. Check Friedman for a fourth."

6. *Assign journals.* Ask students to keep a journal while they are reading for their papers. In the journal, they must not paraphrase the source but must speculate and ponder, apply ideas to themselves, compare assertions from their reading with evidence from their own experience or from other sources. You can set a minimum number of pages or a particular task such as "Pose and speculate about three questions that arise from your reading." You can have these shared in groups for discussion, or you can collect and mark the journals in the same way as the freewrites. The idea is to get students to think independently and to engage in dialogue about ideas. Ignore mechanics and citation form in these journals; concentrate on your role as conversational partner, not your role as judge.

7. *Discuss development of a main idea.* Ask students to write the main idea of their papers, or the questions or hypotheses the papers will address. The students then show their main ideas to peers; the peers, in turn, list the evidence or reasoning by which they would expect that topic to be developed or that hypothesis tested. Alternatively, you can have each student write and hand in a main idea, and then you can select at random two or three ideas from the pile and discuss with the class how these topics might be developed and supported.

8. *Work with outlines.* Outlining may be useful at many different points of the writing process. Avoid giving students the idea that all good writers gather data, construct an outline, then write. Some skilled writers prefer to write

first, then outline what they've written as a check for its organization; some don't use written outlines at all; some progress through several outlines. A writer may end with a final draft very different from an earlier outline.

Chances are, your students don't know these facts about outlining. In high school, they may well have been expected to turn in outlines with their papers. The outlines may have been touted as a planning tool, from which the paper should be written. The role of discovery in the writing process, which may profitably take a writer away from the outline at hand, may not have been acknowledged. Students may have written the outline after the paper was finished and felt guilty about it. Or perhaps the student fixed an earlier outline so that it conformed to the paper. Students and their teachers may not have clearly distinguished between a formal outline, handed in as a guide for the reader of the finished piece, and the outline used as a planning tool for the writer.

You may ask for an outline as guide or suggest that students try out the outline as tool, but you should distinguish: the former must be consonant with the final paper and should be composed after the paper is complete. You can be strict about indentation, numerals, and letters, showing students that when mature writers compose an outline that guides the reader through the paper, they follow one of the standard outline formats.

The outline as writer's tool, however, may follow any system of indentation, numbering, or lettering that serves the purpose of helping the *writer* impose organization on the paper. The outline is a useful tool for some writers most of the time, and for many writers some of the time. A well-written case study by Jack Selzer, which you could show to your students, tells how a professional engineer makes extensive use of outlining. Your students may not be comfortable with outlining as a tool. It's perfectly legitimate to force them to try it, but if you do that, you're wise to explain what you mean by using the outline as a tool and to give students some examples of how tool outlines can serve the writer. Call in the outline before the paper's due date so that students don't return to their old practices of rigging the outline after the paper is done. Make clear that the final paper need not follow the outline if they discover improved ways to organize the paper.

You might ask students to write a page to you, to be handed in with the final paper, on what they learned from the outlining procedure. Or ask them to share that information in class or in small groups. Assure them that if outlining didn't work well for them on this particular task, they're in good company among writers.

Typical outlines will be confusing, jumbled, and incoherent. Common reasons may be that the student has not spent enough time reading and thinking about the topic, does not know how to construct an outline, does not comfortably think in outline form at this stage of the writing process. Further, most students are not very good at responding helpfully to another student's outline, so if you call in outlines, you probably have to respond to them yourself. Your response can cause problems, too. An outline is an awesome production to most students, and if you comment incompletely, they may assume that some parts of it are OK and some parts need to be "fixed," so instead of rethinking the entire approach, as they need to do, they try to salvage as much of the old structure as possible, and get themselves into even deeper trouble.

For those reasons, you may want to respond to confusing outlines merely by a "see me," setting office hours so you can help the student think through the paper more clearly.

9. *Work with alternative planning devices.* You can ask students to hand in any early planning device of their choice—a rough draft or free write, an outline, a rough diagram or list, a web, dummy tables, a polished first paragraph that introduces the paper's topic and line of reasoning, or some planning device useful in your field. Then at least you know that you're responding to a planning device with which the student feels comfortable. Students may not realize the wealth of planning devices available to writers, so you may want to demonstrate the options in class or in a handout.

One option is the web, now coming into wide use in schools. Because it does not impose a tight, linear sequence as the outline does, the web is more flexible than the outline, while providing a way to store and structure information. One begins by writing the topic in the center of a piece of paper. Related ideas are added around the center like spokes of a wheel or strands of a web. Below is an actual web psychologist Susan Robison constructed for a paper titled "The Brain in Writing." She filled about half of it from her current knowledge and the rest as she read further about the topic. This web, from the beginning, had spokes that derived from a single plan—to show misconceptions about how the brain works in writing. Not all webs are so well organized at first. A writer may move through several webs for a single paper. Robison, who composed this web for herself, also teaches her students how to use webs; she organizes lecture notes on the blackboard as webs, and, in class, she demonstrates the development of a student paper topic as a web.

Besides the web, you can suggest planning devices used in your field. For example, in helping students develop a case analysis in a business class, the professor might follow any or all of these planning activities:

a. Students write short answers to six or seven questions about the firm's present operation: What business are they in? What are their resources? What is their market?

b. Students mark any of the above questions about which the company's board or managers might disagree, as revealed either by their statements or by their action in the case material. Students list the opposing points of view and write a paragraph discussing whose point of view they think is more accurate, and why.

c. Students read the case again, listing all the problems that managers and employees *think* they have. They write a paragraph explaining which problem is most real and most important, and why.

d. Students now look for problems that are not directly mentioned by people quoted in the case. Keys to such problems are, Where do peoples' *ex-*

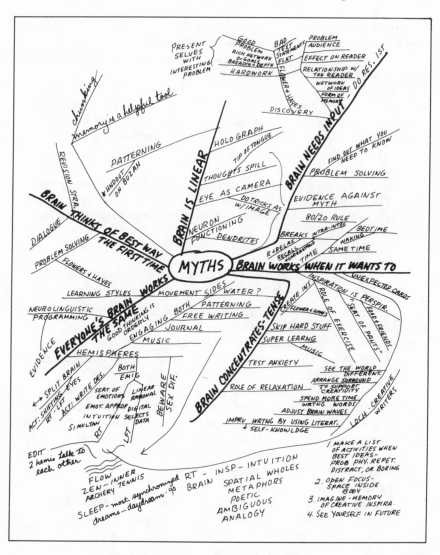

Web for a Paper on the Brain and Writing

pectations about an operation not coincide with reality? About what do people argue or disagree, and why? Which offices of the firm are not doing what they should be doing? What is not being done that should be done? Consider various combinations of departments and lines of authority—what would happen if these combinations were made?

   e. Students are given a diagram of a firm's typical "lifeline," from a beginning business to a mature business. (The lifeline concept is discussed in their text.) Students are asked to locate the firm on this line and to defend their choice.

f. Students must write a single sentence that encapsulates the firm's present status in seven areas—resources, market, and so on.

g. Students write a single sentence that describes the firm's most important problem(s) and their suggested solution(s).

h. Students write a first paragraph that includes the two sentences in (f) and (g). They make a list of the points needed to convince the paper's reader of the correctness of the writer's analysis as stated in the first paragraph.

i. Students arrange their points in sequence and list evidence the reader will need for each point.

j. Students draft the paper.

Until the draft stage, the written products of this planning process are short. They can be read by the professor in a brief time, they can be shared in groups, or the instructor can ask one or two students to read their versions for class discussion.

Helping Students with Drafting and Revising

Some excellent writers produce only one draft. Typically the draft is written slowly and painfully, after much preparatory thought, research, talk, and perhaps other planning devices such as webbing or outlining. The draft proceeds from first word to last word. The writer may scratch out and substitute during the drafting but, after finishing that first draft, revises it only for surface features. At the other end of the spectrum is the writer who begins drafting with no clear idea of what the final paper will look like. The drafting, which may be rapid, is itself a way of working out ideas. Typically, this kind of writer revises many times and in fundamental ways, creating order out of chaos. Most writers, of course, fall somewhere between these two poles. Experienced writers may vary their strategies according to the situation, or a single writer may change strategies over the years.

Your goal is to help each of your students develop the drafting and revising strategies that serve most effectively in a variety of situations. If students were aware of the two ends of the spectrum, your job would be easier. Students tend to believe, however, that good writers pen just one good draft and that revising is a sign of incompetence. Further, research by Sommers and others shows that experienced writers think of revising differently than novice writers. Experienced writers view drafting and revising as ways of finding out what they want to say. Revision to them may mean hacking out large sections of a draft, reorienting the draft, adding new hunks of material, spotlighting a previously peripheral idea. Unskilled student writers, on the other hand, tend to describe revision as mere substitution or excision of words and phrases, or as a process of "fixing" the surface features such as grammar and punctuation.

In addition to students' mistaken notions about drafting and revising, procrastination often leaves a student time for only one draft in any case. Finally, with such weight hanging on the first draft, it's no wonder that some students suffer deep anxiety in the drafting stage.

You can help your students overcome blocks at the drafting stage by increasing pressure to produce a draft but lifting pressure for the perfection of the draft. Below are suggestions:

1. *Structure a draft deadline.* Even if you don't have time to read the draft, make students show it to you, and give credit. They will benefit simply by having had to do it by a certain date.

2. *Explain the zero draft.* Lynn Z. Bloom explains the zero draft in *Strategic Writing* (50–51). Like a free write, the draft imposes no demands for complete sentences, well-phrased ideas, coherent paragraphs, or correct spelling and punctuation, but students must stay on topic. They are instructed to start anywhere—with the idea that seems clearest, or the part with which they feel most comfortable. Drafting should be fairly rapid. The idea is to flush out ideas, not to get them all perfect. The writer may use notes or an outline, or may set aside all aids and let the ideas and facts emerge from memory as they will.

The zero draft, like free writing, helps the blocked writer because it lifts the paralyzing burden of having to write something coherent or correct on the first try. Also like free writing, however, it requires that students learn to refine the ore they've dug. Advise students to write a single sentence that expresses the most promising idea of the draft, then to plan a paper that supports that idea. You might also suggest that they state the main idea of each paragraph, or each relevant idea contained in the draft, then write these on three-by-five cards and shuffle them until a coherent outline emerges.

3. *Suggest taping.* Some students can talk about their topics but freeze in front of a blank sheet of paper. Suggest that they talk out their first draft into a tape recorder, then transcribe the tape and use it as the first draft. This method also works well with students whose speech is more straightforward than their writing—it helps them avoid a pseudoacademic, stuffy draft.

4. *Suggest intermediate planning tools.* Although the requirement to make an outline or web before producing a complete draft can hinder the free flow of thought, some students profit from such tools. Show them how to write a draft, with the outline or web at the right elbow and the stack of note cards or other data at the left. Many books on how to write research papers do a good job of explaining this method.

As crucial as drafting is revising. Studies of revision have indicated that

- Experts do a greater amount of revising than novices;
- Experts attend more to global problems—problems whose solutions would affect the content of a summary of the piece (see Faigley and Witte);
- Writers have more difficulty revising their own text than that of others;
- The ability to detect problems seems separate from the ability to fix them.

(For a literature review, see Hayes et al. 1–5.)

An important body of work by Linda Flower, John Hayes, and their associates adds to our understanding of novice and expert revision (Hayes et al.; Flower et al.). They describe several components of the revision process and delineate some differences between experts and novices in each category:

1. *Task definition* (knowledge of relevant criteria and processes to use for revision in general). Novices need to learn what information they should attend to in the text they revise, how to set goals and make plans for revising, and how to monitor their attentional capacities while work is under way—for example, making several passes through the draft, focusing on a different goal or type of problem each time. Writers must learn to tailor their process plans to the job and to adjust them as necessary; inappropriately narrow task definitions may prevent novices from detecting problems in a text (Hayes et al. 24, 26–27).

2. *Evaluation.* Evaluation is reading one's own text, with attention to both micro- and macro-level issues. Two examples of micro-level issues are decoding individual words and making factual inferences. The more complex macro-level issues are genre conventions ("The report needs a summary at its beginning"), identifying the gist of the text, and inferring the text's function or the writer's intentions and point of view (Hayes et al. 28). In rereading their drafts, novices seem to pay less attention to macro-level issues than experts do.

3. *Problem representation* (how writers represent the problem to themselves). Problem representations range from vague ("Something's wrong with this sentence") to precise ("There's faulty parallelism here"). Experts discover more of the problems in a text than novices do. They are also able to diagnose problems more precisely, though they do not always take the trouble: sometimes they operate from their first vague sense of infelicity and simply write the offending passage over again from scratch. Unlike novices, however, experts are able to select between strategies instead of being stuck with vague problem representations and resulting rewrites.

4. *Strategy selection* (choosing a way to solve the problem). The writer can ignore the problem, delay the effort to solve the problem, search for more information, rewrite the passage from scratch, or revise the existing passage by relying on diagnostic information. The key to success seems to lie not merely in how much a writer revises; some novice writers revise extensively but don't make any improvement. Rather, the secret is to adapt one's revision strategies appropriately to the text and to one's goals (Hayes et al. 47–48). Particularly, novice writers seem to overuse the strategy of ignoring an error, telling themselves that readers won't notice or that it will make no difference; alternatively, they may delete offending passages altogether. They may use the delay strategy and then neglect to come back to the problem. As mentioned above, novices frequently rewrite from scratch, sometimes in successive tries, without having a specific diagnosis or a way of deciding whether the new version is better than the old.

The crucial factors are knowledge and intentions. Students must know a full set of criteria for evaluating a piece of writing, and they must bring that knowledge to bear in revising. In addition, the way revisers represent their intentions to themselves helps them notice certain features of the text and focus their attention (Flower et al. 17).

Students must learn to gear their revisions to the gist of their text and its larger rhetorical concerns, not merely to local aspects. Their strategies must include the ability to diagnose with some precision and to revise the passage at hand, not merely to sense that something is wrong and be stuck with rewriting as their only strategy for change.

All this research suggests that revision as an obligatory stage may help some students but doesn't necessarily produce improvement (Flower et al. 2). The researchers advise, "We may have the most impact on the revising process of inexperienced writers if we find ways to give them flexibility and increase their problem-solving power" (Hayes et al. 57). The suggestions below may help your students exercise the options of expert revisers.

1. *Reduce first-draft polishing.* To help students focus their attention on gist and structure, reduce their commitment to the actual words of the draft. Ignore grammar and punctuation, so they don't waste time merely cleaning up the sentences in a flawed paper. Use word processors if you can; some research shows that students are more willing to revise extensively when they can use a computer, because typing, deletion, and moving parts of the text are physically easier (Bean; but see Collier, Pufahl). You might take a few minutes to have a student who is successfully using a word processor explain to the rest of the class how they can get started and build skills. However, find out whether your school's word-processing facilities are so overcrowded or full of bugs that students are experiencing more frustration than help. If so, be honest with your students about that. Experienced students and computer center staff can offer advice about slack times in the computer center, safeguards against loss of text when the computer goes down, and other ways to reduce frustration.

2. *Reward revision.* Many student papers handed in as final versions can usefully be regarded as first drafts, which could be mightily improved by revision based on the teacher's further coaching. But unfortunately, instead of a structure in which the instructor treats a paper as unfinished and then gives suggestions for further revision, most teachers create a structure in which students have no chance to revise, once they have handed in their papers, and receive no reward for doing so. Thus the instructor's careful comments on a paper seem to the students like treatment prescribed for a patient already dead. So after they see the all-important, unchangeable grade, they chuck their papers, each with its lucid and painstaking teacher comments, into the nearest wastebasket or into their notebooks, which often serve as wastebaskets. If the teacher rewards revision, however, the students are much more likely to make every effort to comprehend their instructor's suggestions and to put them into practice.

To create a structure in which revision is encouraged and rewarded, try allowing or even requiring students to revise their papers after discussing their work with you. This may mean setting deadlines early enough to allow for revision afterward. I have sometimes accepted revisions at any time, up to the last day of the semester. But since such a policy may lead to an unbearable flood of "oh my gosh isn't there something I can do in these last two days to raise my grade" attempts, usually I allow a two-week revision period for each assignment. After that deadline, I accept no revisions. Sometimes, if the revision needs another revision, I'll allow another two weeks.

Once they have a final draft, time to revise it, and reward for doing so, students must be led to full concepts of the task of revising in general. They must look for the appropriate features, especially the gist of a text; have the knowledge to recognize and define problems; and shape appropriate goals and criteria for each piece of writing. Finally, they must know and be able to use appropriate revision strategies. Below are some suggestions:

3. *Provide a checklist.* A checklist is one way of posing the right questions. Writers can check their own drafts, but if peers use the checklist to respond to one another's papers, students may be more likely to see and accept the need for global changes.

4. *Use peer response.* Handling drafts in student groups is covered in chapter 4.

5. *Respond to drafts yourself.* Response to drafts can profitably involve a major time investment by you and/or your assistants. The time for that investment can be stolen from the time normally given to comments on the final paper, which in the new scheme you merely grade. Table 1 shows what your time allotment may look like.

Old way	guiding planning	grading and commenting on final paper	

New way	guiding planning	responding to drafts	grading final paper

Table 1

You can also free time for response by using regularly scheduled class hours. Can you have students cover material by reading or by listening to a taped lecture, while you use the class hour for group meetings, conferences, or written response to drafts? Can you meet with some students while others are working on an in-class exercise? Instructors may answer differently according to class load, discipline, and personal teaching style, but I, and many other instructors experienced in integrating writing into content courses, strongly recommend responding to drafts as a highly productive investment of instructor time.

Helping Students with Visual Aids

A short guide for students in various disciplines—covering the composition and integration of tables, graphs, figures, photographs, and other visual aids—is contained in my student text (*Writing* 439–53). You may want to show your students how to use the instructions in your discipline's style manual or a student's version of it, following the guidelines discussed earlier for teaching citations. Students usually need help learning how to use such guides.

Handing out copies of papers that successfully use visual aids may teach positioning, labeling, and other matters of form much more efficiently than verbal explanations do, especially if the sample paper is also a direct model for what your students will do.

In class, take a few minutes to pass a sample problem or set of data, and ask students to rough out a graph or chart. If you use data you want them to learn, your lecture can both become a lesson in constructing graphs and also cover the course material. Such an exercise helps students learn how to get from data to an effective visual aid.

Perhaps the most important thing you can do is to require "dummy" visual aids early in the writing process, so they become part of the student's thinking and planning about the data rather than a last minute add-on.

Helping Students with Style and Mechanics

The terms *style* and *mechanics* are used in various ways, but here I mean to include aspects of prose style like tone, word choice, and sentence structure, as well as grammar, punctuation, spelling, citation format, ways of handling margins and figures and so on. Chapters 8 and 9 suggest ways of responding to problems of style and mechanics in student drafts. This section discusses methods of guiding style and mechanics other than direct response to drafts.

Style and mechanics are shaped by conventions. Conventions are always social: the only reason *when* is not spelled *whan*, as it was in Chaucer's day, is that today English speakers agree on a "correct" spelling for current use. Similarly, scientists agree on the format of the scientific report and on the specialized language used to write such reports. Those who seek to change conventions must do so within the community of writers and readers, as currently some scientists are trying to push their peers toward a simpler, more direct style with less passive voice. An understanding that conventions are social is an important basis for your attempts to help your students.

Style and mechanics shift not just between Chaucer and us but within various situations in your students' lives. A shift from grandparent to grandchild, from Louisiana to Appalachia, from white to black cultures, from poolroom to classroom, from literary criticism to scientific-report writing—all will affect various aspects of mechanics or style.

If you recognize that language is social and conventional, you must recognize another principle: students do not simply "know" English, or not know it; rather, they have learned through past experience to control the language of the academy more or less well, and in any particular writing situation, they may or may not be able to translate what they know into performance. The social nature of language, the complex relations between knowledge and performance, mean that we must address style and mechanics in sophisticated ways. People learn style and mechanics primarily by being part of the community where certain forms are used—that is, by reading, speaking, and writing the language forms of that community.

It has been conclusively established that the study of grammar, in isolation, does not improve student writing. Yet a knowledge of grammar, though the writer may not be able formally to diagram a sentence or label a preposition, lies behind the control of written grammar, style, and punctuation. Thus the study of grammar, and indeed of all language conventions, must be fully integrated with the students' actual practice (Kolln). Further, students need exposure not just to rules but to real writing that illustrates the conventions they must follow. Finally, we must pay close attention to the factors that affect students' ability to perform at the level of their knowledge. The suggestions below, therefore, represent a variety of ways to address both performance and knowledge and to help your students learn the conventions expected in your classroom. At the end of the chapter, three special topics are discussed—the "basic writer," who is radically unprepared for college-level writing; the speaker of a "dialect" such as Black American English, so different from Edited American English (EAE) that learning the new grammatical forms presents a significant task; and finally the speaker of English as a second language.

Assign Reading

Having students read a great deal of the kind of writing you want them to produce is perhaps the best way to help them write in an appropriate style and control grammar and punctuation.

Make Expectations Clear

Give conscious thought to the level of polish needed for various assignments, and communicate that expectation clearly to students. If you want them to learn how to edit their writing as carefully as they must for most writing in college and the professions, stress your high expectations, make style and mechanics part of the grade, and attach severe penalties for falling below standards. I once taught in an English department where the standard policy was that student papers must be written in complete sentences. Any paper with a run-on sentence, comma splice, or sentence fragment (except fragments used with good reason) would automatically receive an F. While this method has some disadvantages—it may, for example, make writers so afraid of committing an unforgivable sin that they have no energy left for free and joyous expression—it did show me that, if sufficiently motivated—even by abject fear—students are capable of eliminating many errors without direct instruction from the teacher.

Give Encouragement and Remove Threat

Fear should not be the main motivation. Your support should help the students' self-confidence. Students' problems stem from unhappy experiences with writing. Talk with them about past language and writing experiences. Are they anxious about writing, afraid of making errors? Does writing ever seem rewarding and important, or is it in every situation the forced and feared fulfillment of someone else's assignment? Can they identify some rules that they know but do not always follow? Can they suggest ways in which you could create a situation in which writing could be less tense, more rewarding?

Think of ways to encourage students to take pride in their writing. A young boy knows perfectly well how to comb, brush, pick, or braid his hair, but he'll be sloppy about it until some girl lets him know she's interested in him. Are there ways in which you can apply the courtship syndrome to students' writing? For example, is there a format, however informal, for "publication" of student writing, in preparation for which students will carefully polish their papers? Is there a place where good-looking student essays, spiffy and error-free, can be displayed?

Structure Time for Editing

Helping students save time for editing is another useful strategy. Have students come to class with a typed or legibly written draft on a certain deadline date. You can collect the drafts, simply give credit or points to each student who handed one in, and hand them back at the next class session. Without spending time marking the papers, you have both forced students to produce drafts with enough time left for editing and separated them from their papers for a few days, after which they will more easily recognize problems.

You may, of course, want to respond to the drafts; my point here is that even if you don't have time to read them, you can still help students structure their time.

Use Friends and Classmates as Editors

Some students will persuade, hire, or blackmail a friend or typist to fix the mechanics in their papers. You may decide to accept this practice as legitimate; after all, many professional writers have editors and typists who fix their mechanics. You may take the position that in college students must find ways to manage certain logistics such as child care, clean clothes, and well-edited writing. How they do that is up to them.

You may track the editing and convey good habits of acknowledgment if you have students acknowledge their editors. Have them include a separate page or a line on the title page, such as "Edited by Joyce Frederick" or "I am indebted to Joyce Frederick for help with grammar and punctuation."

One can legitimately argue, on the other hand, that though other writers have their writing fixed by editors, students' task is to learn to edit their own writing. Insist that students not have the paper fixed out of their sight; rather, the editor must explain the rule, and the student must be the one who actually pens the correction. The guide to using a writer's network (pp. 50–52) outlines this policy. You can ask students to state at the ends of their papers that they used editors only as teachers. Of course, a few may still secretly have someone fix their writing, but you may decide that you can't police it all.

You can structure peer help within your class. Peer help with drafts should address content, structure, and evidence before focusing on style and mechanics. Once these issues have been addressed, however, when it's time for students to edit their writing, you can ask each student to bring copies of a legible draft to class to be read by a small group for help with style and mechanics. Stress that the draft should represent the writer's own best editing. Each member of the group needs a copy of the paper. If you have time and resources, you can ask for drafts a day or two ahead and make the copies yourself, but most instructors I know who use this system simply ask each student to bring copies to the group meeting. Group members offer suggestions about style and mechanics. They may debate a rule or come to you with questions. Because you may not know the answer to every grammar or punctuation question students ask (I don't), have a handbook with you, as a resource for everyone.

You can arrange peer reading outside of class by asking each student to find a buddy who will read the draft for style and mechanics. You can assign the buddies, but probably a more effective system is to let students find their own—instant popularity for those class members who are good editors. The buddy signs the final paper as "editor." You can help editors check their effectiveness by showing them the marked paper at the end.

Teach Editing Strategies

Students can be helped by suggestions for editing strategies, such as:

1. Read the paper aloud.
2. Read the paper backward for spelling.
3. Have a friend read the paper, following the guide to using the writer's network (pp. 50–52).
4. Type the paper, so problems show up more clearly. Leave time to make a corrected, typed copy or, as necessary, to write in corrections neatly on the typed final copy.
5. Read the paper selectively for problems the instructor has emphasized or mistakes the student makes frequently. More on proofreading and selective reading appears later in this chapter.

Identify Problems Early

At the beginning of the semester, assign students a short piece of writing that does not heavily tax their reading comprehension and that does not ask them to deal with concepts they barely understand (both these conditions will affect their ability to use what they know of style and mechanics). Give them enough time to edit that writing, and make reasonably sure they do their own editing. The results will identify those who have serious problems in producing readable prose that follows conventions of Edited American English. Try to get help for those students from a writing center, tutor, classmate, or instructional guide.

Use a Learning Center

Learning centers are becoming more and more numerous. They may offer drop-in services or handle students only through structured tutorials or courses. Some concentrate only on writing problems; others offer a wider range of subject-area tutoring. They may be attached to an academic department, like English or education, or they may be part of student services. They may be funded by grants or by what people employed in such centers reverently refer to as "hard money."

Whatever its location, type, or status, your learning center probably can be of great use to you and your students. In the center I founded and directed at Central College in the 1970s, we discovered that more students came at the suggestion of faculty members than for any other reason. So you can be fairly sure that both the center and the students will benefit from your referrals and encouragement.

But keep in touch with the center yourself. The research on how students can best master writing skills points not in the direction of hiring more teachers, and not even solely in the direction of hiring more learning center staff members, but rather in the direction of enlisting *you*. Increasingly, we see the necessity of making a team effort to nourish literacy rather than relying on the isolated effort of one unit such as the required English course or the learning center. In a center your students can receive intensive help with mechanics, help that you may not have time or training to provide. Nevertheless the results are better when the teacher and the center cooperate than when the teacher merely passes the problem on to the center staff.

If you are very short of time, if you think you are not skilled enough to deal with mechanical problems, or if you have a number of students with serious difficulties, you may wish to let the center carry the ball for mechanics and spend your own time on other kinds of writing and learning problems. The following steps will help you and your students use the center to best advantage:

1. Early in the semester, give a writing assignment that will allow you to identify students with problems in mechanics. Get the referral process going immediately.

2. Strongly and personally encourage students to attend the center. Let them know that you want and expect them to go.
3. Become at least generally aware of how your center works with students, what its basic philosophy is, and what goals it sets for students in your class. Then continue to back up the center's efforts as you evaluate each student's writing.
4. You might ask the center's director or a tutor to visit your class and spend ten minutes explaining how the center works.
5. Ask a student who has been helped at the center to describe the experience briefly in class.
6. Do anything else you can to help the center combat the notion that only deficient students go there and to enhance its image as a resource for all writers.

Offer Instruction and Example

When a particular assignment requires a particular style or convention, you can instruct by a written handout and by example. Notice how Linda Spencer integrates instruction and examples as she teaches her students the style, wording, and format for a diagnostic evaluation (pp. 43–47).

When the style you expect is distinctive and heavily guided by convention, you can directly help students practice it. For example, hand them a piece of writing with a missing paragraph, give them the information that must go into that paragraph, and have them write it in the style of the model. Then have them read their paragraphs to one another in small groups, with the group voting on the paragraph they think most nearly fits the style of the rest of the piece. You can also give students a model piece, plus the information to write a similar piece, and have them write a new piece based on the model. Again, develop students' ear for style by having them read their pieces to each other. Emphasize that they must imagine their readers vividly and use language that is appropriate and clear for the reader and the situation.

Since students often write prose that attempts a scholarly or high-sounding tone at the expense of simplicity and clarity, warn them against stuffy verbosity. Show them examples of obtuse writing and clear writing. A good sample in science is provided by Robert Kesling:

"Sciensch"	English Translation
Our research, designed to test the fatal effects of XXX on dogs, was carried out by intravenously introducing the drug. In the experiments, a relatively small quantity, 3 cubic centimeters, was administered to each animal. In each case, XXX proved to be fatal, all dogs expiring before a lapse of five minutes after the injections.	The intravenous injection of only 3 cc. of XXX kills a dog within five minutes.

A method, which was found to be expedient and not very difficult to accomplish and which possessed a high degree of accuracy in its results, was devised whereby. . . .	An easy, accurate way to. . . .

Provide samples from other students' writing (presented anonymously) or from your own profession's journals, and have the students simplify the language. For fun, show them clear, simple language and see if they can bureaucratize it. Richard Lanham's *Revising Prose* is an excellent guide to simplification of obtuse, bureaucratic prose.

If students write from a vivid sense of their audience and strive for simplicity and clarity, they will avoid many other stylistic problems, but you may want to point out other features of the style you expect or to counter students' inappropriate ideas. (A science instructor, for example, might warn students that the goal of not using the same word too many times, useful to them in literary and philosophical writing, is inappropriate in scientific writing, where if the writer is talking about an organism, then *organism* is the word to use, as often as necessary.) You might also select the ten aspects or problems of style or mechanics that are most serious in the field, that occur most frequently among your students, or that bug you the most when you find them. List these on a sheet, give an example of each, and hand the sheet to your students as a guide to avoiding your special ire.

Use the Never-Again Notebook

One method I can recommend for use either alone or in conjunction with another instructional program is the never-again notebook. Students purchase standard spiral or loose-leaf notebooks. On each student's paper the teacher marks the two or three most frequent or most disturbing mechanical problems: for example, errors in apostrophe use or subject-verb agreement. Then students must learn to apply the pertinent rules. The explanation may come from the teacher, an assistant, a skills-center tutor, a handbook, or a slide-tape program. Once the rule is clear, students copy in their notebooks all the mistakes they made in those areas, including the way they corrected each mistake and the rule that applies. Then students drill themselves every day on just those rules. In succeeding papers they try never again to make those particular mistakes. Once they master the first goals, the teacher picks one or two new rules for them to work on or lets them make the choice.

The never-again notebook works well alone if the student needs merely to fill in the gaps of a basically sound knowledge of mechanics. For example, the fine points of writing quotations (does the comma go inside or outside? when does one use a comma?) are easily handled in this way, and the explanation can come from any standard handbook on English punctuation. Students with more extensive or basic problems can use the never-again notebook along with a more systematized program of instruction. The problems chosen for the notebook will then be those that appear in the student's papers and that have already been covered in the program. The notebook thus serves to bridge the gap between correctly completing all the exercises in some book and actually eliminating a certain kind of mistake from one's own writing.

You can, if you wish, connect your grading to the type of incremental progress made in the never-again notebook. For example, you may say to the student, "If your next paper has none of the mistakes we've so far put in your never-again notebook, I will give it full credit for mechanics." When the student achieves that goal, you can raise the ante: next time the student must add one more type of EAE usage to get full credit.

The beauty of the never-again notebook is that it focuses directly on students' actual, current problems and provides drill based on their own writing mistakes. Once you've explained the system and had students obtain notebooks, you need only mark in your records what never-again writing mistakes each student is working on. Then you can read for mechanics only to check those aspects and, if appropriate, to pick the next entries for the notebooks. If you wish, you can call in the notebooks along with the papers.

Use a Handbook

Handbooks vary in type, bulk, and levels of difficulty. They may contain one or more of the following: conventions of grammar and punctuation; discipline-specific instruction in citation, style, visual aids, and so on; general guides to clear prose style. Some handbooks or texts for students contain material in all three areas. Some include general advice about the process as well.

You may hesitate to require a handbook that would escalate an already high book cost for your course. However, a saving of $10 or $15, if it will hamper the student's best use of the education that is costing thousands, is foolish. Don't be afraid to act on your conviction that writers in your discipline must control style, grammar, and punctuation and that students must spend the necessary money to purchase instructional guides.

Selecting a handbook may require some inquiry and experimentation. First, ask yourself what your students are ready for. If they differ widely in skills and experience, you might ask your bookstore to carry two or three different types and let your students select appropriately.

Some students may already have a good grasp of the grammatical structure of the language, so that they can comprehend and put into practice most rules stated in the technical terms of grammar. They may have some gaps in an otherwise solid foundation and simply need to add a few missing stones, such as the use of the colon and the use of commas on both sides of an interjected phrase. For these sorts of problems a standard English handbook is a good tool. Typically, handbooks are large, hardcover books with items arranged alphabetically. Oddly, many bear the publisher's name, not the author's (e.g., the *Prentice-Hall Handbook*). Shorter, paperback handbooks are Edward Corbett's *Little English Handbook* and *The Brief English Handbook*, by Edward Doran and Charles Dawe. Find out what your bookstore or library has, or ask what is required in your school's beginning composition classes and thus is likely to be available secondhand. The student looks up the rule in question, examines or completes examples or drills, and then, with the aid of the never-again notebook, learns to apply the rule in writing assignments.

Students may have trouble crossing the bridge between the handbook's alphabetized list of errors and effective editing of their own prose. Guiding students through the process of editing, beginning with the most important problems and offering grammar instruction as needed, is the purpose of my forthcoming short student guide tentatively titled *Ten Steps for Editing Any Writing for Grammar, Punctuation, and Style* (Scott Foresman). The text shows students how to take a draft that says essentially what they want it to say and edit it effectively. The book is self-instructional; exercise answers are included for students to check their own work. If you assign a chapter a week, you hold your students incrementally responsible. For example, on a paper in the sixth week, they are responsible for steps one to six, which include avoiding sentence fragments, choosing and arranging subjects and verbs, subject-verb agreement, verb tenses, pronouns, relating subordinate parts clearly within the sentence, and punctuating to join parts of sentences. In week 10, you ask students also to be responsible for the last four steps—spelling, apostrophe and *s*, punctuating around quotations, and punctuating names, dates, and places.

Some students need a developmental approach, which leads them systematically through the basics of composing sentences and paragraphs that follow appropriate conventions. The learning center can guide such a program, or the student can use self-instructional aids of various kinds in conjunction with the never-again notebook. See if your school owns programmed texts, explanatory texts with workbooks, or programs using filmstrips, slides and tapes, or computers. The discussion here attempts to help you select instructional materials or intelligently to support the approach chosen by your learning center staff.

One approach is the self-instructional programmed text, which breaks down the learning task into small units and gives the student the correct answer at once. Such books are set up in "frames." Each frame presents a bit of information and then asks a question about it. The student answers the question and immediately checks it in the answer column. If it is wrong, some books have the student go back over the same frame; some provide alternative explanations or more drill. After mastering the information in one frame, the student goes on to the next.

The strengths of the programmed text are that it breaks down the job of learning a rule into its smallest components and presents a task from which much of the fright has been removed. The novice doesn't say, "This book asks me to walk to California, and I can't do that," because all the book asks is that the student put one foot in front of the other. After each step the book says, "Great! You took that step just fine. Now here's another step to take."

Computerized learning programs work on the same principle, but instead of uncovering the answer or turning the page to find it, the student learns it from the computer.

The self-instructional texts called "workbooks" usually contain explanations (longer than the frame in programmed texts), followed by exercises and drill. Answers may be in a separate booklet, at the back of the workbook itself, or at the ends of chapters.

Slide-tape or filmstrip programs are useful for students who have difficulty reading or who benefit from the audible reinforcement. Sometimes such a program is used along with a workbook.

In choosing a text, workbook, or media program for your students, watch for the extent to which the text depends on mastery of the elements of traditional grammar. In grammar-oriented texts many questions call for grammatical terms as their answers. The table of contents and the foreword will also reveal an emphasis on grammar. Another type of text teaches as little grammar as possible. It typically begins not with basic grammatical analysis of sentences but with the areas in which unskilled writers make the most errors: spelling, complete sentences, agreement of subject and verb, formation of verb tenses. Attempting to eliminate the student's most frequent mistakes, these texts teach only as much grammar as is absolutely necessary and avoid grammatical terminology wherever possible. This kind of text is probably best for the student who has no previous knowledge of traditional grammar or who is afraid of it. The more traditional text works for the student who has some grasp of grammar or who seems to master that type of material quickly and with pleasure. Whatever you do, be sure that the text does more than teach students to identify parts of speech; it must focus on using that knowledge to teach punctuation and other skills that students need to improve their writing.

Studies have shown that instruction and drill in grammar or in rules of punctuation will be ineffective unless integrated with the students' own writing process (Kolln). Thus if a student is using such materials, work with the same conventions in the student's own writing, coordinating your efforts with the tutor.

One integrated approach to helping inexperienced students control language and language conventions is called "sentence combining" or "sentence composing." The basic idea is to have students write short, basic, subject-verb sentences, then gradually learn to add ideas to that kernel, in the form of phrases, clauses, and modifiers of various kinds. Students learn to punctuate these units as they compose and manipulate them. Traditional grammatical terms, or substitute terms, may or may not be emphasized. (For further explanation of the methods, see the works by Christensen and O'Hare. For evidence of the method's efficacy in increasing students' ability to handle complex sentences—"syntactic maturity"—see Daiker, Kerek, and Morenberg. For a question about the measures of complexity, see Faigley.)

Texts and audiovisual programs differ in vocabulary and reading levels.

If you have a student whose vocabulary is limited or who is a poor reader, make sure you use a simple enough text.

Texts differ, too, in their separability. Some are composed of entirely discrete units, so that the student can easily cut from the herd the section that explains apostrophe use and deal with that beast all by itself. Other texts require the student to go through the entire sequence, perhaps omitting those parts for which a pretest shows efficient mastery of the material, but otherwise following a systematic approach. Again, your choice depends on the needs of the particular student.

Once you've chosen an appropriate handbook or text, make sure students know what's in the book, how it's organized, how to use it. Have them practice using it to perform a relevant task such as deciding whether to place an apostrophe after an *s*, how to label a figure, or how to cite a journal article. Such an exercise also demonstrates to students that you value the text and expect them to use it. Moreover, watching your students try to use the handbook to solve writing problems helps you decide what level and type of handbook they need.

You can further encourage active use of the handbook by assigning a section to be read each week. Write the reading assignment on the syllabus, along with the reading in the subject-area text. Ask in class whether everyone has read and understood the section. Assign a short exercise that will test students' mastery of the material.

Finally, integrate use of the handbook or text with the writing students do for your course. Remind them in class—"Use your handbook to edit your reports, paying special attention to chapters 1–4." Mark papers with chapter numbers or symbols that refer to specific parts of the text (some texts have symbols inside the cover for easy reference). Use every strategy you can think of to show your students that you consider editing a crucial part of preparing any piece of writing for formal submission.

Help the Basic Writer

Basic writer is a term used to describe students who have difficulty with the most basic forms of written English. Here is a sample of a college student's writing:

```
The main point of this topic is that the Children an College students
aren't learning how to read and write for that they will used later in life.
I don't believe society has prepared me for the work I want to do that. is in
education speaking, that my point in being here, If this isn't a essay. of a
thousand word's that because I don't have much to say. for it has been four
years since I last wrote one, and by the time I am finish here I hope to be
able to write an number of essay. (Shaughnessy 14)
```

Mina Shaughnessy, a teacher at City University of New York when it had open admissions, worked for years with students who were radically unprepared for writing at a college level. David Bartholomae's "The Study of Error" builds on her work. These studies show that the typical basic writer is neither stupid nor ineducable and that the "errors" on the page do not drop randomly from the sky. Rather, errors have a logic: they can be divided into features that the writer would readily identify as goofs and features that represent the writer's attempt to make sense of the conventions of standard written English. Typically, such students have spoken a dialect or second language, and they have had little writing practice in their former schooling. Their errors, when analyzed, make sense: they apply half a rule; they apply a rule to a case that's an exception to the rule; they apply the wrong rule for the situation; they universally adopt some features that sound correct and use them in all situations (e.g., a student who's been corrected for "Can her and me go to the store?" will thereafter use "she and I" in all cases: "He gave the book to *she and I*"). Just as teachers of French to English speakers analyze errors for insights into their students' needs, so can teachers of basic writers.

In the passage above, Shaughnessy finds patterns: the inclination to use the comma as a period and to employ the period to mark subordinate structures. Note the word *inclination*, which Shaughnessy uses. Especially in the work of basic writers such as this, one finds not so much consistent rules as tendencies and inclinations. To a trained observer, however, the tendencies indicate a direction for remediation. You may not get deeply into error-analysis skills, but if you ask yourself what led to the error, you can often follow the mind of the learner and offer helpful instruction. But more than the dissection skills, you need the proper attitude—that even a student whose writing is shockingly inept can learn standard written English. It's just that you're starting from way back. Most academics have written and read extensively throughout their lives. It's easy to assume that we were born with pencil bumps on our third finger and hard to imagine how it would be to have read and written as little as many basic writers have. Anger, exasperation, or the assumption that your students are hopeless have no place. You need the attitude of the beginning French teacher, who is not angry at the students for being beginners but sets about to help them learn. The only target for anger, I believe, is your college, if it is accepting basic writers and not providing them with the support and services they need to have a chance to succeed. If you have basic writers in your class and there's no careful sequence of courses for them, no training for faculty in all disciplines who are handling such students, no attention to the problems of motivation and self-image, and no professionally staffed writing center, then anger is appropriate. So is action directed at improving the situation.

If you have basic writers in your classes, early identification and close cooperation with a learning center are crucial. The best guidance for such a student's efforts comes from a teacher or tutor trained in remediation. If your school has no such resource, however, you can use a self-instructional program that offers not only rules of punctuation but also practice in constructing various sentence patterns. The text must begin with the basic sentence, with identification of subject and predicate, and with practice in forming the various constructions that amplify the basic subject-verb unit. The text should be written very simply.

Whatever text students use at this level, you will undoubtedly want to provide a great deal of support and encouragement, for such students have a long, discouraging route to travel before they achieve academic excellence, or even competence. In your course, ask such students to write often but in short units. Have the student use journals for daily writing of responses to class lectures and readings. Any format that encourages fluidity and relaxation will be helpful. You can also use the never-again notebook for sentence-pattern drill. Have students write a series of sentences according to various patterns, starting with the most basic subject-verb units and advancing to more complex patterns. For example, if you found the student sentence quoted above, you might begin by asking the student to write, "This isn't an essay of a thousand words." Then go to other simple subject-verb units following the same pattern. Next the student writes, "If this isn't an essay of a thousand words, that's because I don't have much to say." Then request other sentences that begin with *if* or similar words. Finally, the students might practice adding units: "If this isn't an essay of a thousand words, that's because I don't have much to say, for it has been four years since I last wrote one, but by the time I am finished here I hope to be able to write a number of essays." The three graduated steps of this exercise may roughly match the student's progress through a printed text that works first with simple subject-verb units, then with sentences beginning with *if* and similar adverbial clauses, and finally with sentences that take on additional units by means of a comma plus a connective such as *for*, *but*, or *and*. Try to make the never-again notebook a bridge between the stages of a student's progress through the printed text and the sentences that actually appear in the student's written assignments. Use it also to provide simple practice in putting pen to paper. Remember that a significant part of such students' dilemma is likely to be that they have done very little writing, ever.

In the writing of students who are not sure how to identify or punctuate sentences you will find much puzzling punctuation. You can assume, however, that there is some pattern you cannot immediately see. It is worthwhile, if you have the time, to try to decipher patterns of error, so that you can suggest specific and useful remedies.

Help the Dialect Speaker and the Speaker of English as a Second Language

Most academic writing uses Edited American English (EAE). As the word *edited* implies, EAE is not precisely the language of anyone's everyday speech. Even a white Scarsdale banker's everyday speech differs somewhat from the language the banker would write in a business or academic setting. Further, most speakers range across a variety of language uses—one for the poolroom, another for the classroom. Language choices vary according to a speaker's sense of the audience or of the appropriate level of formality.

Some students have grown up speaking a language close to EAE. Others are much further away; their dialect may present significant problems when they must write EAE. An understanding of how dialect affects writing is essential in handling students' grammar and usage problems. Some initial information about language acquisition may help.

By five years of age, all normal children have learned most of the grammatical patterns of the language(s) they have heard (Langacker). For some native English speakers, however, dialect that they learned as tots and that they continue to use in the neighborhood store and at home is not always one that teachers and employers consider correct. In American society, those whose colloquial speech differs most sharply from standard English are the ethnic minorities and the poor. To paraphrase an old Afro-American saying, if lions had power in our society, roaring would be correct English. But since middle-class whites are the advantaged group, their grammar and usage are regarded as standard.

The lions are therefore at a disadvantage. But that is not to say they are culturally or linguistically "disadvantaged" or "deprived" in the way some misguided philanthropists, educators, and government officials have used the terms. Black students from an urban ghetto are not necessarily linguistically or culturally deprived at all; they belong to an extremely rich culture, whose dialect is vivid, tough, and graceful. Linguistic research has shown conclusively that there is no inherent connection between language competency and race and that every dialect and variety of language is equally capable of serving its purposes (Langacker 98–99). Thus the dialect spoken by a ghetto black from Boston or by a backwoods farmer from Arkansas is just as complex, just as precisely rulebound, and just as useful a tool of communication, in its own setting, as the so-called standard English spoken by a white Scarsdale banker.

Though all languages and dialects are in some ways equal, a particular student who writes for your class may have a greater or smaller vocabulary than others, may be more or less skilled in using the nuances of the language, or may manipulate the complexities of the language with more or less facility. Part of this student's difficulty may be a result of limited mental or verbal capacity. Part may stem from the home environment. Children may grow up speaking in what linguists call a "restricted code," in which language is sparsely functional, or an "elaborated code," in which language is rich and full. These codes may depend partly on class and culture, but wide variations in language skills and habits can be found in students of all cultures and socioeconomic classes.

Furthermore, you can't always tell how linguistically adept a student is. You can perhaps judge with some accuracy the language competency of a student from a background similar to your own: it is, however, much harder to determine the language competency of a student whose dialect and culture differ from yours and whose behavior may be influenced by cultural tensions and perhaps overt discrimination in school. Judgment is further hampered if you misinterpret the habits of stance, eye contact, or response to authority figures customary in the student's native culture. For example, in some American cultures it is considered cheeky for a child or a young person to make eye contact with an authority figure. So in a conference with the teacher, the student will politely stare at the floor, and the middle-class instructor, unable to get the student to meet his or her eye, may conclude that the student is sly, shy, sullen, or stupid. Thus by the time such students come under your tutelage, their language ability may be obscured by feelings of inadequacy, self-consciousness, and frustration developed during years of struggling with the school system.

That dialects can influence even those students whose school writing does not have identifiable dialect characteristics further illustrates the complexity of the dialect problem. One test of college freshmen who showed no recognizable dialect forms in their writing but who were judged to need remedial work for other reasons showed that a high number of them *knew* dialect forms (Crystal). So it appears that even when you have no overt features to guide you, you must realize that a particular student who has for years spoken some dialect has lacked practice in the constructions of EAE.

So how does this information about language affect you as you teach students? First of all, especially if your own spoken language is close to EAE, you will want to watch for grammar and usage that may look wrong to you but that are acceptable in the student's own dialect. Of course, students' writing also contains many examples of grammar and usage that don't belong to any language, that would readily be identified simply as goofs by the students themselves, or that are due to causes other than dialect. If you're not sure whether a particular form might be dialect-related, it helps to know that dialects of English differ most markedly in their verb forms, pronouns, plurals, and possessives.

Let's say that a black student in your class says or writes "I work" where EAE would demand "I worked." You recognize this as a dialect form. Now what? It is important that all your subsequent dialogue with the student proceed from your own recognition that the other person is not writing "incorrectly" and is not "leaving off the -ed ending of the verbs." Rather, the writer is recording the "correct" form of the past tense as heard and learned from childhood. In communicating with students, you will want to do your best to avoid words like "wrong" or "incorrect" and instead employ words that communicate the concept of "appropriateness" or "dialect choice" or "level of formality." You will also want to avoid making any subtle assumptions that such students are culturally deprived or that their race of socioeconomic class has caused them to be linguistically less sophisticated or less able than other students.

The white middle-class teacher should also be careful not to take a patronizing attitude toward "those people." Again, linguistic studies show that people learn to command an astonishing variety of dialects and levels of formality. To assume that a student who does not yet command EAE will not be able to do so is a form of discrimination.

Recognize also that dialect features are a matter of class, culture, and other factors, not solely of race. Some studies show that black, Hispanic, and white students in a given college course will all produce many of the nonstandard writing forms we associate with dialects (studies are summarized in Giannasi 282–83).

Although the dialect issue is full of complexities, you should not simply leave the writers alone. The choice of dialect and the level of formality should be the subject of conscious and thoughtful deliberation for every writer, and those aspects of a writer's work are appropriate topics for student-teacher dialogue. Therefore, you will want to talk with students who, in an academic paper, use "I work" as the past tense. You will want to speak in terms that transmit your respect for the students' own language and your recognition that the problem is one of appropriateness, not of correctness. The discussion will result in some kind of decision about dialect forms and level of formality in the paper.

Such a decision is usually a matter of degree and consistency. Even if you and the students decide that certain dialect forms differing from EAE are appropriate to a particular paper, students will often not have used those dialect forms consistently, but will have mixed them in with EAE forms, since the writing of many dialect-speaking students is already, by the time a teacher sees it, a mixture of their dialects and forms they think will be acceptable to the teacher. Thus you must decide not only whether dialect or informal language is appropriate, but which forms, to what extent, and at what points in the paper.

In making the decision, you may take one of several positions. The students may strongly wish to master EAE. Most students realize that if they wish to earn degrees, get good jobs, and enjoy a number of society's other cookies and gumdrops, they will have to be able to speak and write EAE. Thus many students are happy to have a sympathetic teacher help them learn it.

You may choose to help students learn and write EAE without letting their skill in this area affect their grades. That way the students are not penalized by grade while they are still struggling to master EAE.

Another possible position is to accept only EAE and grade down for use of other dialects. Some teachers justify this stand by saying that, since other teachers and employers will demand EAE, the teacher who cares about students ought to show them graphically what it's like out in the world, where they will be required to use EAE.

Other teachers, though they know that students will be forced to use EAE in other situations, refuse to become part of "the system." Such a teacher can, however, make clear to the student the penalties suffered in American society by one who does not speak or write EAE and can stand ready to help the students master EAE if they wish (for a discussion of the issues, see Giannasi).

For the dialect speaker there are special self-instructional programs that borrow many techniques from foreign language instruction. For example, they have drills in which the student compares dialect forms with EAE forms or translates back and forth from one to the other. An important characteristic of such texts—and one you will want to look for in other programs—is their avoidance of the phrase "correct English." They talk instead about choice of dialects or levels of formality. Such books use words like "error" and "correctness" only in clear reference to correctness *for EAE*. (In matters of spelling and punctuation, which are not features of dialect, the concept of correctness is, of course, more appropriate.) Special texts are also available for students learning English as a second language (ESL).

For dialect and ESL speakers, the most obvious teaching method, in addition to workbooks, is the same method by which students learn any language—exposure and practice. All the reading and listening that you can work into your classroom activities will join with the listening and reading provided in other classes to give students valuable exposure. Beyond that, you can borrow ideas from foreign language teachers. You can also find out how much exposure to EAE your students are getting outside class. Students who socialize primarily with those who speak their own dialect or language might benefit from pairing up each day for lunch with a student who speaks something close to EAE. Sometimes a class in teaching methods for high school English or teaching English as a second language will provide tutors. Perhaps psychologically the best pairing is one in which the EAE speaker also tries to learn the other's dialect or language, so that the sessions involve exchanges between students rather than one-way tutoring. Or move to the written medium: have the student write, in EAE, a page a day about anything at all; then ask another student familiar with EAE to pick out the variant forms. In other words, do anything you can to approximate the kind of language teaching that takes place at the nightly French dinner, the French House, or the French Club. Imitate the ways in which your school goes about helping English students learn another tongue.

Observing the Writing Process

A necessary component of coaching your students is carefully and systematically to observe them and yourself, so you learn more about how you and they write and learn and about how your coaching strategies help or hinder them.

Benefits of Inquiry

There is ample opportunity for publication of such research; teachers and researchers are hungry for information about what happens in classrooms when students think and write. An equally rewarding and legitimate goal is for you to become a better teacher. Information about your students can feed directly into teaching strategies, whose results, in turn, can be immediately studied. The benefits of research into your students' writing and learning, however, reach even beyond a published article or a new teaching strategy. Such inquiry can keep you intellectually alive across years of teaching the same subject matter.

Further, researching your own classroom changes the atmosphere of the class and creates a new relation between you and your students, because they become your partners in the inquiry. Share with them your questions and your research. Encourage them to become researchers of their own and one another's writing and learning processes. You can infuse into your classroom the energy of active learning, shared by you and your students.

Beginning Your Observation

How can such inquiry begin? You may already have a question about your own writing or teaching, or about your students' writing and learning. If so, try to figure out some systematic procedures that will help you explore your question. But don't close too quickly on a question, and don't think that you have to have a well-formulated question or a strict research design before you begin. It is enough simply to begin to observe. You are a good place to start. For one week, collect all your writing and keep a log about it. What motivated it? How did you work on it? How do you feel about it? At the end of the week, study your own writing process. Try to describe it as carefully as you can, categorize its parts, note strategies you used to attack problems, observe what you paid most attention to.

Another good way to begin an inquiry is to keep your own writing log and ask your students to keep logs as they write. You can ask for the logs as an accompaniment to the papers. You will get fuller information if you prod your students with specific questions and topics for their logs. Below are some questions that I have used successfully for years. You may use or adapt them for yourself and your students.

Questions for a Writer's Log
A Student's Guide

1. What steps did I follow in preparing writing the paper? At each step, what mental activities did I engage in? What actual writing, if any, was produced at that step? How much time did that step take?
2. Did I experience periods of discouragement? How did I try to overcome them?
3. Did I seek help from others? In what ways? With what results?
4. How much did I revise after my first draft was written? How much did I revise *during* the writing of a draft? When I revised, what sorts of things did I change? Single words only? Punctuation? Paragraph structure? Content? Organization? How did I decide what to change? Did I change different sorts of things at different points in the writing process?

5. Did I lay my paper aside at any time for incubation?
6. How did I decide when my paper was finished?

(adapted from Walvoord, *Writing* 7)

Another rich and easily collectible record is students' successive notes and drafts, as they work on their papers. Ask students to date and number their notes and drafts—anything they have written that contributed to the final paper. Ask them to attach these materials to the back of the final draft as it's handed in. A log accompanying the drafts will help to establish the sequence and add depth to the record.

Analyzing Data

Once you have your logs and/or drafts, sit down with the record of one student, and try to re-create the story of the student's thinking, learning, and writing. Take notes about whatever catches your attention. Then re-create another student's story, and another. Go over the records several times; insights will begin to cohere. Below are some questions you might ask:

1. What was most difficult for each student? In how many ways did students address the difficult aspects of the task? What were the most common strategies? Do any strategies seem linked to the success of the piece of writing?

2. Does this student's process divide itself into parts? What happens within the parts? How do students compare with one another in the discernible parts or stages of their writing?

3. What kinds of input were students getting from me? from others? from texts? from observation? How does this input affect their writing process?

4. What kinds of revisions did this student make? How many revisions were local in their impact? How many were global? In addition to classifying revision by its impact, you might classify it by operation (deletion, addition, condensation, moving a passage to a different place, etc.), or you might select a particular problem or aspect in the student's writing and analyze how revisions affected that aspect. In one batch of student records from a biology class, for example, students had to deal with the question of audience. They had been told to write to their classmates in scientific format about a scientific investigation they had conducted, comparing two products, such as two brands of popping corn, to see which was better. The instructor thought she was presenting a clear designation of audience, but the drafts show that students struggled with the implied definition of their peer audience—were they to address their classmates as fellow scientists? as lay consumers of scientific information? as consumers who might buy the products? as college students? All those stances occurred. We went through the records to reconstruct how each student arrived at the tone and voice that finally ruled the paper.

These are only a few of the questions that may be asked of logs and drafts. And logs and drafts are only some of the records one may gather. I have suggested them here because they are easy to collect and because they generate many questions about your students' learning and writing processes.

Expanding Your Research Methods

As specific questions emerge, you can turn to other data-gathering methods such as interviews, questionnaires, direct observation of students' behavior as they are researching and composing, or taped sessions in which the student is asked to think aloud while composing.

Depending on your question, your training, and your temperament, you may follow, adapt, or reject an experimental design that involves a control group and strictly controlled variables. It's difficult to conduct research on student thinking and writing by using strict experimental designs, and the questions that can be answered that way may not be the questions you want to answer. Researchers often adapt other methods, especially from the field of ethnography. Such research begins with observation; questions and further research methods arise from the observation and are clarified during the course of the research. The goal is "thick" data that yields descriptions, classifications, hypotheses, and tentative proposals about connections rather than definitive, generalizable conclusions expressed in statistical form. Validation comes through the ability of the research to "triangulate" the data—that is, to support a conclusion by evidence from more than one source. For example, an interview with a student may corroborate or contradict what you observe in the student's notes, log, or think-aloud tape.

An excellent rationale for teacher research that will give shape and justification to your inquiry is Dixie Goswami's "Teachers as Researchers." The first five essays in Beach and Bridwell's *New Directions in Composition Research* (15–126) form a useful starter set on a variety of research methods. Other essays in that volume illustrate methods that can be adapted to study college students. An excellent beginner's introduction to ethnographic methods is Stephen Doheny-Farina and Lee Odell's "Ethnographic Research on Writing: Assumptions and Methodology."

Collaborative Research

Collaborating with a colleague in classroom research can spice the experience for both of you and result in better research. At different times I have collaborated with a biologist, a psychologist, an economist, and several faculty members in business and management. As a pair, I and the other faculty member study the writing processes of students in one of our classes. Such inquiry can begin with observation. The collaborators may look at papers, notes, logs, and drafts. The instructor of the class may keep a careful log of goals, teaching strategies, and observations of students in the classroom and in conferences. The collaborator may sit in on some classes, group meetings, or conferences, observing and recording the students' and instructors' behavior. Here are some questions observers might ask: How must students act to be deemed "competent" in this setting? In what ways does the instructor guide their behavior? How do students get the floor? Who exercises what kinds of power? Who talks to whom? About what? How is writing described and handled in the class? Meet once a week over lunch to shape emerging questions and check your insights with each other. Gradually shape more specific questions, hypotheses, and research methods.

Much of the time, instructors can be a visible team, collaborating with students in the research effort. In some instances, however, you may want to encourage greater student truthfulness in logs by having the collaborator who is not teaching appear in the class as "researcher" to explain and collect the logs. That person makes clear to students that the content of their logs will not be seen by the instructor until after final grades are awarded. Logs and think-aloud tapes are the records most apt to be affected by students' concern that their grade will suffer if they do not describe a "correct" writing process, but you may want to use this strategy for notes and drafts as well.

Students as Researchers

Your methods and questions may engage your students in the role of informants who help you in the task of collecting, interpreting, and recording *their* writing processes. However, you can also send your students out into the world to study how writing goes on there. At Canisius College in Buffalo, New York, for example, instructors from various disciplines have cooperated to design projects in which students study the writing processes of professionals in science, government, or other fields. Each student must find two writers who will agree to two hour-long interviews. In the first interview, students establish contact, learn the basic situation of the writer, and collect several samples of the professional's writing. Then they formulate questions according to some specific techniques, attempting to discover the situations, constraints, and decisions that lie behind the piece of writing. (The techniques for deriving questions from the writing samples are explained in Odell, Goswami, and Herrington, "The Discourse-Based Interview.") Having formulated the questions and practiced the questioning methods, students conduct the second interview and then report on their findings. The exercise takes some supervision, since students must learn the questioning technique, but it provides a wonderful opportunity for them to learn how writing is actually carried on in professions related to your discipline. The results are likely to be a new realism on students' part about the importance of writing and a new sophistication about how writing, and research on writing, is carried on. David Lauerman of the English department at Canisius College is a source of more information about this method. (An article by Lauerman et al. contains some information about the program.)

Summary

This chapter has offered a large number of options for coaching many aspects of the writing process—helping students to understand the process itself, to become involved and interested, to structure their time, analyze the assignment, seek help, write for their audience and context, generate ideas and focus their topics, gather and integrate information, reason and organize, draft, revise, use visual aids, and edit for style and mechanics. The suggestions are meant not to be used in linear order but to be integrated, since the writing process itself is not linear but recursive. Your own and your students' observation of the writing process will be your best guide to gradual improvement in your ability to help your students become good writers.

The next chapter discusses in greater detail one part of coaching the writing process—using peer groups. Following that, a chapter of case studies shows how some instructors have selected, combined and adapted the ideas suggested here.

Chapter Four

Using Student Peer Groups

This discussion will distinguish student groups established primarily for response, where each student produces a piece of writing, from "task groups," in which students cooperate on a single group paper. Both types of groups will usually number between three and seven people.

Response Groups

Constructing the Group

The ephemeral student group formed for a five- or ten-minute exchange during a class hour has already been amply discussed throughout this volume. There are two ways to form these groups: by assigning people to groups that remain constant throughout the semester or by letting groups reform on every occasion, depending on who is sitting where. The advantage of the former is that students in an ongoing group build trust; the disadvantage is that a group that isn't working well is stuck for the semester and that on a given day, when you call groups into session, some groups may be denuded by absences. You have to weigh the pros and cons of permanent groups for your own situation and goals. Groups whose members read one another's drafts may best be kept constant, since the building of trust is crucial to good draft response.

Guiding the Group

Giving instructions. Whenever a group meets, it needs a specific task, a way of getting started, a way of knowing when its task is done, and some guidance about the participation of the members: length, type, sequence. You may also want to warn the group about common pitfalls. Groups will easily forget parts of a lengthy instruction, so write key words on the board. These elements help keep the group from sagging into chitchat.

Below is a sample oral instruction for a 20-minute group session, in which students are given a chance to try out their topic choices for a paper. The instructor says:

When you form your groups, someone be bold enough to begin (or the person sitting toward the windows should begin). That person should take just two or three minutes to describe a possible topic. Then each person in the group should respond in such a way as to help the writer go forward with the idea. You might ask a question about the topic, say what you would expect a report on that topic to contain, or make a suggestion to help the writer narrow the topic. At this early stage, one of the best things the group can do is to get the writer talking, so he or she has a chance to work out ideas. But writers, be sure that you don't take more than five or six minutes on your own topic; then move the group on to the next person. Each person in the group should plan to respond at least once to every other person's topic. If one person in the group is not participating, see if you can help that person jump into the conversation. When each person's topic has been discussed, everybody take three or four minutes to write a few sentences about how your group affected your thinking about your topic. When you're done with your writing, hand it to me; then you may leave. Any questions about what you should do? I'll write the first few steps on the board: [writes] "1. Person toward windows begins; 2-3 minutes to describe topic. 2. All respond (question, expectation, narrowing); 5-6 minutes per writer. 3. Write how group affected your thinking."

Group self-evaluation. Groups benefit from self-evaluation. Ask the group members to take the last five minutes of the group time to write a few sentences telling how they thought the group went, how they would describe their own role, and what they would like to change. These comments can be used as a basis for group sharing, either immediately or at the beginning of the next group meeting. If you collect them, students in the groups may be encouraged to make the group succeed, since they know you will be reading their own and their peers' evaluations of it. The writings are also, of course, a good way for you to become aware of how the groups are doing. If you collect the writings, you may want to encourage candor by allowing students to write anonymously.

Building trust early. When groups are to respond to drafts, give them a chance to meet together in less threatening ways first. The early meetings may last only five or ten minutes and may consist of any exercise that does not call for criticism of anyone's contribution. For example, ask students to describe what they have found most difficult about planning the paper so far, or give each a chance to describe a successful writing experience in the past. Have students write summaries of a lecture or reading and read their writing to one another with no comments. Not only must students learn the material they've summarized, but each will learn from hearing how others summarized it. Yet you do not introduce the more threatening step of group response to an individual's writing.

Structure the group's talk. When you introduce group response to drafts, structure the groups and give them guidance. I have talked with many instructors who tried groups and were unhappy with them, then began to structure the group's task more carefully, and now wouldn't think of teaching without the power of group response. Below is an instruction sheet you can hand to group members to be read before they meet for response to draft essays. You may use or adapt the sheet for your own students and assignments.

Group Discussion of Drafts
A Student's Guide

1. Before handing out copies of the draft, the author should read aloud the first sentence of the paper. The group should then tell the author what that sentence leads them to think is the main point of the paper and what material will make up the body of the paper.

2. Then the author should hand out copies of the draft to all group members.

3. The author should read the paper aloud.

4. There should be two or three minutes of silence to allow group members to digest the paper and gather their thoughts.

5. Group members should then, in turn, voice their reactions:
   a. State the main point of the paper in a single sentence. Who do you think is the audience for the paper? What is the paper's purpose?
   b. List the major subtopics in the paper. If the paper is long, list the subtopics in each major section.
   c. Were there any points at which you were confused about the subject or focus of the paper or its sections?
   d. Consider each section of the paper in turn. Is each developed with enough detail, evidence, and information?
   e. Do the points follow one another in an appropriate sequence?
   f. Is there other material that the author should include?
   g. Are the opening and concluding paragraphs accurate guides to the paper's theme and focus?
   h. Considering the paper paragraph by paragraph, what seems most vivid, clear, and memorable? Where is the language clumsy?

6. The writer should follow these guidelines:
   a. Do not argue with the readers, and do not explain what you meant. You are gathering data about audience response. So, simply gather it. If a particular response does not seem useful, you are free to ignore it when you revise your paper. But for you to spend the group's time arguing and explaining is wasteful and can cause the group to focus on understanding what you meant rather than on responding to what you wrote.
   b. It is usually best for you to remain silent, remembering carefully or writing down what readers say. In addition, you may want to:
      (1) Ask a reader to clarify or expand a statement, so that you understand it thoroughly.

(2)   Ask readers to respond to an idea you have for improvement of some aspect of the paper they're unhappy with.

(3)   Repeat to the group what you think they're saying, just to make sure communication is complete.

In addition to a sheet that tells groups what to do, students may be given a list of the qualities you will look for in the finished paper. An example is Mark Curchack's checklist on p. 47. The group members work from that list as they respond. Alternatively, have the class or the groups design such a list, based on their understanding of the audience, purpose, genre, and circumstances for the writing.

Be available for conferences. You can help allay the anxiety of some students by offering to respond to any draft or plan after the group has responded to it. If possible, hang around for a few minutes as the groups are dispersing. A few students will approach you: "Will you look at my paper?" You can read it on the spot, if time permits, or make an appointment. When you've read the draft, ask first, "What did your group say?" Often the group has given appropriate counsel, and you can simply say, "I think your group gave you good advice," thus helping that student to develop trust in the group process. Even if the group's response seems incomplete or misleading, begin from it if you can. You can also say, however, "I would respond differently," and then explain. Tell your students in class, and in situations such as this, that writing often provokes varied responses from readers and that writers simply have to deal with that experience as best they can.

Provide feedback to the groups. The most common way of managing groups is to have them meet simultaneously during a single class hour. You can disperse them to various corners of your classroom or ask your registrar to send you a list of nearby classrooms that are vacant during your hour. If none are vacant, ask your students to scout for spots that will hold a group: an empty snack bar, some small library conference rooms, or a projection room.

Despite warnings and guidance, groups will need some time to learn to function effectively. How can you speed and guide that process? Below are some suggestions (see also Mary Kay Healy's *Using Student Response Groups in the Classroom*).

You can tape your groups—a step that may initially make them more self-conscious but that keeps them seriously on task. Select taped portions that illustrate where groups did good work, and play them for the class. You can sit in on one group each class period and end the session by offering suggestions about its process (you may also respond to individual papers). You can float during a class period, visiting several groups, again offering observations. Below is a list of things you might look for as you comment on and observe the group's process:

• Is anyone not participating?
• Is anyone dominating too completely?

- Is some praise voiced for each person's draft?
- Is the group's pace fast enough?
- Does the group move smoothly and at appropriate times from one draft to the next?
- Are comments sufficiently specific? (That is, after someone says, "It's a good paper," or "I thought it was well organized," does the group specifically say what is good about it or what makes it well organized?)
- Is the group approaching matters of focus, organization, and evidence first? Do members avoid nitpicking about spelling and punctuation when a paper needs more significant revision?
- When one student has made a comment, do other students voice their agreement or disagreement, so the writer knows whether the response was idiosyncratic or general to the group? Or does the rest of the group just sit there, without revealing what they think of the comment?
- When the group has decided that a draft is well focused and basically well organized, does someone take responsibility for leading the group through a paragraph-by-paragraph examination of the draft? Does the group know what to look for and what to say in such an examination?
- Do any writers spend the group's time making excuses for the paper?
- Do any writers spend the group's time explaining what they meant? Does the group accept the explanation with "OK," giving writers the impression that explaining their meaning is a substitute for revising the paper? Do writers always take responsibility for misunderstandings, or do group members sometimes apologize?
- Do writers ever respond to suggestions by explaining why they wrote as they did? If so, does this exchange help the writer and the group to figure out how to express the writer's purpose better, or does the writer intimidate the group into acquiescence?
- Do group members feel free to disagree with one another?
- Do writers indicate, by verbal and nonverbal language, their appreciation of the group's suggestions, or does a writer become testy or defensive?
- Do writers appear to understand that they must express appreciation in the group but may ignore group members' suggestions as they revise?
- Does the group appreciate and deal fairly with writers who approach the assignment in creative ways, or do they impose too harsh a conformity?
- What standards for evaluation does the group seem to be using? Are the standards appropriate for the assignment, or do students need to be taught what makes a paper "good" in your field?

You can have groups observe one another. Ask one group to pull chairs in a circle and other students to pull chairs in an outside circle around the group that is meeting. The inside group carries on its meeting without interruption; the students in the outside group observe, and later comment on, the group's interaction. To help the observers know what to look for, you can give them a check sheet containing questions such as those above.

Finally, as suggested earlier, you can have members write about their groups and use those writings as a basis for the group's discussion of its own processes.

Require attendance. Since a full complement of group members is needed for successful group meetings, you might want to tell your students that you require attendance on group meeting days and that unexcused absences will affect their course grade.

Keep groups together. When a group is not working well, my advice is to resist the temptation to break it up, even when groups request it. The addition of new members to your other response groups may throw them off, and the troubled group is bailed out rather than forced to face its unproductive interactions. I offer plenty of support and encouragement to the troubled group but make it solve its own problems.

Your Presence in the Group

The instructors may use their presence in the group to guide the group's interaction. One model for your interaction with the group is to restrict your role to commentator on the group process. You sit outside the group circle and remain silent until it is time for you to move to another group or until the end of the group's meeting. Then you take just a few minutes to comment on what you have observed about the group's interaction. Be sure to include praise. Often you can make your suggestions through questions: "Mary, how did you feel after Craig's response to your paper?" or "When John responded to Ginny by telling what he meant to say in the paper, how could Ginny have best answered?" You should leave the group with no more than two or three suggestions for improvement. Give group members a chance to respond to your suggestions; they may perceive a situation differently than you do or may want to argue for their way of doing things.

You can enlarge your role by acting as a group member, making responses to the drafts. The great danger when you assume this role is that soon the group will fall into a pattern: a person reads a paper; everyone looks expectantly at you; you take the bait and give a long response to the paper, which the group takes as the "right answer"; whereupon it seems futile for anyone else to respond, so no one does. Yet there is a legitimate role for the instructor as a responder in the group—you can model appropriate responding, comment on matters the group is not sophisticated enough to pick up, keep the group on task, quicken its pace, and add to the fullness of response that each student receives. A telling argument for your presence is that, since you are inescapably an important part of your students' audience, it seems most honest for you to sit in, letting them know your responses to drafts.

You can fulfill these functions and still allow genuine group participation by sitting back in your chair, by holding your comments until others have spoken, and by directing questions to other members: "Bill, was your response to that paragraph different from mine?" You can also explain candidly to your students that you want to join the group, not dominate it, and that you want their responses to form a large part of the group interaction. Also tell them that their comments should be addressed to the writer rather than to you. Otherwise, they will comment directly to you, referring to the writer in the next chair as "she" or "he." If you find that they all roll their eyes to you as soon as one person has made a comment, deflect the expectation by rolling your eyes back at them, waiting for one of them to answer. Or directly say, "What do the rest of you think?"

Arranging Consecutive Groups

You can offer more guidance if you arrange group meetings consecutively rather than simultaneously. Then you meet with each group for its entire session. Especially with freshmen, or with students unused to group interaction, you may prefer this method to the "float." I follow this pattern with a freshman class that has five papers throughout the semester. The first three or four times, I meet with each group for its full session, gradually playing a less dominant role. By the third time I may be silent for the entire session, commenting only at the end, with a few suggestions or questions for the group. Students learn by my responses how to respond helpfully, what to look for, and how to phrase their comments. I also guide their interaction. But I express clearly my intention of working myself out of a job and my confidence that the group members can learn to respond effectively to one another's drafts. By the time a group is meeting for its fourth or fifth draft response of the semester, I appear only briefly as the group gathers, tell the students I'm pleased with their progress, and say I'm sure they can now function on their own. Then I leave, with instructions where to find me at the session's close, if they need me. I find that with the guidance I have been able to give earlier, their functioning when I leave them is much more sophisticated and helpful than when I had groups meeting simultaneously and could only float among them.

The logistics go this way: I declare certain weeks as "group response weeks." I designate a number of time slots for group meetings, spaced across the week. For a class of 25, I have five time slots of 75 minutes each, spaced throughout the week. At the beginning of the semester, I pass the sheet around in class; each student signs in a time slot. When five people have chosen one slot, the group is formed and no one else may sign. During each group week, I meet individually with each of the groups.

You may cancel regular class meetings during a group week, using the regular class hour for some of the groups, or you may meet the groups entirely outside of class hours. If you use class hours for groups, the work load is reasonable; if you use only outside hours, the load is certainly heavy. However, the instructor takes home no papers. After the third meeting, the groups function on their own, so all those drafts get responses without investment of the instructor's time, except to be available so that any students who want teacher response to a draft can get it.

When I meet with a group, I follow the guidelines above for limiting my dominance. I participate as a group member, offering my response to drafts, and I also, at the end, or sometimes during the session, offer comments to the group on its process. I may, for example, say to a student, "Oops, remember, don't make excuses for the paper" or "When one person comments on a particular aspect, others in the group should say whether the comment reflects the feeling of the whole group, or not." One has to judge which individuals or groups are able to take this sort of check, pick up with a chuckle, and go on. If your ongoing comments on group interaction seem to chasten the group into silence, save your suggestions until the end of the group's meeting.

Task Groups

A task group is responsible as a group for a single finished piece of writing. The final two case histories in the next chapter show task groups in action. This discussion centers on general guidelines for establishing and helping such groups.

The task group reflects a common situation students will meet in the career world. Your students will accept the strangeness and sometimes the frustrations inherent in the group structure if you share with them results of studies that show a large percentage of career-world writing is collaborative (Faigley and Miller).

Task groups may all be assigned the same writing task, such as a report or research proposal, or different tasks. You might even assign each group one aspect of some large class project such as a case study or a research project. One group, or a separately selected editor and assistant editor, would be in charge of pulling the whole thing together.

Task groups present an unusual opportunity for creating "real" writing situations. For example, perhaps your class can offer genuinely valuable services to some department or office in your university or to the public. I have taught a class where students, in groups of three to five, formed consulting firms that the director of academic computing engaged to perform genuine work he needed. One group completed, and reported on, a survey of the freshman class to determine how much computer experience students had on entering the college; another offered suggestions for revision of the student guide to the college's computing service; yet another revised documentation for one of the computers. Community service is also possible. At Loyola College, Andrew Ciofalo offers the service of his advertising students to not-for-profit agencies in the community, who often cannot afford to hire advertising services and are happy to have the students' help. At Towson State University, undergraduate math majors, through a consulting institute originally supported by the National Science Foundation, offer services to local industry ("TSU Math"; "Solving"; for more information, write the dean of the College of Natural and Mathematical Sciences, Towson State Univ., Towson, MD 21204).

Constituting the Groups

Since the groups must collaborate on one piece of writing, the constitution of the groups is crucial to their functioning. Instructors' beliefs and practices about constituting groups differ widely. One physics instructor believes in telling students that they must form groups of three by 10 October and then letting them work it out among themselves. This method may work best for small classes, for classes of majors who already have come to know one another through previous courses, or for small residential colleges; to support it in large classes or with commuting students, however, you may have to give students a class list or provide early opportunities for them to get to know one another. If your lecture sessions for the first three weeks include several small-group activities and if you make sure that the membership of these small groups changes each time, class members can come to know one another's capabilities.

Some instructors who successfully run task groups spend considerable time themselves constituting the groups, on the basis of personality, work habits, and abilities. They try to sprinkle the more able students evenly among the groups, or to provide each group with, say, a student who is good at a certain type of statistical analysis that is necessary to the group's task.

A middle ground is to ask students to express a preference, then make the assignments yourself. Ask each student to fill in the following sheet:

Your name _____

Three people you would most like to work with _____

Three people you would least like to work with _____

You can eyeball these or make up a computer program to construct the groups. You might want to add in factors such as distribution of your class leaders or your best writers.

Of course, you can also assign groups randomly. This system takes the least time and may be just as successful as any you could have agonized over.

The Problem of Shirkers

Anyone who institutes task groups inevitably deals with the problem of group members who do less than their share. They cause conflict and resentment in the group, but often group members will tolerate such a person because they don't have any respectable way to handle the problem, other than routes that seem like complaining or tattling. Thus you'll want carefully structured ways of handling the shirker.

One way is to let the groups know immediately that at the end, in addition to handing in the final product, each group member must send you an anonymous and confidential assessment of the participation of each other group member. You can express these as "went the extra mile," "did a fair share," "did less than others," or "hardly did anything." Such specific phrases help exclude students' evaluation of the *quality* of the member's work—a swamp you don't want to get into. If several of the responses from the same group agree that Sandy did less than her share, Sandy receives a grade or two lower than the rest of the group. This system works well if you announce it before the groups begin their work and if you give groups a chance in the middle to discuss whether any members are not doing their share. That way, people who are perceived as shirkers have a chance to make amends.

Another way to handle the shirkers is to keep the groups at three or less, making it harder for the group to carry a shirker.

Still another way is to allow a group to dismiss any of its members by a majority ballot. The person who is dismissed from a group must persuade that group to reconsider, or must find acceptance in another group, or take an F for the project. You can help groups dare to do this by providing an opportunity, once the groups are partway into their task, for each person to write anonymously the name of any person in the group who is not carrying a fair share. If more than half the group names the same person, that person is out.

Some instructors refuse to try to police or fix the groups that have shirkers. They maintain that there are shirkers in every business and that the groups must themselves find ways of dealing with shirkers. One way is simply to carry the shirker; if a group decides to do so, they are getting a realistic introduction to the world. If a shirker gets carried by the group and receives an A along with other group members, well, the shirker knows who he or she is and must live with that knowledge.

Guiding the Group

Giving instructions. Once the groups are constituted, members need the same information about their task as individual writers do—audience, purpose, context, constraints, standards for evaluation, and so on. Don't neglect thorough instruction in the form of writing the group must produce—the report, the proposal, or whatever. Suggestions about how the group might proceed are also a good idea, especially if you have young students or students unused to group work. You may want to forbid the group to divide the work in certain ways you know from experience will lead them into trouble. You may warn them, for example, about having different group members write different sections of the report, because, although such a procedure might seem most fair to inexperienced group members, such a method often results in a disunified report; groups are far better off if one person writes the final manuscript.

You might ask the group for a plan of action as its first step. Business educators might take this opportunity to have their students practice some planning devices such as GANTT or PERT. For others, a list of the parts of the group's task, together with deadlines, would serve the purpose. The plan may be handed in, or you may meet with each group to discuss its plan.

Checking in. You'll want to establish checkpoints with the groups. You can have the members turn in plans, outlines, hypotheses, dummy tables and graphs, parts of their report, or drafts. One important step is to have the entire group meet with you once a draft of the report, or part of it, is ready. Require a copy of the draft for each group member and for you. Then you can listen to their critique of the draft, add your own response, and help them plan what to do next. A firm deadline for that draft will help the group pace its work.

Scheduling group meeting times. You can give over class hours to group meeting, floating among the groups or making yourself available as a consultant. You can also ask the groups to meet outside of class. If you choose the latter, you may have to factor in the ability of each student to meet in a certain time slot, as part of your group selection process. If they are meeting outside, suggest that each member have a list of all group members' full names and phone numbers and that one person act as convener, to be sure all group members know when and where the group is to meet.

I don't know of any instructors who themselves meet with each task group for its entire session. Students seem able to handle task groups with less direct instructor guidance than they need in response groups, though there's nothing to prevent your setting up sequential group meeting times, as was suggested above for response groups, if you think your task groups need that much guidance.

Group self-evaluations. Midway, you can hold an in-class reporting session, in which each group gets five or ten minutes to explain to the class what it has been doing and what it has planned. Each group will pick up useful ideas from listening to others. You can also take a few minutes in class to feature a particular group's solution to a common problem that others are struggling with.

To help group members express and address frustrations, set aside a portion of one group meeting for the group to discuss how it is doing and what suggestions the members have for a better group. Written evaluations by group members are also useful as a midway self-analysis by the group. Have the groups read and discuss these writings. Occasionally, such an evaluation will result in resentfulness and escalation of hostility, but usually these sessions are therapeutic and helpful to the group's functioning.

Grading Group Work

The most sensible way of grading group work is to give the final project a grade that becomes the grade for all the group members, unless some other factor drags down the grade for an individual. The most common millstone, as mentioned above, is the group's report that the person has not pulled a fair share of the work load.

Kenneth Bruffee has made important contributions both to specific peer-group procedures and to our understanding of the collaborative and social aspects of learning and knowledge. His 1984 article "Collaborative Learning and the 'Conversation of Mankind'" is a persuasive and articulate exposition, and you can work back from there to the body of his work. See especially his "Writing and Reading as Collaborative or Social Acts." For useful insights, see also Newcomb and Wilson's *College Peer Groups* and Bouton and Garth's *Learning in Groups*.

The next chapter illustrates, through case histories, how some college instructors have used the suggestions in all the preceding chapters to integrate writing and learning in their courses in various disciplines, at various types of college and universities, and with students at various levels.

Chapter Five

Course Plans: Some Case Histories

The following case histories tell the stories of actual instuctors who have integrated writing with learning in their courses. Though various disciplines are represented, don't limit your reading to your own discipline; all the case histories contain ideas that can be adapted in a variety of disciplines.

A Core History Course: John R. Breihan

The recipient of students who, he feels, have previously conceived of history as the memorization of dry facts and the narrative recounting of events, John Breihan wants the 30 students in each section of his freshman core history course at Loyola College in Maryland to learn to think and write like historians—that is, to *interpret* the past. He says, "I am continually trying to move students toward argument [where they] advance a thesis, defend it against counterarguments, and support it with evidence."

Seeing that his students were not writing the kind of history papers he wanted to read, Breihan began working out a series of weekly writing assignments that would help them develop the necessary skills. He also began to invest most of his responding time in guiding students' drafts; previously he had spent most of his time writing comments on the final papers—comments in which his own motive was primarily to justify the grade, comments he now believes students did not read carefully enough to justify the time he spent writing them.

Breihan's Sequential Weekly Writing Assignments

Breihan's plan was influenced by David Hamilton, whose work showed Breihan an example of how "contributing skills can be broken down and then put back together again."

Together with their textbooks, Breihan's students now buy, at the bookstore, a set of assignment sheets, with accompanying readings. These sheets give the sequential assignments—usually two a week—for the entire semester. The assignments together count as one-fourth of the semester's grade.

Using a point scale such as 1–5 or 1–10, Breihan quickly grades these short exercises, writing no comments—a procedure he calls "minimal grading." When exercises are handed in, Breihan goes through a batch of 30 in about 40 minutes. "I'm not philosophically committed to reading every word of them," he says, "but I am curious, and I base later lectures on what I read." For the first several assignments, Breihan hands back any papers that are not sufficiently accurate or that are not coherent. The students may get credit only by satisfactorily revising the writing.

Breihan saw that many of his students did not sufficiently value accuracy and that they did not know how to interpret tables. Thus the first writing assignment works on those two skills. Breihan gives students a table of European governments in 1525, showing the type of government and name of ruler for each nation. The assignment is to write a coherent paragraph that answers several questions (i.e., "What sorts of governments were most prevalent?" "Which individuals were most powerful?" "least powerful?" "Why?").

The second assignment works on reading and summarizing skills and on students' recognition that historical writing is an interpretation of history, made by an individual. The sheet begins with short-answer questions such as "Who wrote our textbook?" "What do you know about the author?" "What can you guess?" "When was the text written?" "Published?" Then students are asked to summarize a seven-page section of the text and to write an outline of one chapter. Again, inaccurate or incoherent papers are handed back for revision.

Later exercises develop students' abilities to see the relevance of evidence to argument. For example, students read a chapter in a collection of primary sources. Breihan tells them, "The issue at stake in this chapter is whether Louis XIV was a good king." Then Breihan asks about the first reading: "Who was Bishop Bossuet and when did he write?" and "Bossuet felt that an absolute monarch would be good for his people because. . . ." Later questions, about other readings, ask for a higher level of inference by students: "How can Louis XIV's letters to his heirs be used as evidence about the issue at stake?"

Another exercise asks students to marshal evidence on both sides of an argument. First they write arguments that Louis XIV was a good king, then arguments that he was not. This exercise is the basis for an in-class debate in which teams of students accrue points for making valid arguments on both sides. Following the debate, students write again—what they wish they'd said in the debate.

Breihan's Essays

The three historical essays that students write begin as essay tests, written in class. Students are given the questions ahead of time, so they can prepare; they write on one question only; and after the in-class writing, they revise their drafts at home. Breihan guides this revision process through comments and conferences. For the first essay, conferences are required of every student; after that, conferences are optional. When there is no conference, Breihan responds to drafts with a page of suggestions, returned to the student together with the draft. A word processor speeds this process, and he uses several boiler-plate paragraphs—all-purpose statements about frequent problems such as accuracy and coherence—that he splices into the page of commentary, individu-alizing as appropriate. Students must hand back his comment page with each successive draft, so he can quickly see what he recommended the last time.

Breihan has found that "It's much more fun to comment on papers that aren't done, because the instructor can suggest rather than condemn." Because draft response changes the relation between instructor and learner and because it helps students apply what they learn, Breihan believes that "the notion of responding to drafts is the most powerful thing to come out of the writing renewal of the past ten years. . . . It generates writing that I can be proud to say my students wrote, and they can be proud, too."

In drafts, Breihan pays little attention to mechanics, though he does alert students to persistent errors. On final papers, he refuses to accept papers that don't have mechanics "under control": when he finds more than four errors a page, or serious problems with footnote form, he stops reading and hands the paper back for revision. The student receives no reading and no credit until the mechanics are acceptable. Sometimes a paper goes back four or five times.

Breihan admits, "I spend a little more time [reading and writing comments on papers] now than five years ago," but the extra time is well worthwhile be-cause "I enjoy writing the comments. I have to live with these students and these papers for the rest of the semester. I might as well make it as pleasant as possi-ble, and move the papers forward."

A Sophomore Core Literature Course: Barbara Walvoord

Breihan handles his exercises outside of class and retains lectures as the nearly exclusive classroom activity, except for several sessions each semester in which his students participate in debates over historical issues. He loves to lecture, does it well, and feels it is the best mode of learning for the undergradu-ates in his core history course. An alternative way of building writing into a course is to make exercises the basis for in-class work. I have taken that ap-proach in a core literature class, The Craft of Fiction, taught at Loyola College in Maryland.

The course has 30 to 35 students, mostly sophomores fulfilling their core requirement. Its purpose is only tangentially to introduce students to particu-lar pieces of fiction; a much more central goal is for students to read literature carefully and with pleasure and to express their insights coherently in writing.

In-Class Activities

Outside of class, students read the pieces of fiction, as well as secondary sources. Class time is primarily devoted to having students talk and write about the fiction, and sometimes to minilectures.

The classroom exercises build sequentially through the semester. First we concentrate on plot. For example, students may be asked to read a short story and identify its "turning point." In class, we make a blackboard list of what everyone has chosen as the turning point and ask students to defend their choices. Alternatively, I might gather students in groups of five, asking each group to reach consensus on the turning point and to have a spokesperson defend the group's choice to the rest of the class.

A second exercise, either with that story or with another, will be to list the main events that lead up to and away from the turning point. From that list, students then construct a narrative summary of the story that focuses on the turning point. They can be given time to write the summary in class or as homework. I might have groups of five read their summaries to each other, with no comment, and then give the students ten extra minutes to revise their summaries in the light of good ideas they've heard in other summaries. They could hand the revised exercises in, read them again in the groups, or simply take them home as "notes" for study.

Next we might experiment with alternative developments of the plot. In about fifteen minutes of class time, students write their answers to a question such as "How would the story change if Billy Budd had a limp instead of a stammer?" These writings might become the basis for a general class discussion. I find that when students have a few minutes to write their thoughts even the shy ones are much more ready to contribute in class.

After a couple of weeks on plot, we begin to focus on character, then on theme, and finally on setting. Each week, we discuss the fiction from several different angles, but we emphasize most heavily whichever aspect we're concentrating on that week.

Gradually the writing exercises come more and more to resemble literary-critical papers that argue a point about a story. For example, we might brainstorm a blackboard list of all the ways in which the exotic and fantastical help shape the mood of Joyce's "Araby." Then each student is given 10 minutes to decide which five points are most important, and in which order, for a paper addressed to peers who had read the story but would enjoy a full description of how the exotic worked.

The final stage is to have students develop a paper that argues a debatable topic, such as the role of Captain Vere in Melville's *Billy Budd*. In a 15-minute writing period, I ask half the students to take one side and half the other side, listing all the evidence from the story that supports their side. Then students meet in groups of six, three on each side, and debate the issue. Next, each student must add to the list the points that support the counterarguments. Now students of like positions meet together to read one another their lists and to make changes based on what they learn.

I rarely take these writings home. For the most part, they are handled in class discussion or through peer review. A few students complain that I haven't "graded" what they wrote, but most understand that the purpose of the writing exercise is well served by the modes of response I use.

I have little difficulty with shirkers, even though I don't mark the exercises. Students who do not bring written assignments to class will be embarrassed when they must admit to their group, or to the class, that they have nothing ready. Since so much of the class consists of writing or talking, a student must read the story in order to participate. If ever a class of students began to think it was humorous or acceptable for members of a group not to be prepared or not to participate, I would certainly switch to some mode of reinforcement that used peer pressure in a positive way, or I would collect and grade the writing exercises for a while.

Literary-Critical Papers

For the literary-critical paper, students often choose some topic or approach they've explored in an in-class written exercise. These essays I *do* read and guide very carefully. I handle draft response entirely through conferences, not through written comments, because I would much rather talk to live students than sit home and write comments. So during one week, my "draft response" week, I do not meet the class as a unit. Instead, each student must sign up for a 15-minute conference. If I have 35 students, this takes about nine hours, the same as if I held class for three hours and spent six hours in preparation.

I list 15-minute time slots on a sheet of paper, putting in about 10% more time slots than there are students, to allow for flexibility in scheduling. I pass this list around in class; each student must sign for one conference. Students who *can* come for a conference outside of class hours are asked to do so, leaving the class-time slot for tightly scheduled students who can't come any other time. At the end of the sign-up, I arrange swaps or open additional time slots until everyone has conference time. I tape the conference list to my office door, so students can drop by to check their times or to scratch their names from a time they can't make, and take one of the vacant times I have left.

Students must come to their conference on time and must bring a typed draft of their paper. I read it on the spot, trying to reflect my reading responses so students see my questions, confusions, and delights. I may also get the student talking, or engage in a debate, to generate more ideas for the paper. The student takes notes during the conference and then revises the paper.

Because I have run this system with classes of up to 45 students, and often with several classes a semester, I am strict about students' respect for my time. I explain that only if they are responsible can I afford to run this type of program. If a student is late or does not appear with a full, typed draft, I accept no further drafts and assign an automatic F to the final paper (of course, I make allowances for illness and emergencies).

Don't students hand in sloppy work if they realize they will have a chance to revise? Yes, sometimes they do. I talk seriously with them about that problem beforehand, urging them to get their money's worth out of the conference by having me suggest things they haven't seen rather than repeat things they knew but were sloppy about. Then I turn the responsibility over to them.

Do I grade the drafts? No. I only mark that the student appeared on time with the required full, typed draft. To grade unfinished work seems to me a contradiction in terms.

What about mechanics? I pay little attention to them in the drafts, reinforcing what I want to teach students—that the prematurely "fixed up" paper is a mistake, that drafts must be examined for macrochanges first, and that early obsession with mechanics can block the writer's best work. When I see problems with mechanics, however, I will often help the student anticipate attention to those problems, by a statement such as, "Before you submit the final version, you'll need to pay attention to sentence fragments."

I do require typed drafts because typing makes the structure clearer to me so I can give a better response. I don't require error-free typing—merely readable. However, when slow typists have invested time pecking out a draft, or paid to have it typed, they may be more reluctant to abandon or revise it. You may decide to accept handwritten drafts.

An Introductory Psychology Course: Susan Miller Robison

For her 100-level introductory psychology course at the small, all-woman College of Notre Dame, in Baltimore, Susan Robison usually has 30 to 35 students who attend three hours of lecture and one hour of laboratory each week. Her primary goal is that students should learn, as she says, "to apply the concepts of the scientific method to behavior." Secondarily, students should become familiar with major concepts and terms in various areas of psychology. Robison also recognizes that students will want to apply what they learn to themselves, for "growth, understanding, personal change, and better mental health."

Writing used to be "an assessment device" for Robison. She remembers she had "some vague ideas about writing as learning," but after participating in a writing-across-the-curriculum institute and experimenting for three years with the ideas she was exposed to there, "I'm much more clear about what objectives are being met by what assignments, and how."

Writing in the Lecture Class

Robison has made two major changes in her introductory psychology course. First, she has integrated short writing assignments with her lectures—a development that was hard for her, since she has excellent lecturing skills and tends "to fall back on them." She's convinced, however, that writing integrated with lecture is much more effective for her students' learning. She sometimes uses small-group discussion, dividing her lecture class into groups of five that are constant through the semester, so that trust develops, and she assigns exercises that help students actively learn and process lecture and textbook material. A typical task for the groups is one she sometimes uses in the social psychology unit—the group members imagine themselves, in predetermined roles, in a sinking lifeboat, and decide who is to be sacrificed to lighten the boat. The roles, assigned by the instructor, represent racial groups, religious groups, or people with certain abilities to be saved for society. Groups both write and talk about their choices. Another activity occurs in the unit on developmental psychology: when Robison is about to lecture on pregnancy as a stage in the woman's personal development, she asks students to write a list of all the adjectives they've heard about pregnancy, makes a common blackboard list, then refers to the adjectives as she lectures. In the unit on aggressive and assertive behavior, Robison has students write and then present skits in which someone acts aggressive or assertive in response to a particular problem; after the skit, the rest of the class must classify the behavior.

Writing in the Psychology Lab

In the lab, Robison works sequentially on the skills students need for planning, completing, and writing a psychological study. In the first week, on the scientific method, she has students read a scientific research article; summarize it; write whether they liked or did not like it, and why; and finally write how the article applies to them. Students accumulate points for satisfactory completion of the written assignment. All written assignments may be rewritten for more points, up until the end of the semester. In week 2, on sensation and perception, Robison has students use a piece of equipment in the lab. They then write a description of the piece of equipment, their procedure in using it, and the result. Thus, in the first two weeks students have been exposed to the scientific report format, have summarized and evaluated a scientific research article, and have practiced writing part of what would be the materials-and-methods section of a report.

In weeks 3 and 4, during the unit on learning, Robison has them keep baseline data on an aspect of their own behavior they would like to change, such as smoking. Then students write about themselves as a case history, using APA style, with graphs. Later, during a unit on developmental psychology, she has them interview people at different life stages about child rearing, construct tables from the information gained, and summarize their data. By such exercises, students learn various ways of gathering and presenting data in psychology.

After working with research report format, students experiment with other types of writing that convey psychological information. During a unit on stress management, for example, students are asked to imagine themselves in the career field of their choice. They must write an article for their professional newsletter, on stress management for professionals in that field. In preparation, they must read three articles on the topic and interview one person.

Robison is especially pleased with the results of her policy of allowing students to revise the written exercises. At the beginning of the semester, 25% of the students get the scientific format right the first time they hand her a paper; by the end, 75% of the papers are right the first time they come to her for a grade. The exercises and the revisions teach not only writing but thinking and investigating. Some of the students who find they must rewrite redo their experiments as well as their reports. Through the writing and the revisions, Robison says, "I'm teaching the scientific way of thinking."

Introductory and Advanced Biology Courses:
Virginia Johnson Gazzam

Like Robison, Virginia Johnson Gazzam at Towson State University has students both for lecture and for lab. Her lectures, however, may have 100 students. She lectures and demonstrates to them for 75 minutes, twice a week. Like Robison, Gazzam integrates writing with her lectures. In the middle of most lectures, when students have reached a saturation limit, she breaks for a 10-minute writing exercise that helps them master the lecture material. She'll variously ask students to summarize a point she's made, answer a question, or interview one another about a topic from the lecture and write up the interview. She may ask for recall from previous lectures: for example, when she's covering a phylum a day, she'll ask students to compare two phyla: "How are annelids like mollusks?"

At the end of the semester, students must hand in five of these small writings for a grade. That procedure, in addition to giving importance to the writing, makes students reread their writings—a good way to review course content.

Writing in the Laboratory

In each laboratory section, Gazzam has about 25 students. Here, she explains, she uses writing "to emphasize safety, to allow students to explore feelings, to help me assess my own instructional strategies, and to teach laboratory procedures." To teach safety, for example, Gazzam schedules a lab in which students will draw blood from their own fingers and begins by asking them to write a paragraph on the importance of sterile technique and proper disposal of the blood lancets. Lest students perform a lab exercise without seeing its meaning, she will ask them at the beginning of, say, a microbiology lab, "Why are we using *E. coli* in the lab today?" She won't let them into the lab until they've intelligently answered the question in writing. "That's intellectual safety," she says.

Students also sometimes are given a few minutes in lab to write about their feelings. For example, a priest wrote about how difficult it was for him to view a specimen of a human fetus in the lab.

To help improve her instructional strategies, Gazzam may give students five minutes in the lab to write about topics like "What did you like about seeing the blastula on overhead transparencies?" or "Were there ways this technique made it difficult for you to learn?"

To help students focus on laboratory procedures, she has each lab table design a checklist by which they think she should grade their laboratory behavior. She takes the groups' checklists home and uses them to compose a checklist, which she then uses. Having contributed to the checklist, students are keenly aware of its points.

The Research Report in Advanced Biology

Gazzam's university requires all juniors to take a "writing intensive" course in their major field. To meet this requirement, Gazzam's department offers Biological Literature, which is taken by 95% of the science majors at the university. Students must have had three science courses as a prerequisite, and classes are limited to 15. Gazzam says, "The first year I taught the course, I essentially just assigned a term paper." Now she assigns a variety of writings that help students think and write as scientists.

One of her assignments is an original scientific research paper. Students are instructed to compare two products of their choice (e.g., two brands of popping corn, two types of french fries). They design and carry out an experiment to find out which is "better" in terms of cost and quality. They write up their experiments in scientific report format for an audience of their classmates. The exercise is direct and useful preparation for the type of work many graduates will perform in industrial laboratories.

Gazzam and I have examined in depth the writing and thinking strategies her students employ in fulfilling this assignment. We have asked students to think aloud as they planned and carried out their experiments and wrote their reports; analyzed those tapes; taped students as they interviewed each other; collected and analyzed students' notes and drafts; asked students to keep logs of their progress on the project; and asked student observers to record classroom activities. Gazzam herself has kept a log of her classroom goals and strategies. On the basis of such evidence, we have come to understand more about students' thought and behavior, as they plan and write, and Gazzam has implemented some changes in her teaching strategies.

When we did the research, in 1983, Gazzam was guiding the research projects in the following ways:

25 FEBRUARY: In class, Gazzam made the assignment and guided students through the process of formulating the null hypothesis, which was to be the basis of their experiments. (The null hypothesis assumes no difference between the items to be tested.)

25 MARCH: Students described projects to their small groups. Gazzam floated among groups, offering suggestions.

29 MARCH: Small groups discussed plans for oral presentations and graphs.

4 APRIL: Students brought drafts of Introductions and Materials-and-Methods sections to class for critique by a classmate. Gazzam floated among the pairs, offering suggestions. Students interviewed one another, using a set

of questions she provided—for example, "What has been the hardest part of the project for you?"

7 APRIL: Students brought drafts of the results and discussion sections for review by a classmate, as above.

12, 14 APRIL: Students made five- to ten-minute oral presentations, following scientific conventions, and handed in their written reports.

The procedures used here resulted from Gazzam's thinking about how to guide the writing process, and already they were producing work that she and her students were proud of. The data we collected, however, showed her some better ways to guide her students:

1. She had not emphasized a pilot stage for the experiments, because students already had had three science courses and presumably knew basic experimental procedures. Many students, however, developed no pilot study. A few of the better students did so; for example, one good student, testing two brands of erasable pens, ran the tests with two trial writers first, revised his research design, then ran the improved tests with five other writers to get his final data. Gazzam accordingly has begun experimenting with ways to help all her students structure a pilot stage.

2. In preparation for the class of 4 April, Gazzam asked her students to bring in drafts of the Introduction and Materials-and-Methods sections of their reports. Many students were writing in connected prose about their projects for the first time. The think-aloud tapes of students composing this early draft indicate that they had great trouble reconciling the natural flow of their first extended written description of their projects with the rigid order of the parts of the scientific report. A student will be going along fluently, writing down useful and important prose about the experiment, and will suddenly stop with "Uh, oh, I think that should go into the results section." To avoid such distractions to early flow, Gazzam now lets the parts of the scientific report sort themselves out later and asks initially only for "three pages of writing about your experiment."

A related problem was that, even in later drafts, when concern with the parts of the scientific report form *were* important, students had great trouble deciding what went where, although each of them had read and/or written abstracts for at least ten scientific articles with the same format. Gazzam needed a more effective way to help students understand how to sort information into the sections of the format. She decided to try tactile manipulation as a teaching technique. Now she gives students a scientific article in which the paragraphs have been randomly mixed and has them put the paragraphs into their proper format sections.

3. Most students wrote the 4 April draft after they had completed their experiments. Some, however, if their experiments could be performed in a single weekend, wrote the 4 April draft, then did the experiment, and finally wrote the results and discussion for 7 April. These procrastinators actually profited more from the 4 April draft, because a draft of one's methods, written in the

past tense as though the experiment were complete, forces the experimenter to work out every detail in a thoughtful and precise way. One good student reported, "I have my experimental design all planned." Next day, when he sat down to draft his materials and methods section, he found that in fact he didn't have his experiment "all planned." In the process of writing, he composed his rating terms and scale, added a procedure to his research method, and realized that he must control a variable he hadn't even thought of before. Then he did his experiment, following his already-drafted description of procedure. So this early writing was enormously valuable. Gazzam may now call for this draft much earlier, so that *all* the students write it before they do their experiments.

4. Peer exchange was useful in helping students refine individual operational definitions for specific aspects of the product as "fluffiness." However, peer review was not as helpful in getting students to formulate the larger operational definition—which product is "better," and what does "better" mean, operationally, in the experiment. So she has structured exercises that help students focus on that question.

5. Some students, early in their thinking, decided on inappropriate topics or experiments, comparing products that could not be easily compared, aping TV commercials, or choosing aspects that could not readily be measured. Students' think-aloud tapes show that Gazzam added to this problem by making their first written assignment announce a topic decision. She now asks students to bring to class ten possible topics for group discussion, to help students generate several ideas and then pick the most workable.

Gazzam and I are collecting and analyzing data from the later class where she implemented her improvements. Preliminary impressions indicate that her changes in teaching strategies indeed helped students improve on the performance of her earlier class.

A striking characteristic of all the instructors described in these case histories is that they never stop trying to improve their teaching methods. Gazzam's development shows how, through careful observation of students, a teacher can continually refine ways of guiding the writing and learning process.

An Introductory Sociology Class
and a Word about "Journals":
Michael Burton

Many of the instructors described above have included informal writing as part of the learning experience in their courses. Informal writing, whose main goal is learning, has been discussed widely in the literature as "journal writing" (see especially the work of Toby Fulwiler). Breihan structures a kind of journal writing, with his daily guided exercises; I do another variation when I have students write daily in literature class; Robison and Gazzam integrate other variations of journal writing in lecture and lab. A looser form of the journal is illustrated by sociologist Michael Burton of Loyola College in Maryland, who has his introductory sociology students keep what he deliberately names a "journal." Burton's goal in the journal is to help the students "think like sociologists," but he allows them much more flexibility than Breihan, who structures students' daily writing carefully around specific intellectual tasks. Burton's only requirement is that students respond each day in their journals to what is happening in class, in their reading, and in life around them. He collects the journals periodically throughout the semester. At first he merely gave credit, based on the number of pages they contained, so that judgments about content or quality of writing would not inhibit the students' spontaneity. More recently, he has been giving letter grades to the journals, so students take them more seriously. Burton's reading of his student's journals is both a pleasure and a revelation. He learns what they are thinking and where they are having problems applying concepts from lecture or reading; they are learning to use the sociologist's eye to interpret the world around them. (Assignment, p. 39.)

Task Groups in an Upper-Class–Graduate Course in Marketing Research: Larry S. Lowe

For 12 years, Larry Lowe had taught business courses, requiring each student to hand in a 20-page term paper. However, he became increasingly dissatisfied. One reason was that a class of 100 students would produce 2,000 pages to be read in one week at semester's end. He wanted students to choose areas of their interest, but he did not feel sufficiently familiar with everyone's topic to give good evaluations. He was irritated by what he considered excessive student focus on length, margins, and other mechanical concerns. The threat of plagiarism forced him to be a detective and, in one instance, involved him in a messy, unpleasant situation where a student was finally dismissed from the college. He asked himself, "Is this what I want to do in my marketing class?" The answer was "No." So Lowe abandoned the research paper and went to computer simulations as a way of engaging students actively in management decision making. However, he regretted the loss of writing experience for his students.

Moving to Loyola College in Maryland, which has a strong writing-across-the-curriculum program, Lowe attended a single three-hour workshop in which a colleague reported on a project in which students had worked in groups. That started Lowe thinking. During the following weeks, another colleague served as a sounding board for his developing ideas and helped him work out assignments. The next semester he tried out his new plans. He assigned students to teams of five. Each team was required to design a research proposal (the proposal only; the actual research was not attempted), a form he felt would be directly useful to his students in their marketing careers. The combination of students in groups meant that he had 20 papers to read, not 100. Every student in the group got the same grade, based on the quality of the final proposal. Lowe explained to his students that much writing in the business world is a group effort and that each group member shares the group's rewards or problems. He told them they would have to use their interpersonal skills as well as their thinking and writing skills.

To guide his students through the writing process, Lowe says, "Every 2 weeks I called for something." Each group had to hand in its topic, then its hypothesis, then a bibliography, dummy tables, a draft, and finally the completed proposal.

At the end of the semester, Lowe had met his goals: he had given his students what he considered useful and challenging experience in planning, thinking about, and writing about marketing; he had a manageable number of papers to read and grade; there was no plagiarism. His evaluation of the final papers— one disaster, one poor, most competent, four super. The competent and super papers pleased him most, because their quality was beyond what he was used to getting in "term papers." In the future, Lowe plans to make these changes:

1. Cut the team size to three, to eliminate the "free riders" who were a problem the first time.
2. Allow students to select their teams (the first time, Lowe composed the teams), to decrease sharp personality clashes in the groups.
3. Move preliminary assignments from mid-term to the second week, to allow the groups more time to work.
4. Allow unlimited drafts rather than just one draft, so that more groups can write successful final proposals.
5. Demand a single writer for the proposal instead of allowing a group arrangement where each person writes several of the pages. This change will make the proposals more coherent.
6. Ask for an annotated bibliography, so he knows the material has been read, not just collected.

Assessing his single semester of experience, Lowe notes that "marketing skills and writing skills are very coincident." He believes the project is genuinely helping his students learn both marketing and writing, and he affirms, "I would do it again."

Task Groups in an Introductory History Course:
James Van Hoeven

Teaching an introductory history class, Foundations of American Nationalism, at Central College in Pella, Iowa, James Van Hoeven engaged his freshman and sophomore students in a single class writing project—producing a 45-page booklet on the history of Pella, to be sold at the town's traditional Dutch

"Tulip Time" festival in May. He carried out this project four times during the 1970s, producing four different booklets.

Van Hoeven planned the ten sections of the booklet and divided his class of 40 students into 10 groups, each of which completed one section. Typical section titles were "Early Dutch Architecture in Pella," "Industries in Pella, 1840–1860," and "Scholte's [town founder] Attitude toward Abolition." Van Hoeven handed each group a description of the section it would write, together with directions for finding the appropriate material in the archives of the college or in the local museum or historical society. The class elected an editor, assistant editor, copy editor, and production manager, who belonged to no group. Van Hoeven worked directly with this editorial team, who in turn worked with the 10 groups.

The booklet was printed at the local newspaper office, and students sold it at the festival. The printer did the booklet at cost, as a contribution to the college. Sales typically resulted in a $100 profit, which was donated to a charity of the students' choice. Obviously, instructors adopting Van Hoeven's idea will have to find their own financial bottom line. The point is that he scouted local resources and used the local festival in a creative way.

Van Hoeven announced the booklet at the beginning of the semester, let the groups self-select, and gave each group its task, but he devoted the first two-thirds of the course to lecture and discussion on subjects traditional to American history: Puritan thought, the emergence of the Constitution, the War of Independence, the rise of nationalism. The booklet was the focus of a unit on local histories, near the end of the course. Van Hoeven wanted his students to understand how local histories relate to national developments and to use primary sources to write history, dealing with gaps, contradictions, and divergent meanings, just as all historians do.

The bulk of the research was carried on during a week and a half, when class meetings were spent on group work and trips to museums and archives. Van Hoeven had a skillful and generous partner in Alice Lammers, who had retired as college librarian and was working actively in the college and town archives. She spent many hours consulting with his students as they used archival sources. She kept a record of the books they worked with; Van Hoeven thus had an independent check of students' sources and some idea of the thoroughness of their searches.

Each group received a grade based on the quality of its chapter. The editorial team received grades based on Van Hoeven's estimate of their work with the manuscript.

Students' eager involvement in the project got them past the idea that the study of history is the memorization of dry facts and helped them experience the excitement with which historians pursue and interpret historical sources.

More Suggestions for Specific Disciplines

A wonderful collection of how-to essays by instructors from various disciplines is *Writing to Learn: Essays and Reflections on Writing across the Curriculum*, contributed by faculty at Virginia's George Mason University and edited by Christopher Thaiss.

In addition, journals in composition and rhetoric, as well as in various disciplines, occasionally carry articles about integrating writing with disciplines. Several such articles appear in C. W. Griffin's *Teaching Writing in All Disciplines*; Bruce Peterson's bibliography in that volume is a guide to more. The May 1985 issue (vol. 36) of *College Composition and Communication* has several essays about integrating writing in various disciplines. You can find more such articles through search of the computer data base ERIC. (If your library has DIALOG, ERIC is part of it.) Use the search terms "Higher Education," "Writing," " Interdisciplinary Approach," the name of your discipline, and the inclusive dates (1980 through the present will produce most of what's there). You can also do a paper search. *Education Index* and *CIJE* (*Current Index to Journals in Education*) index articles printed in journals; *RIE* (*Resources in Education*) indexes conference presentations and documents. Don't neglect the latter, since a number of excellent suggestions for teaching strategies by instructors from various disciplines have been presented as conference papers but never published. ERIC indexes not only educational journals but also pedagogical articles published by journals in other fields.

Part Two

RESPONDING TO THE
STUDENT WRITER

Chapter Six

Principles of Effective Response

This chapter will begin by discussing three modes of response: the written comment, the taped comment, and the individual conference. Advantages and disadvantages of each mode will complement discussion of ways of making each mode effective. Suggestions common to all modes, however, are held for the next sections of the chapter. Finally, the chapter treats ways of responding to particular types of writing (e.g., in-class writing, journals). Succeeding chapters discuss response to aspects of writing such as focus, organization, style, and mechanics.

Pen, Tape, or Conference?

Most home workshops include several kinds of saws. When you have wood to cut, you don't just grab the nearest one; you look them all over and choose the one best suited to the job. Likewise, when you want to give students advice about their writing, you won't want to seize the red pen because it happens to be the closest tool on your desk or because so many teachers use it. Instead, consider how you can best communicate your responses to students' writing.

Written Comments

Written comments have the advantage of requiring only a teacher and a colored pen. That basic combination functions on a subway, on a bed, in front of the TV, or at the kitchen table. It may be noon or midnight. The teacher can wear any variety of clothing or facial expression and can attack the stack of papers in any way—read them all quickly before evaluating any; compare them with one another; ponder some, zip through others. Another advantage is that, once inscribed, the written comment is an ineradicable record of the teacher's suggestions; both instructor and student can refer to it at any time.

Written comments may be penned into the margins and at the end. Marginal comments serve several functions. They may illustrate a point that is stated more generally at the end. If you do that, be sure that the terminal comment makes clear to the student that your marginal comments or questions illustrate what you mean in the terminal comment by "choose words more precisely" or "some of your points need more support." Marginal comments may also point out matters that are specific to a spot in the text and hence are not included in the terminal comment. Whatever their function or relation to a terminal comment, marginal comments must be clear to the student. Better to write fewer, if time presses, and make those few clear.

To make only marginal comments may leave the student with no overall picture of what you think about the paper and no way of distinguishing which problems are most important. Be careful not to make marginal comments that imply that the text merely needs cleaning up for punctuation or diction, when your terminal comment urges the students to make major shifts and changes. In those cases, move your comments on style and mechanics to the terminal comment, and place them within the context of the total writing process: "When you've reorganized the paper, spend time editing for verb forms and apostrophes—serious problems in this draft."

To speed terminal comments, some instructors use word processors. If you find yourself writing the same advice or explanation many times, you can use boilerplate paragraphs, adapting them as necessary for the individual and splicing them into your comments. Be careful, though, to make your comment specific to that student's text, so that you don't merely throw a bunch of general maxims at the student.

Written comments can be used successfully for some situations and some instructional styles, but the method has several disadvantages. The teacher cannot be sure comments are phrased so that students can understand them. And red ink makes for chilly communication. It does not allow for dialogue. Finally, writing an evaluation is more time-consuming and cumbersome than offering the same suggestions orally.

If you want to check the student's comprehension, if you want to relate more personally to the student, if you want to join with the student in exploring a paper's problems, if you want to profit from your ability to say more words in five minutes than you can write, then try some other system of communicating with students about their writing—tapes, for example, or individual conferences.

Taped Comments

I've talked with teachers who have made the tape system work at the junior high, high school, and college levels. A cassette player seems to be part of the standard equipment most students own or can borrow nowadays. Some teachers use the school's language lab; others arrange a place where students can use a school-owned cassette player. Then, as the teacher returns a paper to the student, a cassette goes with it. On the tape, the teacher talks to the student about the strengths and weaknesses of the paper. The recording is more personal, you can say more, and the student is more likely to understand you than if you wrote out your comments. One great difficulty arises with immature students. Though many students think they can't go for a five-minute ride in their cars or take out the trash unless they have their favorite singer to entertain them on the cassette, they may never get around to slipping in the tape that will bring your voice to their ears. Either you can try to make tapes that outdo their stars in rhythm or ribaldry, or you can schedule a time for all students to listen to the tapes you have made for them. A system in which revision is rewarded also helps motivate students to listen to your suggestions for improvement. (For more information about using tapes, see Weddington.)

Conferences

Most personal of all and, I believe, most effective, is the individual conference. There you give the student the time you would otherwise spend writing comments on the paper; you read the paper in the student's presence and share in person your pleasure at success and your suggestions for improvement. Together you plan further work.

The conference may last anywhere from five or ten minutes to half an hour; it may be scheduled or impromptu; it may be required or optional. Don Murray, in *A Writer Teaches Writing*, describes how he handled conferences in a high school setting, with a large number of students who had little free time. In a college setting, I simply pass around in class a sheet with blank appointment slots and let students fill them in. If necessary, I use a class hour to meet with students who can come only during that time. I then post the appointment schedule on my office door, so switchers and latecomers can sign up in the remaining blank spaces. You can be as relaxed as you wish about students keeping their appointments. Because I handle large numbers of students in conferences, I am not relaxed. I insist that students keep their scheduled conferences and arrive on time. If they must miss, they are to tell me as soon as possible. For forgetters and oversleepers I do not give makeup conferences; in case of injuries or disasters, of course, I gladly do so. In class, and in writing, I announce my policy and explain that the conferences are a special gift of time from me to them. I expect them to respect my time. This method results in a "show" rate for conferences of ninety to one hundred percent, even with freshmen.

The conference method has many advantages: by watching expression or engaging in dialogue you can tell whether the student understands what you say; you get past the coldness of red ink and into the warmth of person meeting person; you can scotch the old "she just drops 'em on the stairs" myth by letting the student watch you read the paper and respond to it; you encourage students to take responsibility for conducting and planning their own work. The conference does encourage both you and the student to pay close attention, however, and to function at top efficiency. If the acolyte is raptly watching the priestly functions, how can the priest daydream, dash off some muddled pronouncement, or munch peanuts?

One main principle and some guidelines can help the instructor make the best use of a student conference. The main principle is that teachers should not use the conference merely to say what they would otherwise write; the personal conference opens other possibilities, which should be exploited.

One guideline follows from this: the teacher should seize the opportunity to engage the student in a fuller and more personal discussion of the paper than would be possible by means of written comments. When a child brings you a drawing, you do not begin by succinctly pointing out its faults; you begin by responding to what it is meant to be: "Ah! a tree! Is that the same tree you climbed yesterday in the park?" A student's paper, like a child's drawing, is a gift, a self-revelation, an act of communication; the conference provides a rich opportunity to respond to it at that level. When you do so, you help the student perceive writing as a real communication, not as a dead and final *thing* that is either correct or incorrect.

A second guideline is this: the teacher should let the student share the reading and evaluating process. Suppose that the student sits facing you and hands you the paper. You then read it silently, perhaps making your own notes, which the student sees but is not close enough to read. Then, having finished reading, you finally lift your head and deliver your analysis. You have thus made the conference little more than an oral version of the traditional written evaluation. Furthermore, such a process inevitably makes the student sweat through anxious minutes during which your facial expressions and your unreadable marginal notes provoke a painful sense of exclusion. So the student sits there opposite you, chair tilted back in an unconscious attempt to disappear into the wall. Some students nervously begin talking to you, explaining some of their points or self-consciously offering their own guesses about their faults, as if by saying, "I just couldn't get that paragraph right," they can somehow meet and deflect the impending thrust of criticism. Some remain silent, chewing their fingernails or cracking their knuckles, letting their trapped eyes wander across your rows of books, which are at that moment merely the furniture of the inscrutable world from which you will emerge finally to pass on the paper a judgment based on your own inscrutable principles.

Instead of leaving the sinners to stand barefoot in the cold like King Henry before the pope, take them to the hearth and let them participate in what you're doing. Even if you function best reading the paper silently before responding, let the student sit beside you and look on. Or read the paper aloud. Perhaps the best way to exploit the conference is to voice your opinions as you read the paper, even the first time through. Of course, your comments on the student's mastery of information or methodology will mingle with your suggestions about writing, but my examples here will deal mainly with the comments you might make about writing skills. You could, for example, scan the first paragraph and the last, glance through the middle, and say immediately, "All these paragraphs are short and choppy-looking, and your first and last paragraphs don't link together very well. That makes me wonder whether maybe you tried to cover too many different ideas in this paper. Let me read it word for word and see if that's what is happening." Then read. As you work, tell the student what you think each paragraph is about, or point out evidence that your first guess was corrrect, or when a passage shows some lilt of phrase express your pleasure and say why you like what you've read. On display in Chicago's Natural History Museum is a transparent plastic model of a woman; one can watch the heart beat, the lungs inflate, the intestines contract. If you can be the transparent reader, you will grant the student the highly valuable privilege of watching someone respond to the paper sentence by sentence and paragraph by paragraph.

The sight of gastric contractions, of course, is not a sufficient vision for the teacher to vouchsafe. A third guideline: after reading the paper carefully and sharing your impressions, make what in a written evaluation would be a final comment: analyze, summarize, and indicate priorities. Students will not easily remember all you say, so it is often helpful to have them take notes or to tape your comments. Try to group and label strengths and weaknesses, and give the student specific directions for attacking problems.

In recommending this procedure, I should stress that you shouldn't be afraid to do the initial reading of a paper right in the conference, even though this practice can be hard to get used to. When I first began holding such conferences, I was afraid to let my students see me making an evaluation; I was used to forming the evaluation in privacy and then descending like Moses to present to the student the tablets engraved in red ink. I thought, what if I make a mistake? What if I form one opinion during the first reading and then, after rereading, change it? Unwilling to be transparent to my students, I collected all the papers, read them at home in the wee hours, made notes for the conference, and then, when a student came in, I had my evaluation ready. Consequently it sounded canned, and it failed to make use of all the possibilities inherent in the conference system. Furthermore, it took an amount of time that only fire-eyed beginners can give, when they're fresh out of grad school and brimful of zeal and energy. After that early fervor wears off, one must either abandon the conference method or learn to do the initial reading of the paper right there in front of the student. So I did. And I discovered that being "real" to students is highly effective. If I made an evaluation and then changed it, well, that's what sometimes happens when a real human being sits down to read somebody else's writing. If I could not immediately put my finger on what was "off" about a certain paper, I just asked the student to wait a moment while I wrestled with it. If I really was stumped or if I suspected a problem (like plagiarism) that I needed time to ponder, I asked the student to leave the paper with me and come back the next day.

You can conduct a conference in such a way that you become not so much an evaluator as a consultant. Don Murray describes this method in a provocative article, "The Listening Eye." The student's role is to discuss with the teacher successes and problems in the current work and plans for the next stages. The teacher primarily listens, encourages, responds, and gives advice when asked, but the student controls the conference. Such an approach, if consonant with your own teaching philosophy and style, seems to me highly promising and likely to yield results not easily attainable in other ways. It must surely heighten students' ability to analyze their work, to plan their writing progress, and to take responsibility for their learning. The article exudes Murray's particular spirit as a teacher and writer and provides worthwhile reading for teachers in every discipline.

Being a Transparent Reader

Whether you respond to a student in writing, on tape, or in conference, one guideline is highly important: be a transparent reader. Though I have suggested in the foregoing paragraphs some ways in which you can use the conference to let the writer see a reader's reactions, other methods of responding can also benefit from the transparent-reader idea. In using this approach, always remember that writing is not "wrong" in the same way that "two plus two equals five" is wrong. Instead, writing can more accurately be said to fail when it does not effectively communicate to its intended reader. Such failure may result from one of the many decisions a writer makes about content, proof, documentation, word choice, paragraph structure, and thematic organization. Similarly, in matters like comma placement and subject-verb agreement, the writer follows certain conventions to make the paper more easily comprehensible to the reader.

You may use the transparent-reader approach in your comments about content, methodology, and other matters relevant to your discipline, as well as your remarks about writing skills. To remind the student of the audience-centered nature of writing, an instructor might say or write, "I lost the train of your thought here," rather than "This paragraph is not coherent." The second response is not wrong; it just misses an opportunity to remind students that what we call "coherence" is not a mysterious, revealed principle but a way of ordering thoughts so that readers can easily grasp them. Such a statement also helps students understand that "coherence" may differ from essay to essay and that in all cases the test of whether or not a paragraph is coherent is how easily the reader can follow the thought progression. If students think you are picky about commas and periods and quotation marks, your best defense is to point out that as a reader you are distracted and confused by sentences not punctuated according to the conventions that normally govern writing of this sort. "Readers," you can tell your students, "are tough customers. It's dangerous to ask them to work unnecessarily hard just to take in your message. They might figure it isn't worth the effort."

Levels of Response

The transparent-reader approach allows you to respond at several levels. You choose the level that suits your student's ability or your own expertise. At the most basic level, you simply state your own responses as a reader: "I had to read this sentence three times to understand it," or "At this point I realized you were repeating ideas I'd read before," or "I felt bored here." If there is a hypothetical audience, you can mention what you think that audience's response might be, or you may want to set up a situation in which you ask the student's peers to read the paper and respond to it as transparently as they can. At this level, the audience does not analyze or suggest solutions but merely records the delights and frustrations experienced in reading. The responsibility of determining how to get a better audience response is then left to the writer. The beauty of such an approach is that it keeps you from falling into the trap of rewriting the student's paper in your own words. It forces the student to ask, "How can I make this paragraph seem logical to her?" and to find an independent solution. Another advantage is that any attentive reader can use this technique. You need only develop consciousness of your own responses and the ability to state those responses to students. You don't have to be a trained rhetorician, you don't have to know what "coherence" means, and you don't have to tell the student how to fix the problem. You just react. And remember to communicate your positive and pleasurable reactions as well as your negative ones. "This paragraph was clear to me even on the first reading," or "I appreciate your fine note of irony here."

If you think the student is capable of finding solutions to the writing problems that provoke your negative reactions and of repeating the successes that spur you to praise, you may wish to respond only on the first level. As you develop skill in analyzing writing, however, you will want to offer analyses to students who need them. Thus, on this second level, instead of merely saying "I got lost here," you might say, "I got lost here because you did not indicate clearly enough the relation between these two statements," or "This paragraph avoids monotony because you have varied the length and construction of your sentences," or "I had to read this sentence twice because there are two possible ways to interpret it."

Remain at the second level if you think the student can find solutions to the problems. Sometimes, though, it may be wise to move to a third level and suggest some alternatives. For example, you might say, "I got lost here. Try inserting a word or phrase to clarify the relationship between these two ideas, or perhaps turn the sentence around so that the idea I have underlined comes first." Such a comment still leaves the writer with some choices, but it offers guidance about how to amend a transition problem. In another instance you might say, "My reading was held up because there are two ways to understand this sentence. Insert a comma, or try recasting the sentence with *choices* as the subject."

Suiting Response to Purpose

In some situations you will comment on papers that will not be revised. Then your goal is to give the student some advice to remember and use in future writing. You will want to concentrate on general labels or general counsel, using the papers as illustrations so that the students understand what you mean. This may involve commenting on many aspects of a paper's writing and content or on only one or two points you think students can grasp and use at that particular time.

If you are responding to a paper that will be revised, you may decide, especially with more advanced students, to mark everything you see. When there are a great many writing problems, however, or when there is one difficult problem, marking everything may not be useful. (My tennis teacher, fortunately, doesn't mention, at each lesson, all the failings he sees in my tennis game.)

Sometimes the paper will need major structural changes, so the prose will be radically altered anyway. In that case, it may be wise to treat that prose as you would in a paper that will not be revised—that is, offer the student diagnostic summaries, with the particular prose as your example. You might say, for instance, that the paper contains errors in punctuating quotations and that, before writing the final draft, the student should consult a handbook and straighten those out. You may, in addition, rumble warnings about apostrophes, spelling, and capitalization of proper nouns, but you need not mark every transgression of those rules. It is possible to warn even more generally: "I see many distracting problems in spelling, grammar, and punctuation that you'll need to clear up before a reader can move easily through your paper." Then see what problems the student can clear up independently, and concentrate next time on the errors that remain because the student didn't know how to fix them.

A different approach is to ask the student to correct some of the major mechanical flaws before you pay much attention to areas such as organization, paragraph unity, or wordiness. If you put mechanics first, you'll want also to respond to the paper's content in some way, so as to acknowledge the writer's thought and message. It is almost always a mistake to devote all your attention to errors, giving the student the impression that you view the paper not as a communication but as a collection of mistakes.

Whichever approach you take in a given situation, consider the total effect your comments will have, their usefulness to the student, and the message they convey both about what writing is and about your own concerns when you read student writing. We sometimes get so fixed on the paper as a thing to be marked that we forget that our primary aim is not to correct the essay but to help the student learn to write well.

Setting Goals and Rewarding Achievement

Beyond indicating priorities, the teacher who is working with a student on a series of papers or revisions over the course of a semester can set specific goals, thus creating an environment in which the student knows that the first step toward Jerusalem is to make it to the oak tree. That milestone reached, the teacher will be pleased, the student can take heart, and together they can mark out the next objective.

It is even possible to grade on the basis of this kind of incremental improvement. For example, you could say to a student, "If you rewrite this paper so that it has no sentence fragments and no run-on sentences, I will give the paper a C, even though you and I will know that you're still having problems with apostrophes, spelling, and transitions." Or you might say, "In the next paper, if you have arranged your subtopics according to a logical plan, I will give the paper a B, even though you are still having problems with grammar and usage." Once the student has mastered the areas in question, it will no longer be possible to get that B or C just by maintaining that mastery; the student must add another competency just to achieve the same grade. In this way, you reward the student for making progress and save the student who has many problems from the frustration of investing much effort in mastering a particular problem and still getting a D or an F on the paper. Of course, the disadvantage is that either the student or the employers and admissions officers who read the student's transcript may be misled about the actual quality of the writing. Thus each teacher must decide whether incremental grading will work in a particular context.

Whether or not you base grades on a student's incremental progress, you can certainly set priorities and give each student only as much advice as he or she can handle. You can generously praise one who masters the skill you have chosen to emphasize, even though other writing problems are still at large in the paper.

Using Praise

One of the easiest habits for a teacher to fall into is that of silently noting the well-written sections of a paper but commenting aloud or in writing only on the faults. Not only does this give the evaluation an unduly negative cast but it also throws away an excellent instructional method—telling students what they have done right. A student often hits on good writing only half consciously, like the blindfolded birthday child who heads toward the right part of the donkey but honestly doesn't know the tail's going in the proper place unless the audience squeals. The teacher ought to describe a paper's successes, so that the student can repeat them more consciously the next time.

Being Thorough and Specific

Positive or negative, a teacher's evaluation is not much good unless the student understands it thoroughly enough to be able to repeat the success or remedy the failure. When, as a child, I received a coded message from my pal Julie, I raced to my room to get our special decoding key and sat down promptly to translate. Such alacrity, however, is not likely to appear among students who receive from their teacher a paper whose margins contain codes like "Coh,"

"DM," "Trans" and "Frag." If you use such hieroglyphs, you should make certain that the student is strongly motivated to look up their meanings. The code key should be as available and comprehensible as you can make it. I have found it useful to prepare one-page printed explanations and exercises dealing with the most common problems, so that the student whose marginal comment grumbles "trans" receives, in the same fistful of pages with the returning essay, a printed explanation of the way in which one uses transitions to provide connective tissue in writing. It is best, though, to write complete explanations on the student's paper such as these:

> I like this paragraph because there is not a useless word in it. Everything is tight.
>
> You need a transition (a linking word or phrase) to clarify the relationship between these two ideas.

It is better to choose one or two successes or problems on a paper and comment on them in detail than to mark six or seven so briefly that the student understands none of them.

Specificity goes hand in hand with completeness. I once had a teacher who would write, next to a paragraph of my essay, the single comment, "awk." It sounded like Henny Penny, and I could picture my teacher fluttering her wings and squawking in outrage as she read my poor paragraph. But though it evokes a specific image of the teacher, the word *awkward* is not a specific indication of what is wrong with the paragraph or how the writing can be improved. Awkwardness can result from a number of problems: a misplaced modifier, an unidiomatic use of language, a vague conjunction. Sometimes "awk" can tell relatively sophisticated writers all they need to know to make the language smooth, but usually getting back a paper with some amorphous label like "good" or "awkward" or "poorly organized," with no more specific critique and no suggestions for remedy, is like having a mechanic tell you, "The engine doesn't sound right somehow," or a physician say, "Something is wrong with your stomach." Much of the rest of this handbook is concerned with demonstrating how teachers can evaluate successes and failures with greater specificity.

Naming and Summarizing

Naming and summarizing are important services that the teacher performs to help students see forests instead of trees. A three-page paper that comes back with 20 different marks on it can seem hopeless to the student unless the teacher points out, for example, that all the problems fall into three main categories or that most of the problems involve a failure to provide logical links between ideas. Then, too, when you name a fault or a strength, you give the student a way to identify it, remember it, and link it to suggestions from other teachers and readers. For example, I might tell a student, "This passage is too wordy; see whether you can condense it by combining some of the sentences and striking out useless or repetitious words." The student then says to me, with a slightly startled grin, "Oh, that's what Mrs. Parker told me about my writing last year"—as though it were a miracle that any two teachers would have anything like the same response to the same student's writing. I always find such "coincidences" rewarding. I feel that Mrs. Parker and I have made a bit of progress toward giving this student the idea that following certain common, identifiable guidelines can produce writing that will strike most readers as effective.

Grading Writing

In a conference or a written response to a paper that is going to be revised, you may want to indicate a tentative grade to give the student an estimate of the paper's level of excellence. But in recent years I have moved away from that practice, except when the student nervously presses for it. Instead, I regard papers as "finished" and "unfinished," to reinforce the concept that an unfinished product is not yet at a stage to be graded and to separate my coaching stance from my later judging stance. I find that most students work easily with the concepts of "finished" and "unfinished," once they get used to them, and that requests for grade estimates usually come only near the end of the paper's progress, at which time I can usually say with some confidence, "You're working at a B or an A level now, depending on how polished the final draft is." Or I might say, "The paper still isn't well organized, and unless you can achieve tight structure, it can't get above a D."

Here is a dilemma you may sometimes face. Say that in one conference you offer some suggestions. The student then goes off, follows those suggestions, and comes back, expecting that now the paper will meet with your full approval, which means that it will receive an A. But you may have chosen at the first conference to mention only some of the paper's problems—the ones needing first priority. Or you may have marked some things as examples of what the student should amend throughout the entire paper. Or you may not have seen some problems that you later realize do need change. Or the handwriting on the drafts you saw earlier may have disguised faults that show up much more clearly in a later, typed version. A related situation is one in which the student, at an early conference, presses you for the grade he or she *will get* if all your suggestions are followed.

To protect myself against these difficulties, I refuse to predict grades at all, and when pressed to grade a draft, I will either refuse or, if I think the student needs the information, state a range: "The paper is somewhere between a C and a B at this point." Further, at each conference I say something like this:

> Now as you revise this, you will see other things that may need changing, or you will see other instances of some of the things I've marked on the paper, or you will find other problems that I may not have picked up

at this reading. You are responsible for using your own critical sense to analyze this paper and to improve it as you revise. The next time I see it, I will respond as a new reader, telling you what strikes me at that time as successful or unsuccessful. At each reading I try to give the paper a sensitive evaluation, but I don't claim that at any single reading I say everything I will eventually say about the paper.

Eventually, coaching ends and you award a final grade. Here is a set of general guidelines used by many teachers who value writing in their classes. These guidelines apply to papers written outside of class:

A: The paper is well organized, even at the paragraph level. Sentences are smooth and carefully crafted. There are virtually no errors in punctuation or spelling, grammar or usage. Words are chosen with precision. Informal language or dialect is used only when appropriate. The paper avoids triteness and generalizations; the language is fresh and vivid. The paper is tight, not wordy.

B: The work is well organized, but the paragraph structure may sometimes be disjointed. The paper may have a few awkward passages and some errors in punctuation, spelling, grammar, and usage. The language may at times be too general; it may lack the freshness or precision of the A paper. But none of these errors is glaring or highly distracting.

C: The paper is basically well organized, though individual paragraphs may be disunified or misplaced. Generally, however, the paper shows that the writer has followed a logical plan. The writing is competent but wordy, general, imprecise, or trite. Sentences may at times be awkwardly constructed, but their meaning is clear. Grammar, punctuation, and spelling are not highly distracting, but there may be some errors.

D: The paper is poorly organized, though there is a recognizable thesis. Some sentences or passages may be so confused that their meaning does not clearly emerge. Words may be imprecise, incorrect, trite, or vague. In general, however, the paper is understandable.

F: The paper lacks a clear thesis, the language is so muddled as to be unclear in several spots, or the errors in punctuation, spelling, grammar, and usage are highly distracting.

Many teachers ask about the practice of giving two grades—one for "content" and one for "writing." A double grade may at times be appropriate, but I would suggest other labels: one grade for "content and expression" and the other for "mechanics"—grammar, punctuation, spelling, and usage. The handling of mechanics is sometimes clearly distinguishable from other writing skills and may be radically out of keeping with the quality of the paper as a whole. The other aspects of good writing—clear organization, coherent paragraph structure, precise diction, crafted sentences—are so inseparable from content that I have never been able to give separate grades. Rather, I emphasize to my students that knowing and telling are so inextricably linked that in my class, as well as in the world outside, they will not be judged knowledgeable unless they can express their knowledge well. Some teachers take this stand with grammar and punctuation as well and simply never give double grades.

Sample Teacher Responses to Student Writing

To illustrate specifically how you can respond to student writing, here are some critiques that faculty members from various disciplines wrote in response to the student paper printed below. The assignment, in a biology class, was to write a one-page summary of an article about hawks. The audience was the instructor, who wanted students to learn how biologists work and how they present their work to peers and who also wanted students to learn summarizing skills.

Student Summary

Article summarized: Ron L. Snyder, "Some Prey Preference Factors for a Red-Tailed Hawk." Auk July 1975: 547-52.

(1) The purpose of this study was to examine the role of activity in prey selection. (2) The first of three experiments reported herein examined the role of prey activity when a Red-Tailed Hawk (Buteo jamaicensis) was offered a choice between two live prey animals. (3) The second experiment examined changes in prey activity preferences when the hawk was offered two comparatively large prey animals. (4) In the third experiment the hawk was offered two prey of different weights to determine if this would affect the selection against more active prey.

(5) In the first experiment the hawk preferred the more active of the two prey animals when no other differences were apparant between them.

(6) The second experiment varied in its results. (7) If one of the large prey was relatively inactive, the hawk went for it. (8) Over many trials, however, the preference for the less active animal was often replaced by a high-activity preference if the hawk was successful in subduing the larger animals.

(9) Experiment three showed a clear preference for heavier, less active prey. (10) Comparing the data in experiment one, showing a strong preference for the more active prey, with the third where the larger prey was less active

and still preferred, may have demonstrated a tendency in the hawk to choose
the apparently more profitable prey item in terms of relative biomass.

Below are several teacher responses, all based on the assumption that this
paper would be revised. In addition to the overall comments printed below,
teachers made marginal notes about matters like the misspelled word in sentence 5 and the stilted use of *herein* in sentence 2.

First Teacher's Written Response

I would like to see a more complete explanation of the problem these
experiments seek to address. What is at stake? What possible combinations could or could not have resulted? In following through
you need to take another look at some of your sentences (see nota-
tions) for clarity. [Notations were at sentences 8 and 10.]

This teacher's comment calls for "a more complete explanation." By itself, such a statement may lead to a longer paper that is no more satisfactory.
"Clearer" would have been a better word choice than "more complete." After
some intervening words that contribute little, the teacher wisely follows with
questions that should help the student. The second of the two questions ("What
possible combinations could or could not have resulted?") is not as clearly stated
as it could be, but nevertheless these questions are the strongest part of the
teacher's response, because they mirror the reader's confusion, they suggest
remedy in specific terms, and they focus on the central problem of the paper,
which is that information about the three experiments is unclear, incomplete,
and poorly organized.

The teacher's final comment is a good way to summarize some marginal
notes on sentence style. She rightly pulls together those problems under one
label—clarity. Though other sentences are unclear because of the basic organizational problems noted in the first part of the comment, sentences 8 and
10 are unclear because of their syntax. Thus the student would, as the teacher
indicates, correct the clarity problem in sentences 8 and 10 as a follow-through
for the clarity problems noted earlier.

Second Teacher's Written Response

It appears that there are three main factors that you want to discuss
(size, activity, weight) and then want to compare. Am I correct?

If so, write one paragraph for each (T = 4 paragraphs) or one paragraph in which all three factors are discussed.

At present the content of each paragraph is not appropriate.

Can you explain this article using your own words, not the book's?

The first part of the comment tells the student what the reader was able to gather from the report and mirrors the reader's partial confusion—a good first-level teaching technique, simply recording one's own responses as a reader.

The second part of the comment suggests organizational patterns for the paper—a third-level response. One might go on to urge the student, as the first teacher did, to make the decision about organization on the basis of a clearer vision of the significance of the experiments ("What is at stake?").

The teacher's final injunction, suggesting that the student might be better off with a more independent formulation, represents the instructor's guess that the awkwardness of the paper results in part from the use of some half-digested sentences from the original article. This kind of guessing at the process behind a certain writing problem is effective and intelligent.

Third Teacher's Written Response

I had trouble figuring out the prey activity of the hawk. Perhaps if you put each experiment and result together this would help.

Though short, this response is effective. It reflects the reader's confusion ("I had trouble . . . ") and suggests a remedy ("Perhaps if you put . . . "). What is left out is a message to the student that necessary information is given to the reader too late or not at all. It is possible, however, that in reorganizing the paper the student will reconsider the whole question of what information to give about each experiment and where to include it. If you have time to write only a sentence or two, this comment illustrates an effective use of your energies.

Fourth Teacher's Written Response

Your information appears to me to be accurately presented from the source you cite. Your abstract is successful to a point. I like your *preview* sentence.

A few suggestions:
1. Begin with an orienting sentence or two before you state your purpose.
2. Watch your spelling, misused words, redundant words, etc.
   a. apparent, p. 2.
   b. herein, p. 1.
3. Amplify each experiment a bit more.
4. Grammar—if one of the . . . were, p. 3.

Last sentence needs rewriting to act as a residual or summary. Avoid closing without summary.

This comment does something no other does: it finds something to praise. The commendation of the first ("preview") sentence is merited, though I'm a little worried that the remark about accuracy may disguise for the student how seriously muddled the explanations of the experiments are. The first suggestion is puzzling. I'm not sure that the student will know what an "orienting sentence" is, especially since he's just been praised for his first sentence, whose purpose in fact is to orient the reader. Neither am I sure what the teacher means by "state your purpose." The purpose of the experiment, not the student's purpose, is what already appropriately occupies the first sentence.

This instructor rightly points to sentence 10 as problematic, but does not make clear what the problem is. The student's last sentence serves appropriately as a summary of the experiments and an indication of their significance, but the syntax (sentence structure) is poor: there are too many words between the subject ("comparing") and the verb ("may have demonstrated").

The instructor's third suggestion asks for amplification of each experiment. This is a third-level comment without any earlier indication of the reader's inability to understand. The comment would be stronger if the teacher had said what amplification is needed—further information to avoid reader confusion about the weight and activity of the prey in the various experiments.

Fifth Teacher's Written Response

Jack, you do well to begin with a clear statement of the purpose. Next you seem to outline first the *choices* offered in each experiment and then the *results* of each. But the whole section was not clear as I read it. Suggestions:

1. Stick rigidly to a plan that gives *choices* for each experiment, then *results* for each, as now,
   or

   treat all info. on exp. 1 together, then all on exp. 2, then exp.
3. Choose whichever you think would be clearer to the reader.
2. For each exp., give all essential information. Ask yourself, What does the reader need to know, and when? For example, one of my questions was, In exp. 1 and 2, were both prey equally active?
3. Your final sentence rightly presents the results and their significance, but it is clumsy because too many words separate subject from verb.

This comment I consider ideal: it reflects the reader's experience; it uses praise as a teaching tool; it operates on all three levels, as the instructor deems appropriate. In suggestion 1, for example, the teacher goes to level 3, offering specific remedies, but suggests two possibilities and reminds the writer that the choice should be based on reader needs. In suggestion 3, the teacher stops at level 2, identifying the sentence's problem but leaving the writer to find the remedy.

Typical Oral Conference (Same Paper)

TEACHER: *How do you feel about the paper?*

STUDENT: Well, I think I understood the experiments, but I don't know if it's, if they're written very clearly.

TEACHER: *OK, let me read and see whether it seems clear to me. [Pulls near so that both can see the paper.] "The purpose of this study was to examine the role of activity in prey selection." Now that's clear, for sure. I know exacty what the experiments were for. [Student chuckles. Teacher reads first paragraph.] Now I'm lost. I don't understand the differences between the three experiments. [Teacher reads paragraph over again, aloud.] I think what I'm missing is—or, what I don't know at this point is, um, whether the two animals were the same size in experiment 1. And, uh, in experiment 2, you don't tell me whether one of the animals was more active. They are both large, but do they differ in activity?*

STUDENT: Well, I say that later on, in here [points to paragraphs 2 and 3].

TEACHER: *OK, let me read on [reads paragraphs 2, 3, and 4]. OK, now let me see. Paragraph 2 makes the first experiment clear to me, but in paragraph 3 I'm still not understanding what happened in experiment 2. [Reads it again aloud.] I think maybe that "if" clause on the end comes too late. Maybe I need that information earlier in the sentence. Or maybe I need some of this information still earlier, when you first discuss experiment 2.*

STUDENT: Yeah, I see. OK.

TEACHER: *In fact, why do you break up the discussion of each experiment into two parts?*

STUDENT: Well, I don't know, but the first part sort of sets it up, you know, and the second part tells the results.

TEACHER: *So first you tell how all three were set up and then you tell the results of each one?*

STUDENT: Yeah, I guess.

TEACHER: *[Reads first three paragraphs again silently.] OK, now I see what you're doing. But still, I was confused when I read it. How do you think you can fix the confusion?*

STUDENT: Well, I have to give you more information up here at the top.

TEACHER: *How about giving me all the information on experiment 1, then all on experiment 2, and then on experiment 3?*

STUDENT: You mean each experiment, I talk about it just in one place, like in turns, all three?

TEACHER: *Um-hum. I think you could also follow your old plan, but you'd need to give more information in the earlier section. Why don't you just fiddle with it both ways, maybe have some other people read it, and see if you can get it so every reader understands and nobody feels confused on the way through.*

STUDENT: OK, yeah, that's fine.

TEACHER: *Your last sentence is a summary of the results, and that's good, but the sentence is clumsy. Can you fool with it to make it smoother?*

STUDENT: Let's see. [Reads last sentence aloud.] Yeah, I think I can get it better.

TEACHER: *Try. And if you can't I'll try to tell you more specifically how you could fix it. OK. Do you think you can go back now and rewrite it? Do you think you know what to do?*

STUDENT: Yeah, I do. This is good.

The teacher, during the conference, tries to do several things, some of which wouldn't be possible in written comments: to ask questions, to get information about the student's recognition of problems, and to ascertain the student's ability to remedy difficulties. For example, the teacher merely says the last sentence is "clumsy"—a word that one would hesitate to use in a written comment, lest the student not know what to do with such a vague prescription. Yet here, in the conference, there is a way to determine whether the student at least *thinks* he can remedy the problem on the basis of that much guidance.

Responding to In-Class Writing

In-class writing is first-draft writing. Thus, unless you are specifically working with students on their ability to achieve standard written English grammar and punctuation *on first drafts,* you can ignore mechanics and style except when imprecision or awkward syntax muddy the student's meaning. The time to apply high standards for editing is when the student has had time to edit and has had access to a dictionary and a handbook.

If you are working with students on producing first-draft writing that exhibits reasonable control of grammar and punctuation, select three or four of the most pressing problems in a given piece and have the student work on those. Students who have major problems should be working through a learning center or instructional text to develop their written fluency—see chapter 9.

Though you may decide to ignore grammar and punctuation, there is a range of competencies that you can expect from in-class writing. These may include a clear thesis stated in the first paragraph (suggest that students leave a blank page at the beginning and write the first paragraph last); a set of discernible subpoints that support or develop the thesis; thoroughness in covering the announced topic; precision in addressing the question posed; use of specific, relevant evidence; readable sentences whose meaning is reasonably clear; use of appropriate specialized terms. Be sure students know these standards before they write.

The shape of your comments about the competencies of in-class writing will depend on whether the piece is to be revised. If not, then your goal is to give the student some advice to take along to the next in-class writing assignment. Most learners can remember only two or three maxims. Probably a suggestion about process will be more helpful than merely a description of what's wrong with the paper. For example, you might say, "What you've included is well stated, but you've left out two important aspects. [Explain them.] Next time, take an additional minute or two before you write to think systematically through all the reading, jotting down the aspects important to the essay question."

You may want to help students learn in-class writing skills by allowing them to revise their in-class work, in ways discussed in chapter 2. You can have them write the piece over at home or you can take another in-class period to have them respond to the same question(s) without using their first draft but trying to improve on it. Within such a framework, your goal in responding is to suggest some general principles but also to help the student improve that piece of writing.

Responding to Journals

It is possible to have your students do some writing that is not meant to be "worked up"—in journals, for example. When this is the case, expectations should be made clear all around. Your response to the writing will change. You will want to respond personally to the ideas expressed, to prod further thinking, to push toward more creative musing on the next pages of the journal, or to encourage a greater volume of writing.

Let's take, for example, a rambling section from one student's journal, kept for a class in cross-cultural communication.

From a Student Journal

An area that really stands out in my mind is that of social status. If all men are to be equal, why do we even have this social status? Yet I have a better question: "Have you ever seen a poor politician, doctor, or lawyer?" This status kick means nothing to me, as long as it continues to be based on an individual's income level. To change things for the better, I think people should be hired because of their qualitifications rather than status and money. Many of your young, brilliant, and capable people end up doing a gas station job or being a garbage man, simply because they lack enough financial resources to be for instance a lawyer. The example of garbage men and gas station attendants being low in status is also a big hoax.

If this paragraph is not going to be revised, you will want either to listen to the musing without comment or to express appreciation for the sharing of the writer's thoughts or to encourage perseverance in the keeping of the journal. In addition, you may want to respond as you would in an oral conversation, refuting or questioning the writer's ideas so that the student in turn responds; the journal than may become dialogue.

Here are some possible responses that might be used alone or in combination:

1. *Appreciation*: "You're wrestling with some tough questions" or "I'm intrigued."
2. *Clarification and/or restatement*: "You're saying that social and economic background controls one's career options in America?"
3. *Challenge*: "Aren't people hired for qualifications rather than status and money in the US? How about all the 'equal opportunity' laws that guide hiring?"
4. *Personal reflection*: "My son wants to go to law school; tuition at the state school is $2,900 per year. He can borrow all of it. Couldn't the child of welfare parents do the same? I don't know."
5. *Encouragement to pursue*: "How do other cultures we've studied, like Japan, Britain, Mexico, handle entry by the poor into professional fields? I'd like to hear what you can find out?" or "I'd love to read what appears if you write a couple of pages, just on the question of equality and social status" or "This might make a good topic for the term paper."

On the other hand, you may want to encourage the student to "write up" some ideas as a formal essay. If so, you are changing genres, and you should encourage the types of reading, support, and proof appropriate to formal academic papers. You will treat this journal entry as a preparation for an academic paper. Frank Cunningham's "Writing Philosophy" illustrates responses to student muses and drafts that push the student toward formal philosophical essays.

A third alternative is to ask the student to revise and polish the paragraph *as a journal entry*. The student then crafts the writing more carefully but does not change its genre; it remains personal, informal, and conversational. You will want to encourage the student to establish a focus first, since lack of focus is the primary trait that keeps this paragraph from communicating well. Then you will want to help the student develop appropriate ways to flesh out the main idea in a manner consonant with the genre. Finally, syntax, punctuation, and other aspects will need attention. Remember that in informal or personal genres a discursive or stream-of-consciousness organization may be appropriate.

A more carefully crafted version of the journal paragraph might well look like this:

```
I don't believe that the social status of your job should play the role
it does in your life.  My aunt should introduce me to her friends with the
same pride in her voice, whether she can announce: "Dennis plans to go into
law" or "Dennis plans to go into garbage collection."  But then I ask myself,
do I view my own friends differently, even in subtle ways, depending on what
they do or plan to do?  Have my best high school friend Ronnie and I grown
```

apart because our paths are separate now or because I have subtly pulled back

from him, since I'm in college and he's slicing joints at our local meat

market back home? If it is true that in <u>our</u> society we cannot help being

affected by social status, I wonder whether there are societies in which

social status is less influential, or even nonexistent--where Aunt Jane really

would be equally proud, and where Ronnie and I, always invited to the same

parties, would be social equals.

The journal entry has not abandoned its contractions or its personal, mus-ing tone. It has, however, focused on a single idea and developed it with vivid detail. Thoughts are carefully arranged, and the paragraph has a clear begin-ning and end.

Responding to Planning Statements

Responding to a prospectus, thesis sentence, hypothesis, or statement of a problem is a technique that may take some practice on the part of the instruc-tor, the tutor, or the writer's peers. It is useful to begin with a checklist:

- Is the formulation expressed as a complete sentence?
- Does it have a working verb?
- Are the words specific?
- Is it a subject that the student can develop from the available resources?

When you or someone else works face to face with the student, the next step is often best handled as a series of questions addressed to the student, designed to stimulate further planning. Ask the writer, "What will convince your reader of the truth of your statement? What sort of evidence or development do you need to establish your points? What does your audience need from you? What do you want to happen to your reader as a result of having read your paper?" The student's answers to these queries will often result either in recognition of the weaknesses of the plan or in clues for its further development.

If you are not face to face with the student, you can give useful response to a thesis or other planning statement by written comments. Alternatively, you might call together and work with a group of students whose planning state-ments show problems. Or arrange for each student who has problems to get help from two successful peers. The last two techniques will take less time than individual responses.

Whatever form your response takes, it is important not only to describe to the student where the planning *statement* needs change but also to learn what planning *behavior* the student has followed and to suggest helpful planning strategies.

Chapter Seven

Responding to Problems in Focus and Organization

Responding to Problems in Focus

When a paper first comes in, resist the temptation to read it straight through word by word, jumping on the first flaw you see. Instead, begin by scanning it for clues to its thesis and focus. One indication is paragraph length. If the paper consists of a number of very short paragraphs, chances are that the student has tried to cover too much territory and has not developed any of the ideas in sufficient depth. In fact, the paper may actually be nothing more than the first paragraphs of several potential papers.

Another way to determine quickly whether the paper has a sufficiently limited topic is to read the first and last paragraphs of the paper and ask yourself whether they have a common theme and emphasis. If they have little to do with each other, you may find that the student has switched subjects somewhere in the middle and has covered too much. You can sometimes find out where the student went wrong just by reading the first sentence of each paragraph.

If such a quick scan reveals that the writer indeed lacks focus or has tried to cover too much, and if your time is limited, you may perhaps choose not to spend time analyzing the faults in the paint job but to return the paper immediately for a reworking of the whole architectural plan. Begin by explaining that the essay is not a failure but a beginning; that many writers plan first in generalities and then narrow them down to more specific and limited topics. You might request that the student tell you, or write down in a single sentence, the main idea of this draft. The attempt to do so will both show what's wrong and help discover a clearer topic. If the area is still too broad, you might ask some of the unanswered questions, just to show the student how shallow the development is and how the paper too soon scurried on to another major point. Then ask the student to select just one of the topics in the paper or to conceive a single, more limited concept and then write another draft.

In the essay on women's liberation printed below, for example, a scan of paragraph length and a reading of the first and last paragraphs will, in a few seconds, reveal that the student has introduced several ideas outside the one he begins with—that women must accept the responsibilities and hardships that go with equality. The paper does not follow its originally stated thesis, nor does it develop any of its points in adequate depth.

Women's Liberation

I, like most male chauvinists, believe that equality for women is a valid fight, but I also feel that if women want to be liberated, they are going to have to be willing to go the distance. By this, women are going to be exactly equal as their male rivals. This includes, women in the armed forces, hard labor and many other jobs in which men have been more concerned with.

The advantages for women, as equals, except in the cases of equal pay for equal work, is very few. I really cannot see how women could possibly be benefited, by wanting to come out of their protective home, mother, housewife, shells, to work along side a man in some kind of hard backbreaking job. About the only logical advantage that a women would have would be where equal work gets equal pay. If women are qualified and can perform the same work that a man does, she should receive equal pay.

In contrast to the advantages, the disadvantages, I feel would hurt a liberated women than help. For full total equality, women would be subject to the draft and would have to serve alongside men in time of war. Any woman that would be for this, rather than a home life is crazy.

I think that women started the equality fight and have carried it much to far. They have carried the movement to a point where people are either joking or don't think the fighters are to serious about what they say.

It has been said that if women want to become exactly equal as men they will have to give up some of their luxuries. This includes, rights to child support, alimony in divorce settlements, abortion at the demand of the female, and centers for child care.

In the case of alimony, you can plainly see who is the one being discriminated against, yes the male. Alimony laws are unfair to men in the way it lets the women in a divorce settlement collect off her X husband even though the marriage breakup could have been the fault of the women. If equality laws are passed this will be one thing that most women miss dearly.

As for child support, it could be looked upon as the joint responsibility of both parents for the welfare of their children.

In abortion cases, in some states it only requires only the consent of the female to have a medical abortion. This to would change along with other laws.

Some analysts feel that the Womens' Liberation movement is being carried on by white middle class educated females for whom it would benefit the most. The reason for this assumption is the lack of the movement to attract working, lower class, and black women. It can be said then that maybe these women do not want to become liberated. Most women are satisfied with this and have started organizations, such as the Pussycats to denounce the Liberation Movement. This organization is made up of women who do not want to become so-called equals with their men.

I feel that in the long run women are going to have to chose between a protective life, or one that they are asking for, one of total equality. They are going to have to give a little in order to receive a little. In contrast to other liberation movements in the U.S. such as the gay people, blacks and other minorities, the women's libers will probably have a tougher time trying to convince society that their fight is a just and valid cause.

This paper need take only a minute or two of your time. In fact, it's not a paper at all, in the finished sense; it's a spurt of ideas and feelings out of which—with some encouragement, some guidance, and some questions from you—the student may be able to make a coherent, viable statement. When you have scanned it, you can immediately suggest that the student write another draft developing in more detail just one of the aspects touched on—that women must be willing to accept the responsibilities and hardships of being equal or that homemakers have little to gain from liberation or that women should receive equal pay for equal work or that women will have a tougher time than blacks or gays in convincing the American people that their cause is just. The teacher will also want to ask some questions that will lead to more reading and more careful support for whatever statement the student will make. The instructor may also give some warning concerning other problems in the paper: "Read your draft aloud to yourself so that you can hear the patterns—for example, 'in which women have been more concerned with' and 'would hurt women than help.'" But the teacher's essential philosophy is that the student first needs to master the principle of limiting and focusing the topic and supporting it sufficiently. When he has accomplished that, he can concentrate on other concerns, such as the acute problem with syntax or the spelling of *too.*

Don't forget the value of praise as a teaching tool, even in a paper as badly flawed as this one. Paragraph one, though the language is clumsy, sets out a topic and suggests several appropriate subtopics. Although the paper frustrates the reader by not developing as this first paragraph leads one to expect, a seminal plan is present in the opening paragraph, and some of the paper's body begins to develop those points. Your most effective approach might be to emphasize what fits and encourage enlargement, instead of focusing on the chaos of the rest.

In the next student essay the paragraphs are of substantial length, so you don't have the short-paragraph clue to the paper's fuzzy focus. Again, however, it is possible to identify the focus problem quickly. Begin by reading the first two sentences and then the last sentence.

Dostoevsky's <u>Notes from Underground</u>

<u>Notes from Underground</u> has as its original title <u>A Confession</u>, and it appears to be just that. Dostoevsky seems to be revelling against the socialist ideology prevalent in Russia at the time. He once went along with the idea that cruelty is produced by social conditions, and that one can then alter social conditions and forever remove cruelty from the world. An event in Dostoevsky that typifies his early socialist thoughts occurred when one day he was on the way to the School of Engineering that he was attending at the time. He was looking out of the window of a bar when a coach stopped in front of the window and a man stepped out and came into the bar, drank some vodka and left in a rush, getting back up on the carriage and beating the driver cruelly on the neck. Bending over from the blows the driver beat the horses equally violently. Dostoevsky also went along with the idea that if one only allowed him to do it, man would react in his own best interests; this is necessary if socialism is to work.

Dostoevsky was subsequently sent to Siberia a few years later and stayed for ten years; this helped quite a bit in altering his ideas about man's nature. Fyodor devoted his entire first section in <u>Notes from Underground</u> to demonstrate the point that given a chance man would not react in his best interests but would rather do all he could to prove to himself that he has free choice. Avranhim Yanmolissky writes about <u>Notes from Underground</u> in his book <u>Dostoevsky</u> that "Human nature, his hero insists, is not so simple. Man is at the bottom an irrational creature. He not only loves creation but also

destruction, not only well-being but also suffering; he loathes the
mechanical, the predictable, the final. Reason is but part of the self; he
knows what it has succeeded in learning, and some things it will never learn,
all that's certain about history is that it has little to do with reason.
What man wants is not to act rationally and to his own advantage but to act as
he chooses." But what, then, of Plato??? In the Republic, at the end of Book *I'm lost*
I, we have the following passage between Socrates and Thrasymachos: *Is this D's voice or yours?*

Soc: "The just man then is happy, and the unjust miserable."

Thras: "Let it be so", he said.

Soc: "But to be miserable is not profitable, to be happy, is."

Thras: "Of course."

Soc: "Then, O Thrasymachos; blessed among men! Injustice is never more
profitable than justice!"

Seems unconnected.

If one values suffering as well as well-being then it is profitable to *Relate what you're just*
suffer sometimes. We can now see that injustice is sometimes profitable and
justice unprofitable. Perhaps Dostoevsky <u>felt this way</u> partly because during *just*
that time in Russia the courts would let violent murderers go because they
were victims of bad social conditions. *when? as a Socialist?*

It is in this spirit that Fyodor speaks of such things as science which *when does*
was believed to be, at that time in Russia, the miracle that was going to *D spe so, an*
improve social conditions such that people can be happy all the time. The *how related*
author, Chernyshevsky, speaks of the crystal palace that housed the London *to note*
great exhibitions of 1851, an exhibiton of science and industry. Dostoevsky
mentions this crystal tower as being an object of scorn, that man is not
rational and needs an inattainable goal, and one should not accept the
simplest logic (such as two times two is four) because logic builds on itself
and will take over his thoughts in all areas. Man <u>should be</u> free to choose .
his own nature. *I'm confused. Relate to idea that man is or wants to prove his freedom*

<u>Notes from Underground</u> presents a paradox to us because the underground
man sometimes uses the fact that others have persecuted him as a reason for
his own cruelty yet advocates the ability of the human to choose his own
nature. The underground man recalls, when he was in school, his classmates
bothering him; perhaps this is because it actually happened to Dostoevsky when
he was in engineering school. In actuality the entire story is a paradox

because he is trying to explain his reasons for behaving so cruelly to Liza and his very explanation sets up conventions, of the two times two variety, by which he behaves.

Toward the end of the book he sees himself when describing to Liza a scene he had witnessed that morning. He had seen a dead prostitute being carried out, in a coffin, of a basement room and being dropped carelessly in the snow. The underground man is beginning to realize that merely to revel against a mechanistic universe and to cling to one's private whim is death because society no longer cares for you. His crowning cruelty is when he gives money to Liza for her kindness. With this act he shows himself to be totally divorced from life. I can now see why Dostoevsky then turned to Christianity for support, because it offers an inattainable goal during life (heaven) and it also lets you enter into society through love.

The paper is a promising "muse" but not yet a clear communication to a reader. What is your main idea— Notes as refutation of D's early socialist ideas? The contradictions within Notes? If so, which is the central paradox you will treat? Or are you explaining D's turn to Christianity? Compose a single sentence expressing your main idea; then line up your subpoints to develop it.

To help you achieve clarity, try telling your idea or reading your draft to a friend who will stop you wherever she or he gets confused. My marginal notes have shown my confusion about this draft.

To achieve economy, take as an example your first 1½ ¶s. Eliminate information not necessary to your point. Condense the rest, avoiding repetitions or dead phrases. Use these techniques for your final drafts of the essay.

The first sentence proposes one idea—the novel as confession. The second suggests that the paper will treat the novel as a "revellion" (rebellion) against socialist ideology. The last sentence deals with Dostoevsky's turn to Christianity. The body of the paper centers on two topics: (1) *Notes* as a refutation of Dostoevsky's earlier socialism and (2) the contradictions of the protagonist in *Notes*. The paper is a "thinking out loud" piece in which these two questions dominate. The next steps must be to decide on one main point and then to order the body of the paper around that focus, meanwhile improving on the writer's present lack of clarity and his wordiness.

The way to begin is to impress on the student the extent and the nature of the reader's confusion, as I did in my marginal comments. Next, ask what is the main idea. Then ask the student to go through each paragraph, justifying it in terms of the main idea or else omitting it. Such a technique will probably lead to the elimination of the first sentence and perhaps also the material on Dostoevsky's Christianity. The student should revise or delete the material on socialism and on the paradoxes in *Notes*, depending on what the thesis is.

Now ask the student to plan a series of subtopics that will support the main focus of the paper. Finally, work with matters of economy (as I have done in my comment about the first 1½ paragraphs) and with clarity of expression. The clarity problem may take care of itself once the focus is clear, or it may be amended when the student reads the paper to a friend who voices confusion, or it may require your guidance in matters of diction and syntax.

Focus in Research Papers

The bumpy road that leads to and from the long quotation in the previous paper is one example of a common focus problem: the faulty integration of quoted and paraphrased source material. Actually the problem has two aspects: (1) the student may be too dependent on quoted and paraphrased material, and/or (2) the student may fail to integrate quoted material smoothly and logically within the paper's own progression.

In discussing the first aspect, we often use the term "cut-and-paste jobs." The paper is little more than a spliced string of quotations or paraphrases lifted from the sources the student has used. To the student, we may say, "You use too much material" or "More of the paper should be your own thoughts." But trying to add more original thoughts to a paper is like trying to add more chocolate chips after the cookies are baked.

A more helpful approach is to treat the overuse of sources as a problem of focus. You can tell students that they must not be captives of another author's focus but must instead establish their own, using what is relevant from the works of other authors to support their own points and their own direction. They must also meet the needs of their own audience and accomplish their own purpose, not some other author's.

In the student paper below, the assignment was to read part of the anthropology text, select some particular point of interest, and write a short paper exploring and explaining that point. The assignment thus wisely encouraged focus, but the student will need help, in future drafts, to sharpen the focus of this essay.

The Early Years in Anthropology

One of the fundamental aggravations in anthropology is the paradox that this social science rarely employs use of the scientific method as a mechanism in its theoretical explanations. It can't. We cannot reduce explanations of human culture to simple syollogisms with pure deductive reasoning. Characteristic of anthropological field work is the unavoidable subjective viewpoint in theory building, an extraneous variable which Manners and Kaplan use to guage the relative 'immaturity' of anthropology as a science. "Much of what is called theory tends to be circular, tautological and ad hoc." (M & K in 'Notes') Manners and Kaplan point out a second paradox of theory development in noting that greater theoretical demands are made on the social sciences than the hard sciences.

The constant evaluation and reevaluation of theories is indicative of the lack of established laws in the social sciences in explanations of human culture. Constant challenges to viewpoints or methods keeps the discipline on its toes as anthropologists try to explain the why's.

In attempting to explain the first why's in nineteenth century anthropology, theory was employed. Theory necessarily implies some sort of generalization, ansd comparativist anthropology attempted to answer problems by analysis of the associated data which was available.

There could be no theory in the perfect sense of the word derived from pure relativistic anthropology. Manners and Kaplan observe that the relativists leave us with the remainder to study holistically, and to avoid being swayed by our own cultural preconceptions. (M & K, Cult. Th, p. 6) In merely recognizing the uniqueness of all cultures, relativists ignored cross-cultural associations which are useful in analyzing the most important of all the why's; they go no further than 'their own back yard' as though afraid to venture speculation. Manners and Kaplan refer to the destruction of many of the theories of the nineteenth century armchair speculators by the continual pouring in of new facts as a deterrent to forming or trusting generalizations.

The early theoretical generalizations were responsible for the growth of anthropology as a discipline and encouraged the collection of new data to attempt to resolve debated theories or to create new ones in ethnological research. Clearly, comparativism was the real basis for anthropological research. The evolutionists of the nineteenth century "laid down the foundations for an organized discipline where none had existed before," (M & K, p. 43) and utilized the comparative method in analyzing stages of evolution in human culture.

Spencer's rich background in embryology and morphology was the basis for his selection of the biological organism for his analogy in the development of cultures. He also referred to the human body and its countless systems in describing the structure and functioning of the interrelated parts to the whole.

Implicit to the growth of an organism is increase in size and number, with a corresponding increase in structure. Spencer secondly recognizes differentiation of parts after the early stages of integration, and that the vitality of both social and biological organisms increase as fast as the functions within its structure become specialized. (M & K, 27)

Spencer implies a direct unilineal descent in his essay on cultural evolution. He treats his concept of a culture as if it has no interaction with the rest of the world. While Spencer's biological organisms may have been studied in vitro, human culture can not be. There may be contacts between isolated cultures which give society an imput of cultural technology or differentiation before its (evolutionary) time was due.

Morgan, on the other hand defined several stages of evolution. Spencer did not type them but offered that along the line of social evolution, one point was more advanced than another. Morgan's approach was similar to Spenser's due to its overriding unilineal approach to evolution in culture. He sees changes in the Arts of Subsistence as the forerunners to changes in culture. Morgan distinguishes his periods of culture based on its materialistic technology, and refuses to offer the notion that a culture could be trapped between periods, that is having characteristics of two periods. Clearly Morgan and Spenser were easy prey for the diffusionists in implying no contact between relatively simple and advanced cultures. In describing his evolutionary stages, Morgan does not explain the reasons for how the culture advanced to the next period. Certainly, it wasn't predetermined that a culture would have to invent the bow and arrow to escape the title of savage, and achieve the promotion to barbarian. Further, a culture's technology is in accordance with its ecological framework, and conditions may exempt it from Morgan's advancement through technology. A fishing community may have a complex alphabet and writing system with no need for the bow and arrow or smelting technology.

Tylor, however, is the only evolutionist to querry how diffusion may
upset the evolutionary progression. (Tylor, 68) He discusses 'survivals' to
comparatively analyze cultural elements which had their origin in archaic
forms. Tylor also differs in that he used cross-cultural comparisons of
religious complexes rather than materialistic or organic evolutionistic
approaches. He does not adhere to a unilineal progression in his four stages.
In referring to them as stages, he still does imply a natural progression in
complexity from animism to science. Tylor has an interesting approach, but he
places too much emphasis on religion, while ignoring other aspects of culture.
This restricts his analysis entirely too much, and limits any kind of broad
generalizations. All three theorists, and others of their time used the
comparative method to formulate their approaches to evolutionary understanding
of culture. While evolutionism is decidedly not the best theoretical
approach, it initiated a formidable quest for theory in anthropology.

A reading of the first and last paragraphs of this essay reveals that they
have little relation to each other. The first four sentences make the reader expect that the paper will explain the methods of formulating theory in
anthropology—a field in which neither the scientific method nor syllogistic
reasoning is entirely satisfactory. Following this line, we would expect the discussions of Spencer, Morgan, and Tylor to focus on their early struggles to formulate viable theories despite the difficulties inherent in the discipline. The
actual discussions of each anthropologist, however, do not fulfill these expectations. Instead, they are a hodgepodge, consisting either of unfocused summaries of the anthropologists' theories or of unsupported interpretations such
as "he places too much emphasis on religion" or "evolutionism is decidely not
the best approach." In these descriptions of the anthropologists, the student
does not seem to know clearly who the audience is, what the main point of the
essay is, or which of the many available facts about Spencer, Morgan, and Tylor
ought to be included and which omitted.

Interspersed in the discussion of the three theorists, or tacked on to the
end of the essay, are several statements that could serve as thesis sentences but
do not:

- Nineteenth-century theories were destroyed by the inpouring of new facts,
  a process which deterred anthropologists from forming or trusting generalizations.
- Early theoretical generalizations were responsible for the growth of anthropology as a discipline.
- Comparativism was the real basis for anthropological research.

- Evolutionism is not the best theoretical approach but it initiated a quest for theory in anthropology.
- Anthropology progressed from relativism, which ignored cross-cultural associations, to Spencer and Morgan who followed a unilinear approach, finally to Tylor, who for the first time dealt with diffusion.

If I were responding to this student in writing, I would ask for a statement of audience and purpose. I would underline possible thesis sentences and urge the student to choose one of them, or some other statement, as the thesis of the essay. Then I would suggest some techniques for developing the thesis.

In an oral conference, I would ask who the audience is. Then, either as a stand-in for that audience or in my own role as reader, I would voice my confusion about what the real point of the essay is. I would ask for verbal clarification of the essay's thesis and then would have the student make a list of the sorts of information needed to support and develop that thesis.

We can expect that, in the process of rewriting around a clear focus, the student will clarify the explanations of the anthropological theories and smooth out some awkward sentences. Consequently, I would not at this point focus on the stylistic problems, even though they are acute. I would probably voice a warning, however, about problems such as those in paragraph 8, and I might even take a few moments to focus on that paragraph as an example of the kind of revision that will have to be done for the final draft.

If such a paragraph appeared in a coherent draft, I would certainly urge revision of its confused verb tenses, its misplacement of phrases (for example, "in his essay on cultural evolution" should precede "implies"), its confusion of pronoun reference in the second sentence, and its imprecise, jargonistic diction (the term "cultural technology or differentiation" didn't mean anything even to the teacher of the course).

In the next essay, the student has used two or three sources as the basis for an informative essay on the Chisso Company's poisoning of the environment around the Japanese city of Minamata. The sources, not the student, are in control.

                    The Strange Disease

Possible focus— the outward diffusion The chemical company called Chisso poisoned the fishing waters of Minamata, poisoned the aquatic food chain, and eventually poisoned a great *intro* number of the inhabitants. Chisso poured industrial piosons through waste pipes until Minamata Bay was a sludge dump.

As the poisoning continued, fishing in the bay continued and the fishermen knew only that their catches were getting smaller. They ate much of the fish that they did not sell or gave it to neighbors. If a family member became ill, that person received more of the best fish available, for the Japanese believe "a sick body must have the best food we can provide."

Many of those dependent upon the fish and shellfish began to show symptoms of an unusual sickness. Many became severely ill. Some died. The sickness, its cause a mystery, became known as the "strange disease." It was also noted that cats showed the strange symptoms; went crazy and often flung themselves into the sea as "suicides."

The first clear case was reported in 1953. Looking back, it becomes obvious that earlier deaths and illnesses were connected with the "strange disease." One clue comes from the Japanese mother's tradition--disappearing now--of preserving her baby's umbilical cord in a box. Examinations of the cords of children who had the disease would, years later, reveal traces of the cause.

3

Minamata was a restful farming and fishing area, sprawling out from its downtown center to clusters of small homes on the gentle hillsides and along the indentations and cirves of small natural harbors protected by seawalls.

Minamata was also a factory town, dominated by the Chisso corporation, once a mere carbide and fertilizer company, now a petrochemical company and a maker of plastics. Back in 1907, village leaders felt the winds of prosperity when they convinced the founder of the company to build in Minamata.

1

possible focus - moving chisso then being destroyed by chisso

By 1925, Chisso was paying Minamata fishermen a very small indemnity for damage to their fishing areas. Chisso didn't mind. The theory was to continue to dump and to buy off the complainers with the smallest possible pay-off. It was cheaper to pay than to care.

The fishing began to deteriorate. In 1932, Chisso began the production of acetaldehyde (a substance used in making drugs, plastics and perfumes). The process for the production of acetaldehyde required the use of mercury compound as a catalyst. In the 1930's Chisso also expanded into Korea. These days must have been Chisso's finest.

2

The early 1950's saw a strong upward turn in the production and sales of acetaldehyde. The company realized they would need a new factory and new techniques and they raced to make the most possible money from the old Minamata plant.

3

It was early in 1956 that the "strange disease" took on the proportions

of an epidemic and finally became known as the "Minamata disease." In April
of 1956, a five-year-old girl entered the pediatrics department of Chisso's
Minamata hospital suffering symptoms of severe brain damage. She could not
walk. She was in severe delirium.

Among neighbors, an uneasiness developed. Then appeared a fear that the
disease was contagious. The fear soon turned neighbor against neighbor.
People began to notice that the "suicidal" cats - in fact, almost all cats -
had disappeared.

A number of causes were investigated, from alcoholosm to syphillis. No
cause was found.

On May 1, 1956, Dr. Hajime Hosokawa of the Chisso company Hospital
discovered that fish diets were directly related to the outbreaks.
Some investigators began claiming that nearly sixty poisons were being
dumped into the sea by Chisso. Chisso sidestepped the problems and denied
that the factory or the employees could be held responsible. The theories
went even as far as the belief that ammuniation sunk at the end of the war was
the cause.

By July of 1959, a group of Kunamoto University reported that organic
mercury was the cause. Many committees were formed. One met only four times,
then mysteriously disappeared. It had been sponsored by the Japanese Chemical
Association, of which Chisso was a member. Another committee reported bluntly
that the cause was definitely mercury poisoning, and was disbanded the next
day. Chisso was still in charge.

In October, 1959, a carefully concealed series of cat experiments by
Chisso's own Dr. Hosokawa proved Chisso's guilt to its management. He simply
fed some acetaldehyde effluent directly to a cat. He was forbidden more of
the effluent and taken off the experiments. Chisoo had Hosakawa's proof.

In 1959, members of the Fishermen's Union stormed the factory, demanding
further indemnity and a cleaning of the bay. After a bitter fury produced
many injuries, the fishermen gave up.

After 1959, the protest ceased, fishermen returned to fishing, patients
became quiet and still Chisso continued to make a profit. Chisso did install
a "Cyclator" designed to treat waste water, that turned out to be a token
gesture due to the fact that it was often bypassed.

In spite of its many denials, Chisso finally found itself forced into court in 1969 - after a trial lasting nearly four years, the court concluded that Chisso had continued to poison the waters until 1968, when Chisso stopped the mercury method of production because the system had become outmoded.

The pollution had affacted as many as 10,000 people. Some may not even be aware that they are victims, as the mercury silently steals health from the victim.

Were the winds of prosperity really blowing on Minamata, or were they more like the winds of misfortune and suffering?

The story you tell is full of convincing and vivid detail. Now what you need is to find a focus—a reason for telling the story—a dominant impression or idea you want to convey to your reader. Write that focus in a sentence.

Now tell the details in such a way that they support your main focus. You will want to avoid repetition (see my "2" and "3") and to avoid misplacement of material that belongs earlier or later (see my "1"). But you won't necessarily follow my sequence 1, 2, 3. Your sequence will be determined by your focus.

The repetitions may be an initial clue to this paper's problems. It becomes clear that the first four paragraphs are paraphrased from one source and the following material from another, with the result that paragraph 5 starts again at the beginning of the chronology. The confusion about the date and role of Hosokawa's experiments may also spring from the student's having taken two or three versions of the Minamata story and pasted them together end to end. The seams show badly.

It is tempting to focus, in fact, on the seams. But if we merely urge the elimination of repetition and the blending of the various accounts, we do not solve the whole problem. The real dilemma is that the student does not know the audience, the purpose, or the focus for the essay. There are some isolated clues that might eventually be developed into a focus—for example, the first paragraph's emphasis on the environmental diffusion of the poison or the last paragraph's contrast between the village's initial wooing of the company and its eventual destruction by the company. Other aspects of the story could be the center of the account—for example, the eventual cessation of pollution, not because society was able to stop Chisso, but because the mercury process became unprofitable. In a talk with the student, or in a written comment, you should concentrate on achieving a focus, a reason for telling the story of Minamata, a primary impression the writer wants to leave with the reader. Then you can encourage the student not merely to hook together the various accounts but to tell the Minamata story so that it supports the focus and purpose of the essay.

Focus within a Genre Requiring Conventional Sequence

In some types of writing such as lab reports, clinical reports, scientific articles, cases, legal briefs, and so on, there is an accepted order of parts. For example, the scientific report generally begins with an introduction that defines the question and its importance. Then there is a review of the literature, followed by a section on materials and methods, followed by results, and finally, discussion. It is entirely appropriate, when such conventional formats exist, for you to give students explicit instructions about the expected format. But a pitfall for them is thinking that the conventional sequence is the only focus they will need. Into the various required sections they throw whatever seems to them to have something to do with the title of that section. Thus the scientific report emerges with too much detail about one part of the methodology and not enough detail about another, or the introduction does not appropriately support the results and the discussion. The paper resembles one of those puzzles in which, by turning the parts, the child can create a creature with the face of Goofy, the body of Mickey, and the feet of Donald. All the bodily parts are there, but they are not organized around a coherent center. Thus, when teaching students to write in genres that have conventional sequences, make clear that the content of each section must work toward the central purpose and focus of the particular report. It often helps to ask students for written statements of their audience and purpose and for single-sentence summaries of the main ideas they want to communicate.

The same problem can arise when you suggest a sequence for a term paper or an essay test. A possible organizational pattern may be inherent in the questions you ask in your assignment, or you may try to give students a solid start by writing down some possible subtopics. If you give out anything that looks like a set of sections or subtopics, students may assume that the sequence itself is the only focus they need and may believe that if they write something in each section the paper will hold together. It is wise, in phrasing such questions—or in giving such directions on exams, essays, and term papers—to remind students that they need a clear focus to determine the content of their subsections, the order of material within the sections, and the emphasis that any single idea receives.

The case below shows the anatomy of a focus problem within a conventional format. In Virginia Johnson Gazzam's upper-class science course, described in chapter 5, students were being deliberately prepared for the kinds of tasks carried on in industry laboratories. The assignment was to compare two products to discover which is "better"; the results were to be written in scientific format. The student had to consider more than one quality as a component of "better"—in detergents, not just cleaning ability but also aspects like cost, smell, environmental impact, and so on. The focus problem here was to decide what qualities determined "better" for the product, to design tests of those qualities, and to write the scientific report so that only material relevant to the issue was included and so that material was appropriately distributed within the various sections of the scientific report format—introduction, materials and methods, results, conclusion.

A number of students designed good tests of individual qualities but were unable to focus the project as a whole. Karyn (not her real name) is one. In the final paper, comparing a high-phosphate and a low-phosphate detergent, her test of cleaning power was well conceived and well written. However, other elements, especially the issue of phosphate content, were not well integrated; the paper lacked focus. Notes, drafts, and tapes of her think-aloud composing sessions reveal Karyn spent considerable thought on where material should go in the format but did not fully realize the extent or seriousness of her focus problem. It is instructive to see how the focus problem emerges in Karyn's work.

In an early exercise, Karyn was asked to write out her main idea. Below is her text (I have corrected spelling):

Student's Early Planning Statement

Main Idea: To compare cleaning abilities of an all temperature popular laundry detergent, to a generic phosphate free laundry detergent on various laundry stains. Compare other quantitative and qualitative factors such as price, appearance, smell, suds produced, and phosphate content.

The problem is that Karyn's choice of cleaning abilities and other factors to test is not clearly based on systematic reasoning about what will make one product "better." Plans for integrating the factors are vague. Instructor response here could focus on the need to ask "What makes a detergent 'better'?"

In this case, the problem was not remedied at the early stage. Later in the planning stages, Karyn asked herself several questions suggested by the instructor as planning devices. Writing this exercise at home, she first wrote her main idea: "Given various stains, which laundry detergent cleans more effectively and at what temperature." Later in the exercise, she wrote, "It is assumed that phosphate content affects the cleaning ability of the laundry detergent." Still later, however, "The effects of phosphates on our environment has caused this question to be asked." Then she returns to her main idea and writes in "Does the phosphate content of a laundry detergent affect its cleaning ability?" In this case, the exercise that asked students to answer a variety of questions seems to have confused Karyn by raising a variety of issues, among which she did not see the relations.

Her first draft of her introduction shows her still-scattered focus, combining the question of cleaning power with the issue of phosphate content and its effect on cleaning power and on the environment. Students have been told that the introduction must "get the audience's interest and state the main idea." Her attempts to garner interest lead her to fasten in still another way on the phosphate question and to confuse herself still further.

Student's Early Draft of Introduction

The effects of phosphates on our environment is a growing concern. Laundry detergents are a main contributor of phosphate to our lakes. There are local jurisdictions that restrict the use of phosphates [in] streams and rivers. So several manufacturers have produced laundry detergents with low phosphate contents. The main question that arises is whether the phosphate content of a laundry detergent affects its cleaning ability. If phosphates do allow laundry detergents to clean clothes better, is the consumer willing to use a low phosphate detergent to help preserve the environment? This experiment is designed to compare All Temperature Cheer, which has high phosphate content, to Giant Phosphate Free laundry detergent. [Next to the following passage, the student wrote "m & m" (materials and methods).] Seven stains will be washed at different temperatures to determine which cleans more effectively at different temperatures. The amount of suds produced by each detergent will also be measured, since suds indirectly indicate the phosphate content of the detergent.

The student is struggling to determine what material to put in the materials and methods section. But behind that problem of what goes where in the scientific format, the basic problem of focus has not yet been solved, because the relations among the main question of "better," the quality of cleaning, and the questions that swirl around the issue of phosphate content are as yet unintegrated.

An instructor's response to this draft should concentrate on the tight relation that must exist between the hypothesis, the test of that hypothesis, and the main idea as stated in the introduction. The instructor must help the student determine how the issues of phosphate content are related to the hypothesis and the test and to the issue of what is a "better" detergent.

The lesson from Karyn's case, and those of students like her in that class, is that the issue of focus should be addressed early and strongly in papers written to conventional formats. Students may concentrate on the problem of what goes where in the format without realizing the need for focus in the whole.

Focus problems arise, too, when the instructor suggests format. In the following case, an art instructor asks students to report on their semester of student teaching. She gives her students a suggested format: description of the town, description of the school, description of the art department, recommendations for change in the art department. The following draft has no integrating focus, though the student has followed the format. (Names of towns and individuals have been changed.)

An Analysis of Prairietown's High School Art Department

Prairietown is basically an agricultural community. Most of the area is either directly concerned with agriculture or indirectly affected by the farm area. Most of the retail stores are designed to aid the agricultural area by providing supplies for the work done there.

Some of the residents work for industry. Two main industries are established in Prairietown, these being Drow Corporation and United Manufacturing Company. As well as residents working for these two industries, some are employed by smaller industries and also by two major industries in Queenstown: Best Window Company, and Vreelen Manufacturing Company.

[The paper goes on to describe the school, its art facilities, and its art program and then makes several suggestions for improvement, which are, in summary:

A. Place more emphasis on applied and environmental art, which will be practical for Prairietown students as adults.

B. Develop better rapport between the Prairietown citizens and the high school art department.

C. Arrange for more flexible, dispersed seating in the art room, and move more activities outside to avoid a feeling of stifled immobility.]

In your comments about the first two paragraphs of the paper, your main task is to question the student's reasons for including or excluding details about Prairietown, stressing the sketch of the town must be relevant to the main point: suggested changes in the school's art department. Thus your written, taped, or oral comment might go something like this:

Of all the thousands of things one could say about Prairietown, you can include only a few; therefore, you should include or omit details on the basis of whether or not they help you make your most important point clear. Your main purpose in this paper is to suggest changes in the art department. What details about the community would help convince the reader that those changes are advisable? Try rewriting your first two paragraphs so that they prepare the ground for your final suggestions.

In conference you might go through some of the details, asking the student to explain why they are relevant. The two of you would probably come up with an analysis of the paper something like this:

Paragraph 1: The information is relevant because it will help the reader understand why the art department should take a practical approach. It could be improved by making that relevance clearer and the details more vivid.

Paragraph 2: The first sentence may be relevant to the topic, but the writer needs to clarify how it fits in. The rest of the paragraph, in which the writer lists the manufacturing companies and states that some of them are in a nearby town, is not pertinent, unless the fact that some students' parents work outside the town affects plans to build better rapport between parents and the art department. Although the later recommendation makes no mention of this possibility, the writer may wish to add it.

In fact, at this point in the conference, the examination of the irrelevance of the first paragraphs will begin to influence the entire paper. Pondering what to include, the student may remember that the window company gives free wood scraps to many townspeople who have wood-based hobbies. Including this information would lead to the sensible suggestion, later on, that the art department increase its concentration on wood crafts. In addition, the two towns are remarkable in that each has a strong quilting society. It is wise to ask how the art department could benefit from such a tradition. Thus jolted into reexamining the first paragraphs, the student may well come up with an improved set of recommendations at the paper's end.

First and Last Paragraphs

Mismatched entry and exit paragraphs may indicate, as explained earlier, that the paper covers too much ground. If the body does cohere around a single topic, however, those flyaway conglomerations at the essay's beginning and end merely show that the student needs help learning to guide readers efficiently and effectively in and out of the paper.

Opening Paragraphs

Here are some guidelines you can use in helping students write effective first paragraphs.

1. *Emphasize the principle of the "true clue."* A common problem is that the student may begin the paper, or a section of it, with misleading, overly generalized, or irrelevant material before actually saying what the paper or section will be about. One way to explain this sort of poor opening to students

is to compare it to a dog that circles a spot several times before lying down on it. Point out the student's circles and find the spot at which the writer finally drops down on the true topic. That's where the paper should start. Teach your students to check their own papers for circles before handing them in.

Sometimes instead of circling or giving miscues, students write a sentence or paragraph that emphasizes what should be subordinate and buries what should be primary. This opening paragraph is an example:

```
The nongraded school and the graded school are very much alike because so
far a definite destinction has not been made.  The ideal nongraded school and
the nongraded school in practice today are two very different concepts.
```

[The essay continues with a critique of the ways in which actual nongraded schools fail to live up to the idea, and in fact turn out to be much like graded schools.]

The paper, businesslike, rightly begins with matter germane to its main topic; however, sentence structure and sentence order blur the focus. Ask the student whether the real topic of the paper is the comparison between actual nongraded schools and graded schools or the contrast between ideal nongraded schools and actual ones. Another way might be to ask what the real subject is: ideal nongraded schools, actual nongraded schools, or graded schools? What the student should discover is that the paragraph would be strengthened by switching its first two sentences to place proper emphasis on actual nongraded schools as the true subject of the paper. The revised paragraph might read something like this:

```
The nongraded school in practice today is very far from the ideal.  In
fact, actual nongraded schools are not much different from ordinary graded
schools.
```

One special type of first paragraph deserves a separate word—the paragraph that begins with a description of the process by which the writer settled on the subject:

```
When I first read this book I didn't understand it very well, but after
thinking about it I decided to write on....
```

```
For my project in general zoology this term I have been working with
mice, and have discovered that....
```

For some purposes and audiences this approach may be effective, but often it merely delays the establishment of proper focus. To remedy the problem, the student should be encouraged to begin with a sentence that makes a statement about the topic itself, not about the writer's trip toward it:

```
Elaine Roberts' new novel is about how a young girl achieves courage.
```

```
My research in zoology this term showed that mice are affected by
overcrowding in three ways.
```

2. Work for specificity. Often you can encourage students to write good opening paragraphs by suggesting that they avoid the phrase "This paper will. . . . " Thus the writer is forced to move from an opening like example A, below, to the much more specific and helpful example B:

```
A.  This paper will discuss the influence of World War II upon world food
    production.
```

```
B.  World War II resulted in more sophisticated technology for world food
    production, but it also contributed to international tensions that would
    impede distribution of the food produced.
```

3. Encourage liveliness. Students who feel insecure about writing or who believe that they must use 40-dollar words and formal sentences to sound learned will produce nothing but the type of formal topic sentence illustrated by example B above. You can suggest that, depending on their purpose and audience, they introduce their topic in more informal or vivid language.

```
C.  World War II led to the use of bigger and better harvesting machines, but
    it also contributed to the international tensions that kept the harvested
    grain from reaching hungry mouths.
```

A topic need not, in fact, be introduced by a textbook topic sentence at all. It can be broached by a striking metaphor, an arresting statistic, or a vivid anecdote, provided such an opener gives the reader a true clue to the topic. Oft-quoted shibboleths to the contrary, a writer can even use the pronouns *I* and *you* if they seem natural and effective. For example, the paper on World War II and food could open like this:

D. In the years following World War II my mother's relatives in Germany were

harvesting more grain, with bigger reapers, than ever before, but my

father's relatives in neighboring Poland went to bed hungry every night.

Sometimes a student needs to formulate a textbook topic sentence first, as a guide to the paper's focus, but can later change to a more arresting introduction. For example, one student opened the first draft of a paper with this sentence:

The migration of Mexicans across the border into the U.S. is a growing problem

in America today.

The topic sentence was an accurate introduction to the paper, but it lacked spark. Later, the student revised his paper so that it opened like this:

If you think Mexicans are lazy, you should check with the U.S. Immigration

authorities. Mexicans swim rivers, trek hundreds of miles, cross swamps,

evade hunters, cling to the bottoms of trucks, have themselves camouflaged in

loads of hay--all to get to the U.S.A.

Concluding Paragraphs

A concluding paragraph can do an adequate job merely by summarizing the main points of the paper or by stating the conclusion to be drawn from them. Such an ending is especially appropriate for a lengthy, complicated paper, where the reader may need a summary. Unfortunately, however, students frequently attach a long, formal tail to a short, informal dog.

On some occasions, the student's summary will be in proper proportion but will omit some important points. Or the emphasis of the summary may be different from that of the rest of the paper. Or a paper may simply end without any conclusion or with a paragraph that contains what Pooh Bear would call "A Collection of Interesting Thoughts."

Other faults of students' concluding paragraphs include banal, self-conscious statements such as "I found this topic most interesting and I hope the reader has also." Or sometimes the tone turns pious: "A study of the life of Abraham Lincoln leads us to a greater appreciation of the virtues of this great leader."

A remedy for all these problems might be to have the student verbalize just what the conclusion should accomplish for the particular audience. In view of the tone and style of the paper as a whole, could the conclusion be flip, utilitarian, brief, lengthy, anecdotal? In planning the conclusion, the student may find it helpful to write a utilitarian summary of the paper's main points, just to keep on the track. That summary can then be the beacon guiding the actual conclusion—an incident, quotation, question, or fillip that is more intricately carved, more surprising, or more offbeat.

Responding to Problems in Organization

In talking about a paper that is not well organized, you can, by proposing change, encourage the student to describe the organizing principle: "What would happen in the paper if you switched point 5 with point 2?" Just pick any two points, regardless of whether the interchange would be an improvement. In response to your question, the student will say, "No, that wouldn't work [or yes, that would be a good idea] because . . ." and then will state the organizational plan that guides the paper and mandates that the sections come in x order, not y order. The student may not have clearly recognized the need for such a plan, so when you suggest exchanging points 5 and 2, the student needs to race desperately around some inner barnyard of ideas and offer up the first lame chicken that comes to mind. But even so, the writer has now stated an organizing principle, and you have a basis for driving home the necessity of arranging subtopics according to a conscious rationale. Now you are able to discuss other possible organizing principles for this particular paper, settle on the best one, and then use it to order the writer's subtopics.

Here is an example of how a teacher might work with a student on a paper whose subtopics are not arranged effectively (the superscripts refer to the students' footnotes).

Welfare Cheaters

The modern welfare system is certainly misunderstood by the majority of the middle class in this country. One frequently hears the following typical remarks: "People on welfare could work but are too lazy." "They should have to work." "A person on welfare lives more comfortably than I do." "We spend too much on welfare." "Persons on welfare have more kids just to get more welfare." "Most welfare goes to blacks."

I believe the above are typical remarks that the welfare system is credited with, and that they give an overall view of what is thought of the welfare system. The statistics of welfare are quite different however. Welfare recipients have monetary income ranging from below \$1,072 per year for a single person to a ceiling of \$5,722 for a family of seven <u>or more</u>.[1] The two largest categories of welfare recipients are the very old and the very

```
young.  The welfare expenditure in the United States is 6.5% of the gross

national product, which in comparison to European countries of which the

average expenditure is 14% of the GNP, is lower than any two put together.²

The people on welfare for metropolitan areas consisted of 27% blacks. Finally,

only one out of five that could receive aid, do!³
```

You will probably want to point out, first, that the statistics in paragraph 2 appear in a different order from the misconceptions in paragraph 1. To help the student see this, ask whether after reading paragraph 1, the reader would have any expectations about which statistics in paragraph 2 would come first and which would come last. The student should see that the reader expects the first statistic of paragraph 2 to refute the first misconception in paragraph 1. Now the writer is on her way to a rationale by which to rearrange all the facts in paragraph 2. In the process she may realize that she needs some other statistics or that she needs to verify her data more explicitly. She also has a problem with awkward phrasing, but it may be that in reworking to remedy other problems, she will subject her language to sufficient scrutiny to smooth it out; if not, you and she can handle the problem by using the techniques discussed in chapter 8.

Sometimes a student has consciously chosen one ordering principle when another would be more effective. In contrast-comparison writing, for example, there are two basic types:

Plan 1: A1, A2, A3, B1, B2, B3
Plan 2: A1, B1, A2, B2, A3, B3

Knowing that the basic job is to compare two things, the writer should be aware of these two fundamental choices and should consider the advantages and disadvantages of each. In the paper on welfare, for example, we could justify abandoning plan 1, in which all the *A*'s—the misconceptions—are clustered in the first paragraph and all the *B*'s—the refuting facts—are grouped together in the second paragraph. Plan 2 is most useful in this kind of paper, where the *A*'s are not tightly linked in a sequence or logic of their own and where it is important to make immediate comparisons on a small scale. Here the advantage of plan 2 is that one misconception of the middle class (A1) would be immediately followed by the fact that disproves it (B1). Thus the prejudice would not be allowed either to stand in the reader's mind or to become fuzzy in the memory; it would instead be immediately abolished by the quick presentation of a contradicting fact. Even if the student should finally decide to stay with Plan 1, her choice should be based on a consideration of the options. Contrast-comparison papers offer perhaps the tightest set of choices, but other types of writing, too, will exhibit common formulas. Persuasive arguments often follow this order:

- Introduce the issue: Tell what it is and why it is important. Present necessary information or definitions.
- Acknowledge, and respond to, the opposition's major points.
- Present several of the strongest arguments for your own point.
- Conclude.

Reading a student's essay or scanning the scratch outline you have made of it will sometimes reveal that the student has treated the same topic in two different places or that two subtopics are so similar as to be repetitious. A method of talking with students about organization in such cases is to circle the repeated ideas and ask the student to tell you the difference between one concept and the other. The writer, unable to pinpoint any significant difference, will realize that he or she has said essentially the same thing in two separate places and needs to reorganize the paper.

Careful reading of the next paper, written for a drama class, reveals that the student, after a misleading first paragraph, goes on to discuss four ways in which the white women in these very different black dramas are similar to one another: all are lonely, all (except Lula) are naive, all assume that they should control any situation between themselves and a black man, and all believe that the black man will want such a relationship to be sexual. The insights are astute. The writer, however, needs help in crystallizing the points of the essay, avoiding repetition, and providing the reader with transitions and with an introductory paragraph that reveals the paper's real subject. To provide a basis for improvement, you might mark each of the four subtopics as they occur, thus quickly revealing the repetition and scattering of ideas. In an oral conference, you could ask the student to identify the main points about the women and then to assign each sentence of the essay to one of those main points. The result would be a set of jottings similar to the ones already marked on the paper. Once the student has identified the topic of each sentence, it becomes easy to combine sentences dealing with the same topic, to write a single, coherent treatment of each of the four points in turn, and then to write a clear lead paragraph.

The White Woman in Some Representative Black Plays

(1) Only in Bullins' Gentleman Caller, a revolutionary play directed toward blacks, does the white woman fail to triumph over the black man. In Blues for Mr. Charlie and Dutchman, shockers intended for whites, the white woman succeeds as the vehicle of destruction for the black man.

(2) One common denominator for these representatives of the white bitch is loneliness. Lula has trapped herself in a never-ending murder scene and never makes contact with another person. Madame has an ineffective husband

lonely

who is always shaving in the bathroom. Jo married Lyle later than would be
expected. She was the town librarian, the last white virgin in town. Even
after marrying Lyle there are hints of her loneliness. Lyle leaves home alot

naive

to decrease the number of virgins in Blacktown. Naieve fits Madame and Jo.
Neither seems aware of what blacks are like. Madame has some stereotyped
ideas about what to expect while Jo seems to lack even that much. Jo
questions Parnell about her husband and black women but she doesn't really

control

recognize his tomcattin'. At any rate both are certain that they should be in
control of any situation dealing with a black. Madame is the hostess and
guides, or so she thinks, the meeting with the gentleman caller. When Richard
comes into the store, Jo assumes she should be in control and becomes dismayed

naive

when she realizes that Richard has the situation in hand. Lula remains apart
as being the aware one. She is going to enlighten Clay and is far from being

control

naieve. From the minute she sits down beside him, Lula begins her campaign to
draw Clay out of his middle class stupor.

control

   (3) All three women are self-confident toward black men. They are women,
therefore most admired and most beautiful. They assume they should guide the
relationship with black men. The relationship is inevitably sexual. Lula

sex

gives Clay the come-on when she starts up her banter with him, munching away
on her apple. Madame makes a play for the gentleman caller and assumes he's
hot to get in bed with her. She's surprised when he refuses to do anything.
At the store Jo becomes frightened when she sees Richard is not afraid of her.
Jo assumes he's after her, never figuring that Richard might not even want
her. The incident assumes even greater sexual meaning at the trial when Jo
dramatizes the supposed sexual advances by Richard.

*You make four intelligent points, but can you see how scattered
they are? Treat each in turn, with clear transitions and
first sentences. Then write a first paragraph that
introduces the __true__ subject. Your present introduction
is misleading.*

   The next section of this chapter discusses organization in longer, more
sophisticated student papers. If you don't care to read this section skip to the
section on transitions.
   Achieving a careful sequence of ideas is one area in which more sophisticated students can often benefit from your careful critique. In some situations

you may spend a great deal of time with a student who has little idea about how to organize even the simplest writing. At other times, however, you may want to be rigorous and thorough in helping one of your better students, also. Unfortunately, in many colleges the really good students go all the way through school without anyone offering them the kind of detailed critique of their writing that poor writers get all the time. Often no one helps the competent writers to grow into excellent writers. First, for example, let's look at a paper written for a political science class by a capable student majoring in journalism. The assignment was to evaluate Allison and Szanton's book *Remaking Foreign Policy*. Students faced the expected problems of establishing a sufficiently defined focus, writing in the critique genre, and avoiding mere summary in favor of a thoughtful confrontation of the material. The audience was the teacher; the students' purpose was to share their critical analyses with an interested mentor. In several ways the student whose paper appears below responded very well to the challenge of the assignment. He solved the focus problem by concentrating on Allison and Szanton's recommendations for changes in the CIA. To give himself a basis for comparison and analysis, he used two other works—one by Corson and the other by Marchetti and Mark—realizing that those works could be interestingly integrated into his discussion of Allison and Szanton's position. He comes up with a paper that is a creative cross between a critique of Allison and Szanton and a paper on reform of the CIA. As a reading of the paper will show you, however, the ideas are not well arranged; consequently, the paper is hard to follow. That, plus its length, makes this paper somewhat heavy reading. I have chosen an example of this length, however, because it is a length we are often asked to handle, and I did not want to work only with shorter examples. The problems in sequence for sophisticated students often show up in their longer papers. It is worth helping them overcome such difficulties, so that they learn to organize longer pieces.

American Foreign Policy: A Critical Review

Intro.

   Graham Allison and Peter Szanton, in their book, Remaking Foreign Policy,

argue for drastic reforms in government intelligence. Some of the changes

they propose have merit, but others, specifically his plan to split the

Central Intelligence Agency, are shortsighted.

   Allison would separate CIA operations from analytical intelligence and

the Director of Central Intelligence would no longer head the entire

community. Presently, he argues, the DCI "must attempt to command services

with which his own compete." An "Assistant to the President for Intelligence"

would oversee intelligence activities without bias. What Allison is seeking,

through all of this, is a de-emphasis of covert activities, tighter supervision of intelligence and a more accurate flow of information to the President (Graham Allison and Peter Szanton, 1976, p. 210).

1a Allison seems to be most upset with clandestine agents furthering their own interests. The most notable example came during the Vietnam War when President Johnson received biased and inaccurate information from the CIA concerning American chances for success (Allison and Szanton, p. 203).

3 The need for control is obvious. But splitting the CIA into two autonomous organizations isn't the answer. The proposal is not entirely **2** without precedent. Following the breakup of the Office of Strategic Services after World War II there was a hectic period in which many facets of the "Smith plan" were used. The Smith plan, as William R. Corson observed in <u>The Armies of Ignorance</u>, "sets forth quite eloquently the discredited doctrine of separation of intelligence functions from their operational necessities" (William R. Corson, 1977, p. 249).

2a Intelligence operations and analysis are very different, yet very inseparable as Harry Truman discovered in the time preceding the formation of the CIA.

> "...it was clear to Truman that the formula he had endorsed, which
> separated the functions of analytical intelligence and
> operations...was an unmitigated disaster" (Corson, p. 274)

Furthermore, Allison admits that the new agency, "without clandestine programs of its own or supervisory responsibility for the rest of the community" might become "a bureaucratic lightweight, readily elbowed aside" (Allison Szanton, p. 204). Said Dean Acheson, "no committee can govern and no man can administer without his own people, money and authority." (Corson, p. 267)

Allison also makes the argument that

2b
> "the disappearance of the CIA would relieve the nation of a name and
> organization that will otherwise remain a target of derision,
> suspicion, and perhaps attack (Allison and Szanton, p. 203).

The fact is, public support of the CIA and covert operations increased over the past few years (<u>Public Opinion</u>, Mar/May, 1979).

And what effects would such drastic changes have within the community? Certainly there would be resistance. Despite all of the uproar over the CIA,

1c the presidents themselves have been in favor of extensive covert actions,
either by direct authorization or by promising to look the other way, as
Corson describes. President Kennedy did not end clandestine authorization
with the Bay of Pigs operation. Corson reports that later, Richard Bissell,
the Deputy Director for Plans for the CIA got "'chewed out in the Cabinet Room
of the White House by the Brothers Kennedy for sitting on his ass and not
doing anything about getting rid of Castro and the Castro regime'" (Corson, p.
391).

Write Victor Marchetti and John D. Marks in their controversial work, The
CIA and the Cult of Intelligence,

"The CIA has a momentum of its own....They do not want to give up
their covert activities...They believe in these methods and they
rather enjoy the game. Of course, with a presidential mandate they
would have to stop, but the country has not had a chief executive
since the agency's inception who has not believed in the fundamental
need and rightness of CIA intervention in the internal affairs of
other nations" (Victor Marchetti and John D. Mark, 1974, p. 372).

What the community really wants is to maintain the status quo. Said one
observer of the Ford administration, "'the CIA and DOD will love George Bush
and Don Rumsfeld...because neither will make any real waves'" (Corson, p.
446).

3   Still, Allison is correct in his claims that tighter control of
intelligence is needed. The community generally will not disobey a direct
order, but "if lacking precise instructions about what to do and not to do,
1 can be expected to do what it thinks is called for by policy statements"
(Corson, p. 475). It is at this point that, time and again, trouble starts.

The struggle for presidential control of intelligence which Corson
1b depicts in his opening chapter is very real.

"It was only later that Truman and his successors came to
understand that while they might propose policy...(others) could and
did effectively dispose of these policy decisions in accordance with
their own perceptions of America's national interest...Like Robert
E. Lee, Truman and those who have followed him can only issue orders
and hope" (Corson, p. 279).

The community doesn't directly disobey, Corson argues, but will take liberties. "Because they must implement policy which may be improperly drawn or determined, there is a temptation on their part to throw some sand in the gears" (Corson. p. 432-33).

Testified former director William Colby, "'It is entirely possible that some person can do something not authorized'" (Corson, p. 441).

1c Of course, vague orders are often intentional as presidents seek to maintain "plausible denial should activities be uncovered (Corson, p. 475).

3 What is needed, both Corson and Allison agree, is a reduction (not elimination) of covert operations and closer presidential and Congressional supervision.

3 There are no ironclad, foolproof measures to stop abuses of power, says Corson, "but the force of law, especially authorities and effective congressional oversight, would provide a realistic deterrent in almost all conceivable situations" (Corson, p. 459).

3a Neither Corson nor Allison is prepared to abolish covert operations, but both think they should be limited. Corson makes several points, most notably that the operations alert the other government, "thereby complicating the task of getting further intelligence information" (Corson, p. 473). For the future, Corson also emphasizes analysis.

3b "In essence, secret intelligence information would have as its purpose and justification giving diplomacy a better chance to succeed instead of being used to set in motion covert actions which create more problems than they solve" (Corson, p. 474).

3c By giving the DCI more power he should presumably have more control and should also be able to give a more accurate picture to the president. As noted, Johnson had trouble getting good information on Vietnam although it might be pointed out that Johnson did receive some CIA reports which were not so optimistic (Allison, p. 196-197). Often, perhaps, presidents listen to *1c* what they want to hear. Dissenting reports are always available. Writes Corson,

"The president can if he chooses require the inclusion of dissent in preparation of written intelligence estimates, or invite the testimony of the proponents and dissenters when an estimate is being

considered for acceptance as the basis for a policy decision at the
highest levels" (Corson, p. 456).

3d   A role for Congress would also keep the CIA in line without severely
hampering the president's decision-making powers.

> "It would...make clear to the Congress the ambiguities inherent
> in the intelligence estimating process concerning the capabilities
> and intentions of potential and actual opponents in impending
> crises. Second, it would provide a sound basis for what has
> euphemistically been referred to in the past as 'prior consultations
> with the Congress.' And third, it could conceivably dampen
> Congress' carping criticisms of presidential foreign policy
> decisions by giving the SSC a much better appreciation of what is
> known and not known about the consequences of a presidential
> decision" (Corson, p. 457)

Of course, Congressional involvement raises the question of combining the
requirements of democracy with the need for secrecy (Corson, p. 447). Many
would argue that letting Congress in on secrets is as good as making them
public. Yet as [name of instructor] remarked, "Congress can keep its mouth
shut when it wants to."

Although current director William Stansfield is moving toward the above-
mentioned goals, many, including Senator Daniel P. Moynihan, feel that
Congressional involvement is poorly set-up. Presently, eight committee look
at parts of the intelligence scene (Orr Kelly, 1979), pp. 27-32). A single
committee such as Allison proposes would have more effective authority,
involve less bureaucratic slow-ups, and get a better idea of what is going on
(Allison and Szanton, pp. 209-210).

Conclusion   Thus, Allison is correct in his call for CIA control. Future
intelligence targets, writes, Corson, require

> "sources who are capable of knowing the meaning and significance
> of equations written on a blackboard and not sources who only know
> how to blow up a bridge or are adept at 'silent killing'" (Corson,
> p. 482).

But that control can be accomplished without all of the severe measures
Allison proposes. We don't need an intelligence agency so crippled that it

becomes just more bureaucratic fat, powerless to act quickly. In other words, the "committee urge", which Corson found in the Smith plan, must be avoided. It's

> "a recurring phenomenon in government, especially among career administrators who, when faced with the fact of inept of indifferent leadership by elected and appointed officials, favor an organizational or interorganizational response to offset that leadership void...Rarely do these actions achieve their intended purposes because regardless...There is no substitute for direct and concerned leadership on the part of elected and appointed officials" (Corson, pp. 267-268).

[The paper concludes with a bibliography.]

Both the first and the last paragraphs state the student's thesis: some of Allison and Szanton's recommendations for limiting the CIA have merit, but, as Corson's book illustrates, their plan to split the CIA will not work. However, though the initial and concluding paragraphs maintain focus and though the paper contains appropriate material for a strong essay, the reader is confused because points are not well sequenced. Below is an outline the student might logically have followed in analyzing the suggestions of someone with whom he partly agrees and partly disagrees or in describing a problem for which he is going to reject some solutions and embrace others:

Introduction: statement of the student's thesis, plus summary of Allison and Szanton's plan.
1. Student agrees with the authors that there are major abuses. Analyzes categories of abuse and reasons for abuse.
2. Student disagrees with the authors' plan to split the CIA and tells why it will not work.
3. Student agrees with Allison and Szanton, and with Corson, that tighter control is needed and suggests some specific measures.
Conclusion: summary.

It would probably be a mistake to give the student this outline. Instead, ask him to outline his paper or to list the main points of all its paragraphs. Then get him to identify his three main points and arrange his material accordingly.

Another way to approach this paper is to express your confusion and your awareness of repetition. For example, when you first begin to lose the train of thought, write "I don't follow; you are presenting ideas helter-skelter." Next to paragraph 3 you might write, "Here and again later at several points, you mention abuses. Why split up the discussion of that subject?" Questioned about the dispersion of one point, the student will have to reexamine his entire plan.

After reexamining the paper, he may come up with a plan somewhat different from the one I have suggested. In fact, he may try to justify something close to the plan he has. If so, you can then discuss the relative merits of various organizational schemes. You will also need to stress the need for connective material and for signposts that tell the reader what the writer is doing. In addition, emphasize the need for paragraph coherence. For example, paragraphs 5 through 8 are choppy and disorganized; the student should combine some of them and write better transitions and topic sentences.

The next example is a review of Robert Ardrey's *The Hunting Hypothesis*, written by a young man who later won a Danforth Fellowship. A teacher could make a significant contribution to the training of such a highly talented person by working with him here on the sequence of ideas, which is not quite as tight as it could be.

A View of the Hunting Hypothesis

(1) In many ways man is a unique creature. He kills his own kind and yet can exhibit an intense care for them. He has a complex social organization far above that of any other species in its versatility and complexity. Man has developed tool use to a high degree not found in any other animal. Robert Ardrey, in The Hunting Hypothesis, seeks to answer the question of why man is what he is. He would answer with the statement than man is man because of his evolutionary past as a hunter.

(2) During the Pliocene the great forests of Africa began to recede. Under extended periods of drought the lakes and streams began to dry up. Africa became predominantly savanah. In this period of time our ancestors were forced from a fruit-eating forest-dwelling life into the dry plains of Pliocene Africa. Ardrey states that they were poorly adapted for scavenging, they could not digest the grains of grasses, and thus they were forced rapidly into the hunting life. Gradually their feet adjusted, their stance became more erect, and they discovered the value of tools in the hunt. For millions of years our ancestors faced a selective pressure pushing them to become more effective hunters. Ardrey believes that the movement toward improved hunting was not merely a physical change, but is reflected in our mental heritage as well.

(3) In the early 1950's Dr. Raymond Dart was finding Australopithecus, a segment of the human evolutionary line, in South Africa. With the fossil

remains Dart found evidence that Australopithecus had hunted armed. This
means that three million years ago man subsisted as a hunter.

(4) The idea that man has a talent for hunting with a mind that leans in
that direction contradicts many modern philosophies. Rouseau's peace-loving
uncorrupted man becomes somewhat unlikely. The "Tabula Rasa", or blank sheet,
which is the mind of an infant suddenly is given a built in propensity and
talent for violence. The belief in the power of economic goals which is held
by Marxist and Capitalist alike is weakened if man is by nature a hunter.

(5) Evidence has been found to support the hypothesis. In caves
inhabited millions of years ago have been found bones and weapons used by the
ancestors of men. Alternative theories such as man the scavenger and man the
seed-eater are disputed by Ardrey. Early man, claims Ardrey, could not have
been a successful scavenger. His feet were not adapted for the speed to reach
a kill first, and his sense of smell was too poor for early detection of a
kill. He was a creature too weak to drive off other scavengers or predators
from a kill. Ardrey turns to biochemistry for some of his points. Man could
not have been a seedeater, Ardrey claims, because man can not digest many
seeds raw. "None of our vegetable staffs of life - our wheat, our rice, our
maize, our beans - can be eaten raw in any quantity at all without remarkable
digestive uproar," (Ardrey, 1977). Cooking is required to make these foods
digestible. Man did not have fire until 40-50 thousand years ago.
Furthermore, in the analysis of coprolites, fossilized fecal material, there
have been no grains found, although evidence suggests that if present they
would be preserved.

(6) Our behavior also lends support to the hunting hypothesis. Man tends
to work well in groups of about ten. This is about the size a good hunting
pack would be. The coordination that groups of humans exhibit and the fact
that one member of the group functions as a leader also lend themselves well
to a hunting life. The territoriality we exhibit, not so much individually
but as organized groups with a deadly efficiency, suggests the protection of a
hunting range by its owners. Ardrey points out that these traits are not
necessary to the degree they are found in man unless man has a background of
meat-eating and hunting. Our ability to cooperate to the point of building a
society such as we have is not necesssary to a vegetarian who must merely

search for edible plants. It is this ability to cooperate in moving toward a single tangible goal which has given man the ability to create a culture based on goals. A vegetarian or a scavenger exists on a much more regular set of actions; the first hunting for grains, the second hunting for a kill from which it can drive the owners.

(7) Ardrey also believes in the development of art as a survival trait. "We would not have survived without art," he says. According to Ardrey, art arose from magic. Magic for early man was a way to ritualize hunting. The two together (art and magic) provided both instruction and a ritual procedure for obtaining luck. It was a way of maintaining enthusiasm for the hunt between actual hunting expeditions. Art also becomes a sublimation of the hunting urge in man.

(8) In modern times hunting for a living is generally maladaptive. Ardrey believes that anything which sublimates hunting is a valuable activity. The competition we face in virtually all facets of life is foundthere because of our need for the hunt. Without the chase and kill in some form or other man becomes bored. Perhaps this urge to hunt is a part of the problem of a search for meaning which the race of man continually wrestles with. Yet many men have found meaning in the pursuit of a business career. In business men are willing to spend inordinately large amounts of time in the pursuit of business goals. These goals - the fight for a contract or the financial destruction of a rival (driving him off of one's own territory) - are easily explained as sublimations of hunting. The delight which man takes in hunting for sport does not make sense for a vegetarian. Ardrey points out that what is of survival value is made pleasurable. Hunting has no real value to a vegetarian.

(9) The writer does not have the background of information to measure the truth of Robert Ardrey's rhetoric. It is convincingly presented and the information I do have available does not contradict it, in fact it supports his conclusions. If we accept the hypothesis as valid there are some conclusions to be derived from it in understanding ourselves and our roles in our technologicl society.

(10) A biological urge has been frustrated. There is little room for the hunt in Tokyo. But the urge is still there, pushing for something which is an

impossibility. For some it can be sublimated in business or sports, perhaps a somewhat passive viewing of television violence will suffice. But our society consists of a large range of individuals. For some the sublimation is only partially successful, for others it is almost useless. And for few will a substitute activity provide equal satisfaction. This frustration will have the effect of increasing stress in man. In a culture in which stress is already high because of other factors this effect can hardly be doing much for our racial happiness and sanity. *Is this the idea you want to highlight?*

I felt lost here— what is the connection? → (11) The freedom and right to own a gun <u>is one of the more hotly debated issues of the present time.</u> The guns are dangerous. It is only necessary to read the paper to find instances of a child being killed or wounded by his father's gun in an accident. We do not wish to lose the instrument symbolic of hunting. If that symbol and possibility of hunting is there, if that self image as a hunter can be had by a gun, then its' possession makes the loss of real hunting a little more tolerable.

(12) The pursuit of an activity as horrible as war seems such a pointless and painful action. But where else in our world can a real hunt be had? One is pitting one's life on the outcome of the hunt. The odds are not much different than they were millions of years ago. Yet the danger is obviously there. There obviously are many aspects of it which are hated. Few would admit to enjoying the actual killing. But the idea of war, the training for it, and the fascination with it in books and movies point to it as a substitute for hunting.

(13) Many aspects of the hunting hypothesis seem rather negative. However, in our talent for cooperation and our ability to pursue a goal lies the hope for escaping some of our hunting tendencies. The key point here is that these urges are only tendencies. They can be escaped, and our minds which evolved for the pursuit of the hunt have the capability to find that escape.

There are two points at which the sequence of ideas could be improved in this essay. One is in paragraphs 4 and 5, where material about modern philosophies interrupts an otherwise smooth flow between the information about fossil remains and the other evidence, much of it biochemical, with which Ardrey refutes theories about man as seed eater or as scavenger. The second point is in paragraph 6. Repetition arises from the organizational plan the writer has chosen:

I. Behavior that lends itself to the hunting life
   A. Working well in groups of 10
   B. Coordination among groups and leadership patterns in groups
   C. Territoriality

II. Behavior necessary only for meat-eating hunters
   A. Cooperation not necessary to plant searchers
   B. Cooperation toward a goal different from actions of vegetarians and scavengers

My comments to the student ask him to justify the interruption and the repetition. With a student at this level of ability, such questions should be enough to start the search for better alternatives, without my having to suggest specific solutions. I expect that paragraph 4, if it survives at all, will appear either just before or just after paragraph 9. The student will probably reduce paragraph 6 to what is presently point ii in my outline. If workable, the questioning technique is sounder because it prevents the student from blindly following the teacher's suggestions to move a paragraph to spot X or to integrate the two halves of paragraph 6.

There is a third problem in paragraphs 10 through 13, which seem to me not to hold together very well. The theme of frustration is nicely developed in paragraph 10, but then the reader needs some transitional material to indicate how the paragraphs on gun ownership fit in. To jog the writer into revision at this junction, I might do two things: first, reflect my difficulty in following his train of thought from paragraph 10 to paragraph 11 and, second, question the present first sentence of paragraph 11, which provides no transition and no clue to the true focus of the paragraph. It is not the debate about guns we are primarily interested in; it is the fact that many people cling to so dangerous an expression of their hunting instinct. A sentence that makes a transition and also leads into the subject of paragraph 11 might read something like this: "If our stress is not sublimated in relatively harmless activities like sports and TV, it may emerge in more dangerous and deadly forms. For example, many Americans, in the face of hot debate, stoutly maintain their right to own and use guns. The guns are dangerous."

In addition to making these comments on organization, I would, in a full critique of this paper, probably also point out some mechanical problems and some aspects of diction, just to help a fine writer learn to polish his writing to even greater perfection. Praise, too, would form a significant part of my response—praise for the interesting first paragraph, for other felicities of phrasing, and for the points at which the essay effectively and accurately summarizes Ardrey's points.

Transitions

I have just suggested some approaches you can take if the paper does not follow a discernible outline because the student has not arrived at sufficiently developed and effectively ordered subtopics. Sometimes, however, the student does have a sensible organization in mind but cannot make it clear to the reader. So again, but for a different reason, the paper fails the acid test: can a reader perusing the paper reproduce, without the use of ESP, the writer's outline? When logical thought patterns are present but not clearly evident, the student needs to learn how to give clues to the organizational plan of the paper. Usually this is a matter of learning to supply accurate topic statements and smooth transitions.

You should emphasize that it is the writer's responsibility to provide you, as the reader, with enough clues so that you can reconstruct the outline as you read the paper. You can tell the student that when a paragraph first engages the reader's eye, it must rapidly announce what it is about and how it fits into what the reader has just read. The paragraph may start right off with a straight topic sentence of the good old rhetoric-book variety, or it may use more subtle or more imaginative markers. But it must not let the reader wonder or wander. Like airplane pilots on foggy nights, readers need to receive enough bleeps so that they always know where they are.

Students sometimes need reminders about the ways a writer can indicate a shift from one point to another and can spell out the relation between two ideas. Here are some common transitions:

- *Single words:* because, but, therefore, however, next, nevertheless, since, moreover, and so on.
- *Structural devices:* repetition of key words, parallel structure, use of pronouns.
- *Phrases or sentences:*
  The second major impact of radiation exposure is. . . .
  After having gained the person's trust in all these ways, the interviewer must now. . . .
  The same duality that appears in Freud's theories appears again, somewhat altered, in those of Adler.
  Can such a cycle of self-defeating actions be broken?
  Proponents of the bill, on the other hand, base their argument on Labor Department statistics.

The following paper illustrates the sort that results when a student has a logical outline in mind but fails to make that outline sufficiently clear.

Men's Roles   *Clarify relations between sentences.*

(1) Men suffer the effects of traditional gender roles more than women. ||

Behavioral patterns that are innate come into conflict with the assigned roles that culture attempts to instill in its youth. || Culture expects boys to mature

faster than girls even though boys actually mature slower than girls. An act

of opposite sex behavior carried out by a boy is frowned upon to a greater

degree than if performed by a girl. Similar behavior of a boy and of a girl

is often met with scorn for the boy and acceptance for the girl. The concept

that only men must achieve and be aggressive is a prime cause of their

suffering.

I'm lost. How does this relate to what I've just read?

(2) If it is true that the central nervous system differs between males

and females, then it should cause differences in the behavior of male and

female children. There should be differences in behavior patterns even before

the force of cultural environment takes hold on the two sexes.

(3) It is difficult to conduct a study of young infants under six months

of age because of their lack of body control and inability to communicate

good transition

effectively. (Therefore,) the study subjects must be at least six months old in

order to perform a relevant study.

again provide transition

(4) A study of infants which was conducted by J. Kagan and M. Lewis

(1965) produced the following results of innate differences.

6 months

	Male	Female
1)	"Greatest cardiac deceleration (a measure of attention) to an intermittent tone."	"Greater cardiac deceleration to complex jazz music"

13 months

	Male	Female
2)	Preference for the low complexity stimuli	Preference for high complexity stimuli
3)	Slower language development	Earlier language development

(5) Girls mature faster than boys even though society expects the

opposite. It enables girls to conform to the cultural standards of behavior

as well as avoid the stress that accompanies conflict with cultural standards.

Since culture views infantile behavior as feminine, boys are pressured to

abandon their innate behavior and to conform to the assigned masculine role.

The high percentage of males with psychological problems reinforces the claim

that men suffer more than women because boys are forced to change their

behavioral patterns which creates physical and mental stress. Culture does
not force girls out of their infantile behavior because culture views it as
feminine. Therefore, girls seldom experience the stress of altering their
role.

Let me know you've begun your second point,

(6) A tomboy is barely noticed by others, but a boy who is reserved and
passive is branded as a sissy by his peers. I have a tomboy and a passive boy
on my bus route. After transporting her home, she often climbs a tree on her
yard in order to show off for the others on the bus. The students on the bus
do not respond with any negative reactions. ‖ The boy is often ridiculed for
being a girl for insignificant acts such as not being able to open his window.
This results from his age and physical capacity, but not from his personality
or personal traits. He tends to be moving towards a state of insecurity while
the tomboy seems to be unaffected. Culture is responsible for his insecurity
because it forced a sex role that conflicts with his natural personality.

and what that point is, before you get into tomboys and sissies.

Fine transition and topic sentence.

(7) Culture is especially disruptive when it inhibits an act by one sex
while encouraging similar acts by the other sex. A six year old boy on my bus
was teased about not being a man because he was crying after bumping his head
on a seat. A young girl on my bus was encouraged by her older sister to "let
it out" when she was crying. Boys are always trying to prove their
masculinity by feats of strength and fighting. Girls are scolded by their
older siblings as not being "ladylike" when they engage in physical
confrontations. Society teaches males to be "nobody's fool" while it implies
that females are "emotional fools."

(8) I was insecure in my youth, because culture tried to force me to be
(aggressive) and competitive. My personality has always leaned toward being
reserved and cooperative. I felt insecure in regard to boys because I thought
they were superior if they displayed aggressive traits. My insecurity in
regard to girls stemmed from my concept that I would be inadequate for a girl
since I did not possess the aggressive trait that girls valued highly. I
suffered greatly from the feeling that I was below standards in the eyes of
girls. If society had been less rigid in defining what a boy's role should
be, then I would have fit into society more confidently.

(9) Society has succeeded in deceiving the children on my bus into
believing that males should be active leaders who will control and operate the

country while their "love objects" remain at home to cook, clean, and get
pregnant. The males suffer the problem of achieving their active leadership,
but the girls, whose only goal in life is to get married and have kids, find
it easy to get pregnant. Males who completely accept their assigned roles
become very aggressive, independent, and competitive in order to become a
"success." The importance of "success" causes severe stresses for men that
women who are at home do not experience. This competitive stress reduces
men's life expectancy, enjoyment of life, and ability to relate to others.

(10) The male dominated society has brought males short-run benefits with
high long-run costs. Men will continue to suffer more problems in life than
women unless we open up all areas of our culture to both sexes. If we
increase opportunity for all, then both sexes will have equal footing in
society. The evolution of society from one of barriers to one of
opportunities will make all our lives more enjoyable and long lasting.

Your essay is well organized, but you have to give readers more connections and more clues to reveal that organization.

On first reading, this paper seems disjointed, but further scrutiny reveals
that the sequence is carefully arranged. The first sentence announces the topic,
and the rest of the first paragraph outlines the four main sections. The rest of
the paper develops each of the four in turn. Very logical, very well organized.
But the writer has not provided connective tissue and clues about organization
to enable you, the reader, to grasp the plan of the paper as you read it. You feel
as if you're led along blindfolded. The guide may be heading straight to the des-
tination, but you still feel lost and insecure.

In working with a student who has this weakness, you can approach the
issue like so many other aspects of writing, by talking about reader expectations. My written comments show how you can do this if you are writing your
response to the student. In a conference, you might read aloud the first and second sentences of the paper and voice your confusion about how the second sentence is related to the first. Do the same for the rest of the first paragraph. Then
move to the second paragraph and read its first sentence. Again voice your confusion: "How does this business about the central nervous system relate to the
topics mentioned in the first paragraph?" Your goal in this questioning process
is to help the student see that the essay is tossing the reader one isolated statement after another, with nothing that helps the reader understand how all this
material fits together. Then ask the student to revise the paper, providing the
clues and the transitions that readers need. Perhaps the writer will come back

with something like the paper that follows. The new transitions and topic statements are underlined, and I have left the essay's remaining flaws alone, in the interests of concentrating only on the addition of connective tissue. You will often find, though, that the student, in revising to correct one problem, makes other improvements along the way. If not you will want to deal with stylistic problems, handling of data and quotations, and so forth—either along with your comments about transitions or at some later time.

Revised Version of "Men's Roles"

(1) Men suffer the effects of traditional gender roles more than women. <u>One reason men are so disadvantaged is that</u> their innate behavioral patterns come into conflict with the assigned roles that culture attempts to instill in its youth. <u>For example,</u> culture expects boys to mature faster than girls even though boys actually mature slower than girls. <u>A second reason for the difficulties of boys is that</u> an act of opposite sex behavior carried out by a boy is frowned upon to a greater degree than if performed by a girl. <u>In addition,</u> similar behavior of a boy and of a girl is often met with scorn for the boy and acceptance for the girl. <u>Finally,</u> the concept that only men must achieve and be aggressive is a prime cause of boys' suffering.

(2) <u>Society expects boys, more than girls, to overcome their innate biological characteristics.</u> If it is true that the central nervous system differs between males and females, then it should cause differences in the behavior of male and female children. There should be differences in behavioral patterns even before the force of cultural environment takes hold on the two sexes.

(3) <u>Such evidence of differences does in fact exist,</u> based on six-month old infants. <u>The reason for</u> using six-month olders is that it is difficult to conduct a study of young infants under six months of age because of their lack of body control and inability to communicate effectively. <u>Therefore,</u> the study subjects must be at least six months old in order to perform a relevant study.

(4) One such investigation of six month old infants, which was conducted by J. Kagan and M. Lewis (1965), produced the following results of innate differences.

6 months

Male	Female
1) "Greatest cardiac deceleration (a measure of attention) to an intermittent tone."	"Greater cardiac deceleration to complex jazz music"

13 months

Male	Female
2) "Preference for the low complexity stimuli."	"Preference for high complexity stimuli."
3) "Slower language development."	"Earlier language development."

(5) This study indicates that girls mature faster than boys even though society expects the opposite. This enables girls to conform to the cultural standards of behavior as well as avoid the stress that accompanies conflict with cultural standards. However, since culture views infantile behavior as feminine, boys are pressured to abandon their innate behavior and conform to the assigned masculine role. The high percentage of males with psychological problems reinforces the claim that men suffer more than women because boys are forced to change their behavioral patterns which creates physical and mental stress. Culture does not force girls out of their infantile behavior because culture views it as feminine. Therefore, girls seldom experience the stress of altering their role.

Pressured to transcend their innately slower rate of maturation, boys also experience greater disapproval than girls do for opposite-sex behavior For example, a tomboy is barely noticed by others, but a boy who is reserved and passive is branded as a sissy by his peers. I have a tomboy and a passive boy on my bus route. After transporting her home, she often climbs a tree on her yard in order to show off for the others on the bus. The students on the bus do not respond with any negative reactions. However, the boy is often ridiculed as being a girl for an insignificant act such as not being able to open his window....

Certainly there are still flaws in the essay. One of this student's primary writing problems, however, was his failure to provide transitions, a fault that obscured for the reader the actual logic of the student's organization. A teacher who helps students command that particular skill does them a great service.

This chapter has emphasized response to problems in focus and organization, including related issues such as first and last paragraphs and transitions. The next chapter emphasizes response to issues of style; the last chapter, issues of grammar, punctuation, and spelling.

Chapter Eight

Responding to Problems in Style

Analyzing the Situation and Setting Goals

Once you turn your attention to style, consider first the probable origin of the language that concerns you. Then shape your goals: ask "What will best contribute to this student's learning, with the most efficient use of my own time?"

Several situations are common:

1. Part or all of the paper is thinly paraphrased from a source. What bothers you initially may be the student's own language, much more awkward than the paraphrased parts. You don't want to discourage students from writing their own language and make them rely even more readily on paraphrase. You may, in fact, want to attack the ubiquity of the paraphrase and work with the students' language only when there's enough of it to make a viable piece of writing.

2. The student has not understood the material from which the paper is written. Hence the paper is an only half-digested concoction of facts and sentences adapted from the reading material. Attacking individual stylistic problems is fruitless; you'll want to work on the understanding first and then, as time permits, on whatever stylistic problems remain.

3. The student was tired, drunk, depressed, or under the influence of drugs when the paper was written. The paper is not evidence of the student's stylistic competence. Time spent in detailed stylistic analysis will only tell about matters the student could have cleared up if writing in a better frame of mind.

4. What you are seeing is first-draft writing by a student who was too busy attending to structure and content and just slapped down any words that approximated the meaning. This student could substantially improve the paper's style by taking time and care. Again detailed stylistic analysis will probably only repeat what the student already knows. You will want to demand and motivate careful editing.

5. The student is adopting a pseudoacademic, stuffy, or cute tone, thinking it is appropriate to the situation. You will want to address first not individual words and sentences but the student's vision of the reader's expectations and the underlying problems of voice and tone—treated below as aspects of style.

6. The student is attempting to use words and sentence patterns beyond his or her confident control. Such an effort is bold and investigative; it embodies just the attitude of exploration we want in our nation's finest minds. You want

to help the student gain control, but above all you want to support and encourage experimentation with language.

7. The student, even when writing with a clear sense of audience and an understanding of the issues addressed in the paper, and even after careful editing of the paper, forms sentences in awkward ways. This student will benefit from direct instruction in aspects of style. Your goal is to give only as much instruction as the student can handle at this time and to explain the points you do approach clearly enough to help real learning take place.

Only in the last three instances does it make sense directly to critique style. The other situations have been addressed earlier—helping students become involved, helping students structure time, and so on. Yet in the appropriate situations, the analysis of style is vital. A lamentable aspect of much instructor response to student writing is that the competent writer receives a B or A on the paper, the comment "good," and little help in moving from competence to excellence. Many of your students may never have had detailed, focused help with writing style. The rest of this section suggests how you can analyze some common stylistic aspects of student writing and how you can help students learn to write more effectively.

Some aspects of style may vary with situation or discipline; I concentrate here on aspects that are generally valued in most writing. In various disciplines or situations you may emphasize one or the other more strongly.

My own student guide, *Ten Steps to Editing Any Writing for Grammar, Punctuation, and Style*, discussed on p. 97, will help most freshmen and those upperclassmen still having difficulty with basic sentence awkwardness. More advanced guides to style, useful for both faculty and students, are Williams; Cook; Lanham, which concentrates on simplification of obtuse, bureaucratic writing; and Strunk and White, the old faithful many of us have used. Any of these will enhance your sensitivity to your students' style and your own, and any can be assigned to your more advanced students. In the discussion below, I concentrate on responding to students' style.

Responding to Tone and Voice

Before you begin marking individual aspects of style, ask yourself whether the stylistic problems stem from the student's adoption of an inappropriate tone and voice. Below is a paragraph from a philosophy paper. The student assumes a pseudoacademic tone that renders the writing nearly incomprehensible—even to the instructor of the course, its intended audience. The student has misjudged the instructor as reader.

Student Paragraph for a Philosophy Paper

In order to remain responsive to the continually developing nature of

human society, beliefs must be examined in light of questions pertinent to the

times in which they occur. It is in the interest of attaining an authentic
rather than a prejudiced conceptual outlook on the world that man searches his
beliefs through such questions for a basis in the assumed qualities of
authenticity: attentiveness to the world of factual experience; intelligence,
or the interpretation and organization of raw sense data; reasonable testing
of these interpretations for validity; and responsibility in acting in
accordance with the belief itself. To search out these qualities in belief,
then, what questions should modern man ask?

A major problem in academic writing is stuffy, bureaucratic, jargonistic language. You'll remember Kesling's ridicule of scientific journal writing (p. 00). Different situations call for different styles. Sometimes technical language is necessary for precision, sometimes it qualifies as unnecessary jargon, depending on the audience and context. Current style in most fields is moving toward language that is more simple and clear (see Goldfarb and Raymond). You must judge, and teach your students to judge, what style is most appropriate for your writing assignments. Lanham and Williams both address the issue of bureaucratic language and give examples, as well as showing how to simplify.

When you decide that your student's language is too bureaucratic and that the problem is pervasive in the paper, your most useful response is not to mark all the individual sins of style but to voice your confusion as a reader and to drive the writer back to speech. Writers are best advised to rewrite the passage from scratch; trying merely to fix the obtuse language usually doesn't produce enough change. The writer should picture the intended reader sitting down to read the piece, then ask, "What do I really mean?" and say it as simply as possible. Linda Flower describes this to students as the "WIRMI" strategy—"What I Really Mean Is" (*Problem-Solving* 28, 31).

In a written comment, suggest that the student turn on a tape recorder and just explain simply, as though to a listening reader, what he or she means. Those taped words can then be transcribed as the first draft. In a conference, ask the student, "In simple terms, what do you really mean here?" Write or tape the student's words, which can then serve as a draft. Sometimes a student is helped by having to address a few paragraphs of the paper to a child or a high school student. You can also suggest having the paper read by fellow students who do not know the subject matter and who will tell the writer whenever they feel confused. The paper below, for example, was to have been written to classmates.

Opening of a Student Paper

A national government has several responsibilities that are accepted to
be inherent duties. Among these are maintenance of national defense, setting

of standards and measures for the nation, and the establishment of a stable economic system.   In recent years, this last duty has gained importance as our United States economy has fallen to shambles.

Prior administrations have chosen to use fiscal (tax) policy to try to manage our nation's economy.   This system attempts to regulate the economy by affecting its demand factors through taxing policies.   Obviously this policy has been ineffective.   (Walvoord, *Writing* 10)

Instead of attacking individual elements of style in this paper, encourage the student to adopt an appropriate voice with which to address her classmates in a discussion about tax policy. Asked to picture her classmates reading the paper, the student wrote this revision:

Revision

In the past few years, "inflation," "recession," and "the economy" have become the main topic of dinner table conversations, cocktail party chatter, and presidential campaigns.   Most Americans have felt the pressure of our troubled economy.   College tuitions are soaring, and part-time jobs are harder to find.   Small businesses declare bankruptcy regularly.   Even large corporations such as Chrysler have faltered.   The tax policies aimed at improving our economy have been ineffective.   (Walvoord, *Writing* 11)

When bureaucratic style is not pervasive in the paper or when your suggestions to the students that they adopt a more straightforward tone and stance don't work, then turn to an analysis of the specific stylistic qualities that contribute to bureaucratic prose. Particularly, focus on

- using the subject and verb to express the central idea;
- using active rather than passive verbs;
- depending on verbs rather than nouns (e.g., *progressing*, not *making progress*);
- shortening sentence length;
- placing sentence parts in clear relation to one another.

More about these below and in Williams, Cook, Lanham, and Strunk and White.

Responding to Incoherent or Confusing Prose

If you can't understand what the student meant and if the passage seems a genuine attempt rather than a case of inadvertently omitted words or some other scribal problem, ask yourself first whether this student is normally comprehensible in speaking. If the answer is yes, the student probably could speak a sentence whose gist was clear. So drive the student back to speech. Simply write, "I couldn't understand your meaning. Say out loud what you meant, then write it down." In a conference, the student can say what he or she meant, and you can write down or tape the words that were spoken. You might suggest that, from now on, the student dictate a first draft into a tape recorder, then write those words down, or have them typed, as the first draft of the paper.

Help speakers of English as a second language find a classmate who will read the paper and suggest "We would say it like this. . . ." Response-group members make good helpers, and the group's closeness makes it easy for you to say, "I wonder if the members of the group would give Yung their phone numbers so she could call on them to read her drafts, and help her phrase things so the reader can understand them." If you do not have response groups, ask for volunteers from the class. ESL speakers frequently are isolated and hesitant to approach American students for aid or friendship. Your help in making the arrangement may be important.

If the writer of badly confused or incoherent written language is a native speaker of English who frequently has trouble writing sentences whose meaning is understandable, this student needs not *in situ* stylistic analysis but a comprehensive program of progressive practice with the written language. Such programs frequently rely on "sentence combining," a way of building competence at short, elemental "kernel" sentences, then gradually increasing the student's ability to write and to punctuate more and more complex forms. Such a program is best guided by a writing center. If your school does not have one, your student may profit from a self-directed writing text (see pp. 97–105). Whether your students are working in the writing center or with self-instructional texts, motivation and self-image may well be the most important aspects of the effort. Offer such students praise for comprehensible sentences and firm evidence of your belief that they can learn to write more clearly.

The next four sections help you respond to individual sentences and paragraphs. They help you specify what is wrong with a passage that seems awkward and offer specific suggestions for amending the problem.

Responding to Problems of Emphasis

When reading a student's writing, ask whether the paper accurately reflects the relative importance of various ideas. There are two main ways of emphasizing ideas:

1. By the *position* of words and phrases in the sentence or paragraph. Minor ideas are relegated to subordinate clauses, to modifiers, or to unobtrusive places in the sentence or paragraph. The most important words or ideas appear in spots that receive most attention—main clauses and at the beginnings and endings of sentences and paragraphs.
2. By the type of *structure* in which an idea appears. Important ideas are usually treated in a main clause; the writer avoids making a whole sentence out of a subsidiary idea that should be merely a modifying word or phrase.

The following, from a paper on the influences that shape men's roles in our society, illustrates both methods of indicating relative importance:

```
(1) The masculine role is developed at an early age.  (2) Parents shape
this role to a large degree.  (3) This is evident by the different way parents
treat their children.  (4) Fathers tend to play rougher with boys, while
mothers nurse, handle, and verbalize less with boys.  (5) This was found in a
recent study.
```

The student is writing about the masculine role—its origin and effects. In this sample paragraph, he is beginning a section on how the masculine role is shaped, first by parents and then by the media and the schools. Thus his first sentence in this paragraph appropriately states the thesis for this whole section. The next sentence also does its job well: it indicates that the writer is now about to discuss the parental influence. But though the paper as a whole and this paragraph as a part of it show a definite organizational plan, the writing is clumsy. In working toward a remedy, the instructor would do well to analyze the causes of the awkwardness. In this instance, the problem lies partly in the way the student has indicated the relative importance of various ideas. The most striking fault is that "This was found in a recent study" is not important enough to merit a full sentence or to deserve that climactic spot at the end of the paragraph. It offends in both position and structure. The fact should instead be presented in a subordinate phrase relegated to an unobtrusive place as in this example:

```
(4) Fathers, according to a recent study, tend to play rougher with boys,
while mothers nurse, handle, and verbalize less with boys.
```

There is another point in this paragraph at which the writer could better indicate the relative importance of two ideas. The beginnings and ends of sentences or paragraphs tend to be prominent. In sentence 2 the writer has not properly used these spots to distribute emphasis.

```
(2) Parents shape this role to a large degree.
```

Ask the student which of the two marked phrases is more important or forms the basis for further development later in the paragraph. The answer is "shape this role," since the rest of this paragraph and several succeeding paragraphs tell how parents shape children's roles. If "to a large degree" were the main idea developed by the rest of the paragraph, then the placement of "to a large degree" at the end of the sentence might be justified. Such a paragraph might look like this:

```
Parents shape this role to a large degree.  Lesser influence, however, is also
exerted by the schools.  Television has its impact, too, as does magazine
advertising.
```

The student's paragraph, however, does not develop the "to a large degree" idea but rather the "shape" idea. Therefore, "shape this role" could better have the prominent place at the end of the sentence. The revised version would thus read:

```
(2) Parents, to a large degree, shape this role.
```

As this example illustrates, the whole question of where to insert clauses, phrases, and modifiers needs to engage the attention of the writer. The first instinct of most beginning writers is to state the subject and the verb and then to stick modifiers on at the end. Though this structure can be effective, it also can produce sentences that trail off into confusion or trivia or that waste the climactic end spot on a relatively unimportant idea. Many beginning writers need to be reminded that sentence elements, like railroad cars, have couplings. One can often detach an element and insert it in a different spot. Phrases, clauses, and one-word modifiers can frequently be slipped into any one of several positions in the sentence, and the skillful writer makes a conscious choice on the basis of where the emphasis should fall. Further examples appear later in this chapter. But meanwhile, let us consider another, closely related aspect of writing.

Responding to Problems in Indicating Relations

Good writing style depends a great deal on clearly indicating the relations among ideas and words. The writer has three important means of pinpointing these relations:

1. By the *position* of words, phrases, or sentences.
2. By *words and phrases* that accurately specify the relations between ideas.
3. By *grammatical construction*.

Position

Look again at the paragraph about how parents shape their children's gender roles. The paragraph improved after the student made two changes to clarify the relative importance of ideas. But more possible improvements become apparent when we ask whether or not the writer has clarified the relations among ideas. The altered paragraph reads like this:

```
(1) The masculine role is developed at an early age.  (2) Parents, to a
large degree, shape this role.  (3) This is evident by the different way
parents treat their children.  (4) Fathers, according to a recent study, tend
to play rougher with boys, while mothers nurse, handle, and verbalize less
with boys.
```

One problem with this paragraph is that some ideas are placed where their relations to other elements are unclear or ambiguous. One example is sentence 4.

```
(4) Fathers, according to a recent study, tend to play rougher with boys,
while mothers nurse, handle, and verbalize less with boys.
```

When the word *less* appears, readers must go back and change their initial understanding of the beginning of the "mothers nurse . . ." clause. When a student has made you retrace your steps through a passage of writing, you should feel gypped, take your complaint straight back to the writer, explain as clearly as you can why you had to backtrack, and ask that the problem be solved. One way to show the student how this sentence has set the reader up for misunderstanding is to read the sentence aloud to the student, modulating your voice or supplying elliptical phrases so as to emphasize the misreading that can occur: " 'mothers nurse boys, handle boys, and verbalize less . . . ' oops! Now I see that it should be 'mothers nurse boys less, handle boys less,' and so forth." If you are making written comments, jot down in the margin the misreading to which the reader is vulnerable, or ask a question that will allow the student to recognize the possible misreading: "Do mothers nurse boys or nurse boys less? Let me know early in the sentence."

Sometimes a problem of this sort will need merely the insertion of a comma, but often, as here, the remedy calls for a rearrangement of words or groups of words in the sentence. A revision of this sentence might read this way:

```
(4) Fathers, according to a recent study, tend to play rougher with boys,
while mothers less frequently nurse, handle, or verbalize with boys.
```

The problem of ambiguous placement also emerges in sentence 3 of the paragraph, where imprecise diction compounds the difficulty:

```
(3) This is evident by the different way parents treat their children.
```

The position of the word *different* and the use of the word *children* make the reader unsure whether parents treat their own children differently from other peoples' children or whether they treat some of their own children differently from others of their own children or whether different parents treat their children in certain ways. Thus the reader is forced to go back and puzzle out the meaning. The teacher should again read or explain the sentence so that the student sees the reader's possible confusion. Then the student should revise until the result is something like this:

```
(3) This is evident by the way parents treat their boys differently from their
girls.
```

Words and Phrases

Though sentence 3 is now better, it is still not quite right. It reflects another common problem: relations between two ideas cannot be accurately expressed in inaccurate words or phrases. For example, the phrase "this is evident by" does not really indicate the true relation between the two ideas it connects:

Idea 2	*Idea 3*
`Parents . . . shape this role.`	`. . . parents treat their boys`
	`differently from their girls.`

In working with the student, try writing these two ideas in separate columns, leaving a space between them, as above. Then ask the student to tell you the relation between the two ideas and to write that in the middle. Or ask what the writer means by the phrase "This is evident by." Either of these exercises should help the student see that the phrase "is evident by" is not accurate. What the writer really wants to say is that parents shape roles *by means of* their different treatment of sons and daughters. Thus a revision of the sentence might look like this:

```
(2,3) Parents to a large degree shape this role by treating their boys
differently from their girls.
```

Getting words and phrases right may require not only substituting better choices but also adding words or phrases for clarity. The paragraph with which we are working might be improved by the insertion of a transitional phrase such as *for example* between sentences 3 and 4 so that the reader realizes immediately that the recent study about mothers and fathers is an example of how parents shape gender roles by treating their sons and daughters differently. Here is a revision:

```
(2,3) Parents to a large degree shape this role by treating their boys
differently from their girls.  For example, fathers, according to a recent
study. . . .
```

The final improved version of the entire paragraph now looks like this:

Original	Revision
The masculine role is developed at an early age. Parents shape this role to a large degree. This is evident by the different ways parents treat their children. Fathers tend to play rougher with boys, while mothers nurse, handle, and verbalize less with boys. This was found in a recent study.	The masculine role is developed at an early age. Parents to a large degree shape this role by treating their boys differently from their girls. For example, fathers, according to a recent study, tend to play rougher with boys, while mothers less frequently nurse, handle, and verbalize with boys.

The paragraph could probably be further improved by substituting the simple phrase *talk to* for the more academic *verbalize with*. But regardless of the remaining faults, the paragraph has been greatly improved by a more accurate indication of (1) the relative importance of ideas and (2) the exact relations between those ideas.

This discussion of clarifying relations between ideas by choosing appropriate words and phrases would not be complete without a mention of the ubiquitous *and*, so often used as a connector when the writer needs a more accurate word. For example, one student writes:

```
Most activities in the rehabilitation center take place in the blue room, and
one large group is conducted twice a week in an adjoining room.
```

This sentence illustrates a common failing: the *and* indicates that the two activities are parallel, but they are not; the second is an exception to the first. Ask the student to explain the relation between the statement that most activities take place in the blue room and the statement that one large group meets in an adjoining room. If you can provoke the recognition that the second is an exception to the first, then the writer can choose a connecting word that specifically conveys the concept of exception—a word like *however, but,* or *although.* A revision might read:

```
Most activities in the rehabilitation center take place in the blue room, but

one large group is conducted twice a week in an adjoining room.
```

Grammatical Construction

The third way to show connections is through grammatical construction. An idea may be embodied in a main clause or merely in a single adjective. Sometimes the ubiquitous *and* needs this remedy; one of the statements linked by the inaccurate *and* should be changed to a dependent clause, a phrase, or a single word to more accurately indicate the relation between a main idea and a dependent or subordinate idea. In the following example, the words in question are italicized:

Original	*Revision*
The catfish's mouth is surrounded by sensitive barbels, **and** these help in orientation and food gathering.	The catfish's mouth is surrounded by sensitive barbels **that** help in orientation and food gathering.
Chavez met with the grape workers **and** he decided to send six organizers to help them.	After meeting with the grape workers, Chavez decided to send six organizers to help them.
The sea turtle has flipper limbs **and** with these it rows itself along.	The sea turtle has flipper limbs **with which** it rows itself along.

In the examples above, relations are indicated by the use of subordinate structures. Parallel ideas are often revealed by parallel grammatical construction—a technique with which students often need help. The principle is this (and you can write it this way on student papers): parallel ideas should be expressed in similar forms. Successful writers may modify this principle, but it is a useful guideline for amateurs. Its clearest application is in lists, where equal elements should be stated in similar forms. For example:

Original	*Revision*
My hypothesis was that rat #9 would	My hypothesis was that rat #9 would
dominate, be inclined to a high	be dominant, highly active, and
level of activity, and always get	combative.
into fights.	

When working on something larger than a short list, the writer also can express relations through parallel grammatical construction. When students are faced with a number of elements or statements, you might urge them to break sentences or passages into individual units and then try to line them up. For example, here is one student's sentence:

```
In 1918, sixty percent of House members supported the measure, but it was
opposed by sixty percent of them in 1919.
```

A way to work with the student on a sentence like this is to identify the "fulcrum" of the sentence (in this case the word *but*) and then identify the elements on each side.

date	*percent*	*verb*
In 1918	sixty percent of House members	supported the measure

fulcrum: but

verb	*percent*	*date*
it was opposed	by sixty percent of them	in 1919.

By arranging the units in columns, the student can recognize departures from parallel form and can then revise. In this example, probably the best plan is to arrange the units in exactly the same order on both sides of the fulcrum, in the order date, percent, verb:

Original

date, percent, verb	In 1918, sixty percent of House members supported the
fulcrum	measure, but
verb, percent, date	it was opposed by sixty percent of them in 1919.

Revision

date, percent, verb	In 1918, sixty percent of House members supported the
fulcrum	measure, but
date, percent, verb	by 1919, sixty percent of them opposed it.

Here is another example of writing that lacks parallel structure (the superscript numbers in the writing sample refer to end notes in the students' papers):

total	A statistic that speaks most favorably for Patuxent is its recidivist rate. A study showed that out of 210,
percent, who, verb	80% of the repeaters had been released from Patuxent
by whom, fulcrum	by the court while
who, by whom	those who had been released by the staff of Patuxent
verb, percent	(who considered them ready) made up only 20% of the
total	210 recidivists.[16]

In this example the elements labeled "total" and "who" need not be repeated because they do not change. We can simplify this passage by gathering common elements in one spot—at the beginning. "A study showed that out of 210 repeaters. . . ." Now the writer can line up the contrasting elements in parallel order:

total	A study showed that out of 210 repeaters,
percent, verb	80% had been released from Patuxent
by whom	by the court,
fulcrum	while
percent, verb	20% had been released
by whom	by Patuxent staff (who considered them ready).

The comment you make to help the student move from the first to the second version might simply be "parallel structure," if your students understand the term. If they need a longer explanation, you might say, "This is hard to follow. Use the same order for the elements on each side of 'while.' "

A related error is the misplaced sentence elements that can cause either confusion or a ludicrous misreading. We've all chuckled over some of these:

Reform school staff created much antiprogressive thought in the public's minds by telling stories of policies and case decisions which documented the permissive and chaotic state of administration to the press and magnifying them.

Like many such student sentences, this one starts out just fine. In this case it's the modifying clauses and phrases tacked to the end of the sentence that cause the trouble. I frequently handle this kind of problem by circling the offending elements ("to the press" and "magnifying them") and writing, "Is this placed correctly in the sentence?" Here is the resulting rearrangement:

```
Reform school staff created much antiprogressive thought in the public's minds
by telling and magnifying, to the press, stories of policies and case
decisions which documented the permissive and chaotic state of administration.
```

Here's a slightly different problem. This student is discussing her response to a stage presentation of *Cat on a Hot Tin Roof*:

```
There are so many opportunities for Maggie to express her "cattiness" on stage
that I simply did not picture when I read the play.
```

The *so* and *that* in this sentence may be misread at first as the familiar *so many . . . that* construction, in which *that* introduces a consequence of *so many* (e.g., "There are so many opportunities that I don't know which to choose"). The latter structure is so common that readers are likely to expect it here and then have to go back and reread the sentence. The remedy is to change the sentence order beginning with what is now the last clause and making the *that* clause into a main clause. It's also helpful, of course, to delete the weak intensive *so*:

```
When I read the play, I simply did not picture the many opportunities for
Maggie to express her "cattiness" on stage.
```

In the next example, the ambiguity of the last phrase can be remedied by inserting a word or two to clarify the relation of the phrase "rather than the Japanese" to the rest of the sentence.

```
Because of the Communist group, the Allies were constantly faced with the
problem of restraining Chiang from using the aid sent to him against the
Communists, rather than the Japanese.
```

Here, the first step is to add *against* so that the relation of the last phrase becomes clear:

```
using the aid sent to him against the Communists, rather than against the
Japanese.
```

If you want to do something about the slightly clumsy placement of "sent to him," you might suggest substituting *their* or moving the idea to an earlier part of the sentence:

```
Because of the Communist group, the Allies were constantly faced with the

problem of restraining Chiang from using their aid against the Communists,

rather than against the Japanese.
```

or

```
Because of the Communist group, the Allies, who sent aid to Chiang, were

constantly faced with the problem of restraining him from using it against the

Communists, rather than against the Japanese.
```

In the next example, the run-on sentence results from insecurity about handling a long parallel construction.

```
The Japanese were unpredictable, at times staying away from their prisoners

completely, then at other times they would descend on the men, shouting orders

and violently attacking them.  At other times, they would share their

cigarettes and food with the men and act in a civil manner. [13]
```

I would not mark this "run-on." Instead, I would say something like "Put these three parallel ideas in similar form, separated by commas." The revision might read:

```
The Japanese were unpredictable, at times staying away from their prisoners

completely, at times descending on the men, shouting orders and violently

attacking them, and at other times sharing their cigarettes and food with the

men and acting in a civil manner. [13]
```

You may want to urge a dash instead of the first comma, or you may decide that the sentence is too long and that it should be broken up.

Because the problems I've just been discussing are so often intermingled, I've preferred to hold off most examples until now, when I can analyze sample student pieces that demonstrate several stylistic faults in indicating the relative importance and relatedness of ideas. The first example illustrates the need for parallel structure as well as the usefulness of a connecting word more accurate than *and*. The writer is comparing several experiments to determine the prey preferences of hawks. Experiment 1 showed that, when offered two prey animals of equal size and weight, the hawk preferred the more active. Experiment 3, however, showed that, when offered a small, active animal and a large, inactive one, the hawk preferred the inactive prey. Here is the student's conclusion (I have underlined the *and*):

```
Comparing the data in experiment 1, showing a strong preference for the more
active prey, with the third where the larger prey was less active and still
preferred, may have demonstrated a tendency in the hawk to choose the
apparently more profitable prey item in terms of relative biomass.
```

In working with this student, you might first try to find a more accurate connective than *and*. The writer might come up with something like "the larger prey was less active, *though* still preferred." Next, suggest that the student use parallel structure in describing the two experiments. The revision might look like this:

```
Comparing the data in the first experiment, showing a strong preference for
the more active prey, with the third, showing a preference for the larger
though less active prey, may have demonstrated a tendency in the hawk to
choose the apparently more profitable prey item in terms of relative biomass.
```

You and the writer might judge this sentence too complicated for maximum ease of reading, because the subject *comparing* is so far away from the verb *may have demonstrated*. If so, the student might clarify the subject-verb relation by revising the sentence to read:

```
Experiment 1 showed a strong preference for the more active prey, while
experiment 3 showed preference for the less active though larger prey. In
comparison, the two experiments may have demonstrated a tendency in the hawk
to choose the apparently more profitable prey item in terms of relative
biomass.
```

This revision, which holds closely to the student's own wording, still is not as precise as it could be, since it is not the comparison itself that demonstrates the hawk's tendency, but the third experiment in the light of the first. Thus the student might place the emphasis on the third experiment by making it the subject of the second, and most important, sentence:

```
Experiment 1 established the hawk's preference for more active prey.
Experiment 3, by showing the hawk's preference for the less active though
larger prey, may have demonstrated a tendency in the hawk to choose the
apparently more profitable prey item in terms of relative biomass.
```

In the next example, the writer wastes the final sentence—a high-emphasis spot—on a subsidiary idea that should have been integrated earlier as a subordinate clause or phrase.

```
Another person who feels the program is too extensive is Antonio G.
Olivieri, a democrat from the upper east side of Manhattan and a leader of
campaigns to end solitary confinement in juvenile prisons and halt the
incarceration of neglected and abandoned children and other nondelinquent
children who merely need supervision.  He thought that abolishing all juvenile
institutions was too radical for New York.  "Realistically there's no chance
of doing that," he said.  "We need some closed detention facilities."  He is
in favor of shutting down the state juvenile training schools.31
```

In analyzing this paragraph, I would focus on the final sentence, asking the student whether the information it contained should be given that late in the paragraph and whether that information deserves the climactic ending spot. Clearly the answer is no, so the student now moves the information to an earlier point, indicating its relative unimportance by making it a subordinate clause and clarifying its relationship to the rest of the sentence by adding *although*. (A problem that remains in the paragraph, of course, is the switch from present to past tense.)

```
Another person who feels the program is too extensive is Antonio G.
Olivieri, a democrat from the upper east side of Manhattan and a leader of
campaigns to end solitary confinement in juvenile prisons and halt the
incarceration of neglected and abandoned children and other nondelinquent
children who merely need supervision.  Though he favors shutting down the
state juvenile training schools, he thought that abolishing all juvenile
institutions was too radical for New York.  "Realistically there's no chance
of doing that," he said.  "We need some closed detention facilities."31
```

The next example is from a report on hermaphrodites: what the types of hermaphrodites are, how they are identified at birth, how they are raised, and what can be done medically to help them adjust. At the end of the paper, the student uses this information to offer an opinion on the case of a hermaphrodite she had personally known.

```
In conclusion, I would like to express my learning of this to my
experience of growing up with my classmate.  I would have to say that she
would have been a lot happier if she would have been brought up as a male
```

```
rather than a female.  Her height would not have been so put down if she was a
male, her breasts are not fully developed, and she had to have an operation.
The doctors, I feel, made the wrong decision and should have consultanted
specialists.
```

While I would discuss the problems in diction in this essay—particularly *express my learning of this, put down,* and perhaps *a lot*—and the confusion about verb tenses, I would first address the student's problem in indicating relations among ideas—a problem that could be remedied by correcting a false parallelism. The writer strings together three clauses with commas—the clauses about height, about breasts, and about the operation. Yet they are not stated as results of being raised female, as the first part of the sentence leads the reader to expect. So I would ask for a fuller explanation of what each clause means and then suggest that that explanation be the basis for the revision of the paragraph. The result might look like this:

```
In conclusion, I would like to relate my investigations to my experience
of growing up with my classmate.  I would have to say that she would have been
much happier if she had been brought up as a male rather than as a female.
Her height would not have been ridiculed, the incomplete development of her
breasts would not have mattered, and her operation would have been simpler.
The doctors, I feel, made the wrong decision and should have consulted
specialists.
```

The next sample shows how placement of elements in a paragraph can create a false emphasis, or focus, and mask the true meaning. The student is discussing the maturation of Esther in Sylvia Plath's novel *The Bell Jar.* To be consonant with the rest of the essay, this paragraph, though it summarizes part of the story, must focus not on the plot but on Esther's stuggle to become independent of others' expectations. Despite this imperative, the paragraph gives too much emphasis to the chronology of the events and too little to their meaning.

```
(1) After returning to the suburb and learning that she did not make the
writing course Esther decides instead to learn shorthand and write a novel.
(2) By learning shorthand Esther would still be clinging to the need of
meeting others' expectations (that of her mother); however we see that she is
making progress when she gives it up.  (3) After one day she decides to put
off writing the novel until she has been to Europe and had a lover feeling
that she has had no experiences worth writing about.  (4) And in a different
```

```
sense from this, because Esther has always merely met others' expectations,
she has no true experiences to write about.
```

I would begin by praising sentence 4 because the student has used a sophisticated sentence structure, inserting the *because* clause before the main subject and verb, thus effectively saving the main idea for the last, climactic spot in the paragraph. I would urge revision of sentences 1 and 3 because they place primary emphasis on chronology. I would suggest that in sentence 2 the writer reconsider the order of the last two elements: *she is making progress* and *when she gives it up.* It would perhaps be more effective to hold the *progress* for the last place in the sentence or otherwise to emphasize that idea more prominently. Also in sentence 2, clumsiness results from having three preposistional phrases in succession: (1) *to the need* (2) *of meeting others' expectations* (3) *of her mother.* When puzzled about a clumsy passage, check the number of prepositional phrases; I find that method often explains clumsiness that I otherwise can't quite put my finger on. Working on the basis of these three suggestions and remedying as well the unnecessary *from this* and the verb-tense problem in sentence 1, where *has not made the writing course* would be a better choice, the student might revise the paragraph in this fashion:

```
    Still struggling with her need to meet others' expectations, Esther,
after returning to the suburb and learning that she has not made the writing
course, decides to learn shorthand and write a novel.  When she gives up her
mother's expectation--shorthand--we see she is progressing toward maturity.
After one day on the novel, she decides to put it off until she has been to
Europe and had a lover, feeling she has had no experiences worth writing
about.  And in a different sense, because Esther has always merely met others'
expectations, she has no true experiences to write about.
```

Now the paragraph establishes a focus in accord with the paper's thesis, and it structures and arranges its sentences so as to develop that focus.

Encouraging Economy

Economy in writing means that every word should pull its weight. In some contexts, extra words may heighten emphasis, clarity, or vividness or even contribute a baroque richness necessary to the particular author's purpose; such passages are economical, even though their ideas could be presented in fewer words. Beyond what serves good purpose, however, all ideas should be expressed as briefly as possible.

The economy of the paper as a whole is closely tied to organization: the writer must eliminate or condense irrelevant, repetitious, or inflated subtopics.

Once the overall focus of the paper is clear, the student must strive for economy in each paragraph and sentence. The best way for writers to achieve economical prose is to express accurately the relations among sentence elements, as discussed earlier, and to "write with nouns and verbs," as I explain in the next section, "Encouraging Precision, Concreteness, Vividness." In addition, when you are analyzing a student's prose, you can look for three enemies of economy: inflation, repetition, and the passive voice.

Inflation

Easiest to spot is the inflation that results when a student uses filler words that can simply be omitted. One learns, after a while, to spot those most common to student writing: "the fact that," "in order to," "proceeded to," "the one who," "in the case of." In the examples below, the revision appears in parentheses.

> The governor went to the flooded area in order to observe the damage that existed.
> (The governor went to the flooded area to observe the damage.)

> It seemed to me that the new holes were larger.
> (The new holes seemed larger.)

> One of the biggest points of difference between the two organizations is in the matter of structure.
> (One of the biggest differences between the two organizations is their structure./The two organizations differ markedly in structure.)

> In comparison with the rat study, many things evident in that study were also observed with mice.
> (Many things evident in the rat study were also observed with mice./The mice reacted in much the same way as the rats.)

In other instances, the writer uses roundabout or attenuated grammatical constructions. Here are two of the most common:

The verb to be:

subject +	verb *to be*	+ predicate adjective
	or synonym	or predicate noun
The room	is	a cheerful place.

Try changing this to a noun plus an adjective: "the cheerful room."

> The room is a cheerful place and encourages creative activities.
> (The cheerful room encourages creative activities.)

Clauses beginning with words like that, who, *or* which: A writer may use a clause beginning with *that, who,* or some similar word when an adjective would suffice. In the following examples the revisions are shown in parentheses:

An experiment which was successful. . . .
(A successful experiment. . . .)

The authors also discuss briefly the later chapters and what they will contain.
(The authors also discuss briefly the contents of the later chapters.)

His attitude was one that conveyed hostility.
(His attitude was hostile./He was hostile.)

Repetition

Sometimes a student will repeat one word—or a word and its synonyms—several times in a sentence or paragraph. The teacher can mark or list all the words that express a single idea. Then the student should revise the passage so that fewer repetitions appear. For example:

I have been working with mice and the effects of crowding on their behavior.

(I have been working with the effects of crowding on the behavior of mice.)

Of all Mr. Jones's articles of equipment that he uses, his rifle is most important to him.

(Of all Mr. Jones's equipment, his rifle is most important.)

Passive Voice

Often the use of the passive voice adds unnecessary words and makes the passage indirect and muted. There are at times very good reasons for choosing the passive, but students universally overuse it, so you'll often have to urge them to switch to the active voice.

In helping a student, you'll usually find that before you can warn students about the passive voice, you'll have to teach them to recognize it. If the student can pick out the subject and verb in a sentence, your task will be easy. Simply say that in the active voice the subject of the sentence *does the acting*: "The girl threw the ball." In the passive voice the subject of the sentence *is acted upon*: "The ball was thrown by the girl." The ball does not do the throwing; therefore the verb is passive. Ask your students to go through their papers and label all the verbs passive or active. Next, they should try to justify all passive voice verbs. If they can't, they should change them to active.

The passive voice appears extensively in scientific writing, though even there its popularity is fading. In the next example, while the style is a bit wordy and clumsy, the student logically and legitimately employs the passive to impart objectivity to his writing and to avoid ascribing a cause or an actor to some action described in a verb.

> The next part of the information gathering will be a compiling of records on the individual students. Height and body weight will be recorded for each student. These will be accompanied by a subjective description of each individual concerning their general physical appearance and condition. The attendance records of each child for his past years in school will be recorded. The teacher of each child will be asked to evaluate each child participating in the study. The evaluation will consist of academic, behavioral, and attitude ratings.

In contrast to the straight scientific use of passive illustrated above, this student uses the passive unnecessarily in describing the process of detasseling corn plants:

> When the area supervisor decides to start detasseling, the main office is informed to start lining up contractors to meet at the field. At this meeting 2 or 3 contract supervisors and contractors assemble. Supervisors distribute contract forms and contract lists, while contractors are asked how many contracts they want. Contractors are informed of the size of the contract and are allowed to read the contract. If the contract is satisfactory it is signed by the contractor and the contractor is also shown the plot. At this time the contractor is also shown how to properly pull tassels, and directed on the use of the fruit jars. This process is repeated until all contracts are filled.

The use of passive voice here depends on purpose. If this essay is attempting to describe the interesting process of corn detasseling for a general audience, then most of these verbs should be put into the active voice. Any passive verbs that remain might serve to retain the emphasis on the *contractors'* experience— *their* view of the corn-detasseling process. This was in fact the aim of the student who wrote the paragraph but it proved possible to eliminate most of the passive verbs and at the same time enhance the paragraph's vividness and its emphasis on the contractors' experiences.

```
Contractors first hear about the advent of detasseling time when, at the
area supervisor's instigation, the main office starts lining up contractors to
meet at the field.  At this meeting, contractors assemble with 2 or 3 contract
supervisors.  Supervisors distribute contract forms and contract lists.
Contractors decide how many contracts they want.  They learn the size of the
contract and have a chance to read it.  If the contract is satisfactory the
contractor signs it and then views the plot.  At this time the contractor also
learns how to pull tassels properly and how to use the fruit jars.  This
process is repeated until all contracts are filled.
```

In writing papers students often use the passive voice awkwardly in affecting a pseudoacademic or an obtuse style. Here is an example:

```
The creation of new alternatives was approached by the department by
having therapeutic and humane homes instead of the custodial institutions.
The use of small community-based programs instead of large institutions, and
the purchase of services from private community groups rather than state-
operated programs were also incorporated into the reform.
```

The revision makes *department* the subject all the way through the paragraph—an appropriate choice, since the department was in fact the instigator and since the essay emphasizes its role in changing juvenile services.

```
As new alternatives, the department created therapeutic and humane homes
instead of custodial institutions.  It instigated small community-based
programs in place of large institutions, and it purchased services from
private community groups instead of using state-operated programs.
```

Coaching the Verbose Student

Whether verbiage results from overuse of the passive voice, repetitions, or inflation, it is one area in which teachers can legitimately suggest alternative wording. When a student's writing is verbose, I have found it helpful to write out the condensed version of the sentence or paragraph, to illustrate how it can be tightened. This is often an eye-opener that enables the student to practice economy throughout the rest of the paper. Here is a paragraph I chose from a longer paper as an example of the student's wordy style; I condensed it into an economical version and then asked the student to do the same for the rest of the paper:

> Toni's Restaurant owned and operated by Anthony Rocco is an example of a firm which did not design a marketing strategy plan. This plan consists of two guidelines: selecting a target market and developing the most appropriate marketing mix for the target market. Anthony Rocco failed to follow these guidelines and as a result it took several months for his business to become profitable.

The ¶ is wordy. It could read "Toni's Restaurant took several months to become profitable because owner/operator Anthony Rocco did not design a marketing strategy based on two guidelines: selecting a target market and developing ... mix." Can you revise the rest of the paper in the same way?

A teacher can sometimes achieve the same effect by editing:

> Toni's Restuarant owned and operated by Anthony Rocco ~~is an example of a~~ *because the owner* ~~firm which~~ did not design a marketing strategy ~~plan. This plan consists of~~ *based on* two guidelines: selecting a target market and developing the most appropriate marketing mix for the target market. ~~Anthony Rocco failed to follow these guidelines and as a result it~~ took several months ~~for his business~~ to become profitable.

Another method is to mark repetitions in some special way, using a different color ink or distinctive circles or boxes. Then you can ask the student to compose a second version, eliminating some of the repetition.

> Toni's Restaurant owned and operated by Anthony Rocco ~~is an example~~ of a *deadwood* firm which did not design a marketing strategy plan. This plan consists of two guidelines: selecting a target market and developing the most appropriate marketing mix for the target market. Anthony Rocco failed to follow these guidelines and as a result it took several months for his business to become profitable. *Can you eliminate the repetitions and deadwood?*

If a student needs more explanation and drill, you might suggest that he or she study a pertinent chapter in a writing text.

Encouraging Precision, Concreteness, Vividness

Various types of writing, or passages within a single piece of writing, may call for various levels of abstraction or concreteness, or various degrees of vividness. Nearly all writing requires precision. There are several ways to help students achieve these qualities. One of the best ways for students to produce concrete, precise, simple, vivid prose is to "write with nouns and verbs." Most students think that when you get fancy, when you really spend time over your writing, you add more adjectives. Not so. If you build a fence and the posts aren't solid enough, the wood not hard enough, or the holes not deep enough, you're going to have to prop the fence up with extra boards. Students often build their sentences that way. It's important to get them to use strong, vivid nouns and verbs rather than weak or abstract words that then need the support of modifiers. A student, for example, will sink that vague verb *went* into a shallow hole and then prop it up with *slowly* instead of using *shuffled* or *dragged* or *meandered* or some other verb more precise, concrete, and vivid.

To see what makes for a bland paragraph, try reading just the verbs, then just the nouns. Are there many vague nouns like *thing*? Are there instances where *beast* or *carnivore* or *dog* would be better than *animal*? In scientific writing are all terms as specific as they can be? Are there catchall verbs such as *go, run, do,* and *is* where more specific terms would be more accurate or livelier?

In teaching students about this aspect of writing, you can talk about the ladder of abstraction. Take a word like *mutt* and go both up and down with it. More abstract are *dog, carnivore, animal*. More concrete is *Fido*. When you find overgeneralized writing, circle the offending words and ask students to find more specific alternatives. Here are some examples:

```
The car went down the hill.

(The Fiat whizzed down the hill.)


You don't lose your own culture when you come into a new one.

(You don't lose your own culture when you enter a new one.)


Her statement about U.S. TV programs is that there is too much emphasis on

violence and not enough on creativity.

(Her criticism of U.S. TV programs. . . .)


Maddox said, . . .

(Maddox argued, . . .)
```

In addition to substituting words lower on the abstraction ladder for words higher up, writers can achieve concreteness and vividness by using an example in place of the general term:

```
A veterinarian must be ready to handle any kind of animal.
(A veterinarian must be ready to handle everything from a cat's torn ear to a
mare in breech birth.)
```

```
In Cuba Mrs. Rio was able to make friends in all areas of her daily life.
(In Cuba Mrs. Rio was able to make friends at the grocery store or outside
while working in the yard or waiting for a bus.)
```

```
My teacher can tell you something about almost all fields of knowledge.
(My teacher can tell you about the Crusades, binomial theorems, and chemistry
equations.)
```

The following example illustrates the fuzziness of meaning that results, in scientific writing, from inaccurate use of words. Reporting his observation of nesting behavior, the student writes:

```
Two chicks remained in both of those and one of the suddenly abandoned nests.
```

The remedy is to substitute the word *each* for *both* and to add the word *in* to clarify the place of "one of the suddenly abandoned nests" in the total sentence structure:

```
Two chicks remained in each of those and in one suddenly abandoned nest.
```

The next example suffers from imprecise diction as well as from several of the other problems we have discussed.

wordy – find one word for all this   *word choice*

```
The porifera seem to provide a paradox to observers in the way a current
of water is able to move through them, seemingly in one direction. This
                                               a
study, made by Vogel, seeks to show evidence for some type of valve system to
be present in sponges which prevents two-way flow.
        cp.
Vogel sites earlier information supporting the idea of a one-way channel
through sponges, water entering through ostia and exiting through osculum. He
    word choice
also connects this flow to the current of the water surrounding the sponge.
                       word choice
It is here where he tried to connect the seeming need for valves since the
```

```
ostia facing downcurrent cover a bigger surface area than the osculum; thus
the flow from a reduction of pressure should encourage more water to exit
through these ostia than through the osculum.
```
this is clearly stated

word

```
    Vogel outlines two experimental set-ups, one with a mechanical model and
```
word

```
one with live sponges.  His results support the idea of some type of built-in
valve system located in the dermal membrane and probably associated with the
ostia, yet the particular valve-like structure has yet to be found.
```

You can encourage your students to use more precise and concrete language. You can have them read vivid language, or you can read it to them. Select a paper or a paragraph that uses definite, sharp words and read it in class. It may be a descriptive passage or a piece of scientific writing that simply uses great precision in its word choices, to make the meaning absolutely clear. Your goal in the reading is to make your students live for a moment surrounded by bright colors so that they will be dissatisfied with their own pastels. A related technique is to praise the specific language in a student's own writing. You can even mention the more generalized or vague word the student might have used, just so the writer becomes conscious of the choices available and can repeat the success. Your comment might read: "I'm glad you chose this word instead of a more vague noun like 'statement.' "

Another method for increasing precision is to circle generalized, vague, or inaccurate words and write some message you're sure the student will comprehend, like "word choice" or "Be more precise."

Sometimes, in a sample paragraph, you might suggest alternative wording for individual terms to illustrate what you meant. I would not use this technique except in a sample passage, however, lest you appropriate the paper and encourage students to believe that there is a set of "right words" in your head that they must guess. Below is a sociology instructor's final comment, together with a sample passage in which the instructor illustrated how the student might revise. Elsewhere, the instructor wrote "vague" or "wordy" next to particular passages, to call the student's attention to problems. As a basis for the paper, students had viewed a film about the Holy Ghost People, members of a religious sect centered in Appalachia. They were asked to analyze the religious behavior from a functionalist perspective and from a structuralist perspective.

Instructor's Final Comment

This is a thorough, thoughtful, and insightful analysis. I enjoyed reading it.

But I was *patient* because I could see that you have a good grasp of sociological concepts, and that you are a sensitive and thoughtful observer.

Unfortunately, the effectiveness of your essay was weakened by the indirect, vague, and wordy prose. See examples by my comments in the margins. Also see my example of how you can attack this problem—namely, by cutting words, rewording, and striving to replace the abstract with the concrete.

Sample Passage Marked to Show Student How to Revise

Try to use
fewer   *Holiness Church said they couldn't*
*words: ....*Members of the ~~Holy Ghost expressed feelings of never being able to~~ go on
& more   *Holy Ghost*   *vague*
exact. without the ~~Spirit~~. They felt safe from any harmful substance or being. ~~This~~
          They demonstrate this by   *ing*
~~is evident in their acceptance of being able t~~o drink poison and handle
          poisonous   *energetic rituals?*   *ing*
vague ~~dangerous~~ snakes. Through the ~~forceful movements~~ of the ~~entire~~ congregation,
                                    extra encouragement to live with
          an almost blind woman was given ~~much needed emotional~~ support. *her handicap.*

Problems of style frequently touch as well on problems in grammar and punctuation, which are treated in the coming chapter.

Chapter Nine

Responding to Problems in Grammar, Punctuation, and Spelling

I will use the word *mechanics* to refer to the three areas on which I will concentrate most heavily: grammar, punctuation, and spelling. Related conventions such as citation form and manuscript format, sometimes also classified as mechanics, may be handled by similar strategies.

Analyzing the Situation and Setting Goals

If you are looking at early drafts that still have major problems with focus, structure, and evidence, you'll want to ignore mechanics, except to warn students about problems they will have to fix before the final draft. For example, you might write or say, "There are lots of sentence fragments and problems with commas and apostrophes here. Before you hand in the final paper, you'll want to remedy those." In a conference, you can ask whether the student knows how to fix the problems you see. If the answer is no, then a quick explanation, reference to an instructional text, or referral to the writing center is in order. If you're not in a conference, you might add to your written comment, or announce in class, "If you don't feel sure about editing your papers for grammar and punctuation, see me" (or "Here is information about the writing center," or "A departmental assistant, Sandy McReady, will be in the departmental seminar room every evening from 7 to 8, to help").

When you respond to final or near-final drafts for which you have required formal polish, you will want to deal with mechanics as an important part of the success of the writing. If the drafts you see are to be revised, your goal may be to help students catch and solve every problem in mechanics. If such a goal is beyond your students, you want them at least to catch the most serious problems or to make progress in knowing how to edit for some problems. If the drafts are not to be revised, you want to give the students something they can take to the next writing experience. For each draft or final paper you see, decide on your goal for this student at this time.

Even if your goal is to help students catch every problem, don't assume you need to mark every error or explain every convention in every situation. In many cases, to do so is merely to waste your time telling students what they already know. Many mechanical problems are performance-based problems, not knowledge-based problems. For much the same reasons as were set forth in the previous section on style, the language you see may not represent the students' actual ability to command mechanics. Thus, first try performance-based remedies—they are less time-consuming and are often effective for many of the students' problems.

Addressing Performance-Based Problems

Many remedies for performance-based problems involve the entire course plan, the building of class morale, the value you have placed on writing, and the students' pride in their work. These have been discussed earlier. When you have students' writing in front of you and you suspect that you are not getting their best editing work, here are some possible responses:

Return the Paper

A number of instructors simply stop reading with any page that has more than four departures from Edited American English (EAE) grammar or from conventions of punctuation, citation, or spelling. Draw a line where you stopped reading. Write, "I will finish reading this paper when you've met my needs, as a reader, for grammar, spelling, and punctuation." Then see whether the student can come up with a revision that meets your standard.

You will have to decide, with this method, whether you will also allow revisions in content. If you do, you may be giving the student an unfair advantage over students who have exhibited control over mechanics and hence have not received their papers back with a chance to revise. An option, of course, is to allow all students to revise their papers if they wish but to give students who do not control mechanics a mandate to revise, at least for mechanics, if they are to get a passing grade.

Incorporate Mechanics in Grading

Incorporate mechanics as part of the grade, and write a terminal comment, "Your paper's quality suffered because of mechanics." I believe this is better than a double grade, since the double grade gives students the idea that mechanics are separate from the "real" writing of the paper. When you give one grade and let students know that an element in that grade is mechanics, students more clearly understand that a writer cannot communicate ideas effectively without following the conventions of EAE.

Edit for Publication

Ask the students to edit their papers for some sort of "publication"—either distribution to the class, inclusion in a booklet of the best papers, or sharing in a group. Pride in the appearance of the writing may be enough to help the student amend problems in mechanics.

Address Proofreading Skills

A common performance-based problem is faulty proofreading. Try offering help in the following ways:

1. *Suggest a text.* Give the student a study-skills or writing text that offers instruction in the process of proofreading. (My own *Ten Steps* is an example.)
2. *Use marginal checks.* Put a check mark in the margin next to any line that has a problem in mechanics. This method helps the student locate problems but takes little of your time. Use it when you think the student will be able to fix most problems once they're pointed out.
3. *Use computer editors/spellers.* If the student has access to word processing on the computer, suggest an "editor" or "speller." The program flags any word or group of words that does not match the computer's store of "correct" patterns. The student then decides whether the flagged language is a problem or not. Such programs typically also offer stylistic analysis, telling the student what percentage of verbs in the paper are passive voice, and so on. Spelling programs usually are capable of emendation, so that the student can add words such as the specialized terms in your discipline, gradually making the program less likely to flag legitimate words the student uses.
4. *Mark a sample.* Mark the problems on a sample page, and let the student find the problems on the other pages.
5. *Focus on selected problems.* Select two or three major problems in the paper, mark a sample of each, and have the student search for other examples of those problems (i.e., sentence fragments, ambiguous pronoun references, and apostrophes). In this method, you mark only samples of the three or four major types of problem you find. Use this approach when the numbers and types of problems might be overwhelming to the student and when you judge it pedagogically preferable to attack only the most serious problems first.

Watch for Disability

A perception problem or disability can only be diagnosed by someone with training, but you should suspect one if the student commonly transposes letters (*gril* for *girl*) or introduces new errors when copying a passage. Both severe proofreading problems and disabilities are best handled as a team effort by you, the student's other instructors, and a writing specialist.

Addressing Knowledge-Based Problems

Some students may need help with both performance-based and knowledge-based problems. Once you've addressed the performance-based and believe that you're seeing language where the students have done their best editing work, then you can offer instruction in areas the students do not know.

Use the Writing Center

If your institution has a writing center or tutors who will help students with mechanics, use your best arts of persuasion to get that student to the writing center. A personal word to the student before or after class is better than a note alone. Follow up a week later—"Kim, have you started in the writing center?" and later, "Kim, how's the writing center going?" You might offer points for work in the center or agree to structure grades around specific goals worked out by you, the student, and writing center staff.

Set Priorities

Whether in conjunction with a center or on your own, your next step is to select one or two aspects of mechanics you want each student to learn during the semester. One way to set your priorities is to allow students to choose the problems they partly know, find most disturbing, or feel most ready to tackle. Alternatively, select the problems in priority order, using the order in my *Ten Steps*, or your own priorities. Of course, if your students are working in a learning center, select priorities in conjunction with center staff.

Use the Never-Again Notebook

Make sure the student has, and is using, a never-again notebook (see pp. 95–96). With the returning paper, identify, or ask the student to identify, as many conventions to be learned as you think the student can handle at this time. Make your own record of what the student is working on. For example, in your grade book, next to Mary's name, may appear "frag, apos." That means Mary has sentence fragments and apostrophes as "never-again" problems. You'll read her further papers only for those aspects, until she gets control of them, then select other aspects. If Mary doesn't take this seriously, try increasing her motivation by talking with her, awarding grade points for success, or—a drastic step, to be used carefully—refusing to accept papers that offend in the problem areas.

Offer Instruction

Needed instruction may be offered in several forms. In some cases, merely fixing the problem right there on the page will teach students the rule. Such cases are relatively rare, however, since the single instance does not necessarily illustrate the boundaries or conditions of the rule. Further, when you "fix" students' papers, they are tempted mindlessly to copy your correction rather than to learn the convention.

For some problems, you might pen a short explanation of the convention right in the margin of the paper or on a separate sheet. You might have such explanations of common problems boilerplated on your computer, to be spliced into your final comment, or you might have photocopied sheets of explanations to attach to the paper as you hand it back. Another method is to refer students to the relevant section of the handbook you've asked them to use. As much as possible, follow up on these sources of explanation to discover whether students were able to understand and follow them. Amend or replace explanations that give your students trouble.

Help the Basic Writer

For conventions that do not depend on a complex understanding of grammar or for students who already have a framework of grammatical understanding, a single explanation plus some exercises may be enough. Some "basic writers," however, are very inexperienced in handling the grammar of written language. Also, some problems have deep roots in the grammatical system of the language. Most difficult are verb forms (*I run, he runs; I carry, I carried; lie* and *lay*), choice and consistency of verb tenses, punctuation of sentence boundaries (run-ons, comma splices, fragments), pronoun case (*he* or *him, who* or *whom*), subject-verb agreement, and pronoun-antecedent agreement. Because these problems require grammatical understanding, your student may not be able to learn to amend them quickly, or in isolation. If two different textbook explanations of sentence fragments don't help, try hard to get the student into a systematic developmental program, preferably under the guidance of a writing specialist. Alternatively, choose a self-instructional text (see pp. 96–99) based on sentence combining, and give your student the encouragement and reward necessary to spend time each day working systematically through the book. Students who are very inexperienced writers may be better off focusing not on eliminating a particular error such as sentence fragments but on more confidently using several types of sentences. Shape your goals from the text the student is using and from your own observation of the student's developing competence with written language.

Helping with Spelling

A special word about spelling. Poor spellers are the students who are perhaps most likely to become discouraged, sometimes feeling like the only ones on the ward with an incurable disease. It takes forever for them to get their papers ready to hand in because they have to look up every other word in the dictionary, and occasionally they don't even know enough of the spelling to find the word. Tonics for poor spellers come in two basic types, and both taste awful, but there's no sugar-coated alternative that works. One approach is to have the student learn the rules that govern English spelling. Several workbooks and programmed texts take this approach, and for some students it is helpful. The problem is, of course, that there are so many exceptions to the rules that when you get done you may have as many chickens still running around the barnyard as you've managed to shut up in the coop.

A second approach is to rely primarily on memorization of the most fre- quently misspelled words or the misspelled words that are most likely to dis- tract readers. Texts and workbooks that rely on this method present the two or three hundred most commonly misspelled words and ask the student sim- ply to drill and memorize, with perhaps a little guidance from some obvious or simple rules, like "*i* before *e* except after *c*. . . ." Your student may or may not be misspelling the same two hundred words as the other students in the national sample, however, so a pretest might help.

The never-again notebook is an excellent tool for spelling because it al- lows students to concentrate on their own spelling errors, not just on the words in the workbook. Select five words for the notebook from the student's own writing. Once those are mastered, never to be misspelled again, choose five more. Base your choice on misspelled words you think would be most disturb- ing to readers.

Encourage Experimentation

With any student, watch for problem solving by avoidance. A student criticized for run-on sentences may address the problem by keeping all sentences very short. A student not sure how to spell a word will use another; one not sure how to punctuate a clause will rephrase the idea. The great danger of iden- tifying individual "errors" on any student paper is that you dampen the stu- dent's willingness to experiment with language, and you fix the student's attention not on the attempt to write in more competent and sophisticated ways but on the attempt to avoid errors. You can fight this tendency by making sure that all response to student writing deals significantly with content and that appropriate, sophisticated language is specifically praised, both by you and by response groups in your class. Remind students that in drafting they should boldly say what they mean in the most precise way they can; worry later about punctuation and spelling. When you find a student who seems nevertheless to be focusing primarily on error avoidance, you might try creating a "safe zone," in which penalties for error, even on final drafts, are at least temporarily lifted, and language experimentation is rewarded.

Your goals in responding to students' problems with mechanics are, first, to identify and help the student eliminate performance-based problems and, then, to attack remaining problems in such a way that the student does not feel overwhelmed, and does not have the paper "fixed," but increasingly learns to control the conventions of written language more confidently with each paper, each semester.

Summary

If you've read this book straight through you've been bogged down for a long time now in clauses and colons. But in the total view, my advice to those who want to help students write more effectively can be summarized in just three statements. First, writing is the yeast of the learning process, not merely the frosting. To integrate writing as a significant element in your course is to enrich students' learning, and the thoughtful teacher can increase the yield by careful attention to the types of writing students do, the purposes writing fulfills, and the way assignments are explained to students.

The second tenet of this book is that the teacher should become a coach of the student writer rather than merely a judge of the written product. Third, the wise instructor, instead of merely marking errors simply because they're there, analyzes the writing as a communication by a writer to a reader. In communicating to the student about a paper, the teacher should concentrate on the writing-learning process the student is following and should tailor the response to the individual student: what the student already knows, what the student is able to learn in the particular writing exercise, and what the student needs for optimum learning—praise as well as criticism, help in setting priorities, and so on.

If teachers practiced these three principles across the curriculum, I believe that we would significantly enhance the quality of writing—and, more broadly, the quality of learning—that takes place today in institutions of higher education.

Works Cited and Selected Bibliography

Note: This list contains very few discipline-specific articles. The Griffin and Thaiss volumes and the May 1985 *College Composition and Communication* (vol. 36) contain a number. To locate others, search ERIC, using the descriptors "Higher Education," "Writing," "Interdisciplinary Approach," the name of your discipline, and inclusive dates (1980 through the present should net most of the available material that makes use of recent theory and research). ERIC (part of DIALOG) indexes articles published not only in journals of education and English but also in journals in other fields.

Anglin, Jeremy M., ed. *Beyond the Information Given: Studies in the Psychology of Knowing*. New York: Norton, 1973.

Bartholomae, David. "The Study of Error." *College Composition and Communication* 31 (1980): 253–69.

Beach, Richard, and Lillian S. Bridwell, eds. *New Directions in Composition Research*. New York: Guilford, 1984.

Bean, John C. "Computerized Word-Processing as an Aid to Revision." *College Composition and Communication* 34 (1983): 146–48.

Berthoff, Ann E. *The Making of Meaning*. Upper Montclair: Boynton, 1981.

————, ed. *Reclaiming the Imagination: Philosophical Perspectives for Writers and Teachers of Writing*. Upper Montclair, Boynton, 1984.

Bisconti, Ann S., and Lewis E. Solomon. *College Education on the Job: The Graduates' Viewpoint*. Bethlehem: College Placement Council Foundation, 1976.

Bloom, Benjamin S., et al. *Taxonomy of Educational Objectives. Handbook 1: Cognitive Domain*. New York: McKay, 1956.

Bloom, Lynn Z. *Strategic Writing*. New York: Random, 1983.

Bouton, Clark, and Russell Y. Garth, eds. *Learning in Groups*. San Francisco: Jossey, 1983.

Brannon, Lil, Melinda Knight, and Vera Neverow-Turk. *Writers Writing*. Upper Montclair: Boynton, 1982.

Britton, James. "The Composing Processes and the Functions of Writing." Cooper and Odell, *Research* 13–28.

————. *Language and Learning*. Harmondsworth: Penguin, 1970.

————. *Prospect and Retrospect: Selected Essays*. Ed. Gordon M. Pradl. Upper Montclair: Boynton, 1982.

Britton, James, et al. *The Development of Writing Abilities (11–18)*. London: Macmillan Education, 1975.

Bruffee, Kenneth A. "Collaborative Learning and the 'Conversation of Mankind.'" *College English* 46 (1984): 635–52.

————. "Writing and Reading as Collaborative or Social Acts." Hays 159–69.

Bruner, Jerome, R. P. Oliver, and P. M. Greenfield. *Studies in Cognitive Growth*. New York: Wiley, 1966.

Camp, Gerald, ed. *Teaching Writing: Essays from the Bay Area Writing Project*. Upper Montclair: Boynton, 1983.

Cannon, Walter. "Terrors and Affectations: Students' Perceptions of the Writing Process." Conference on College Composition and Communication. Dallas, March 1981. ERIC ED 199 720.

Christensen, Francis. "A Generative Rhetoric of the Sentence." *College Composition and Communication* 14 (1963): 155–61.

Coe, Richard M. "If Not to Narrow, Then How to Focus: Two Techniques for Focusing." *College Composition and Communication* 32 (1981): 272–77.

Collier, Richard M. "The Word Processor and Revision Strategies." *College Composition and Communication* 34 (1983): 149–55.

Cook, Claire Kehrwald. *Line by Line: How to Edit Your Own Writing*. Boston: Houghton, 1985.

Cooper, Charles R., and Lee Odell, eds. *Evaluating Writing: Describing, Measuring, Judging*. Urbana: NCTE, 1977.

———, eds. *Research on Composing: Points of Departure*. Urbana: NCTE, 1978.

Corbett, Edward. *The Little English Handbook*. 3rd ed. New York: Wiley, 1980.

Crystal, Daisy. "Dialect Mixture and Sorting Out the Concept of Freshman Remediation." *Florida FL Reporter* 10 (1972): 43–46.

Cunningham, Frank J. "Writing Philosophy: Sequential Essays and Objective Tests." *College Composition and Communication* 36 (1985): 166–72.

Daiker, Donald, Andrew Kerek, and Max Morenberg. "Sentence-Combining and Syntactic Maturity in Freshman English." *College Composition and Communication* 29 (1978): 36–41.

Diederich, Paul. *Measuring Growth in English*. Urbana: NCTE, 1974.

Doheny-Farina, Stephen, and Lee Odell. "Ethnographic Research on Writing: Assumptions and Methodology." Odell and Goswami, *Writing* 503–35.

Doran, Edward, and Charles Dawe. *The Brief English Handbook*. Boston: Little, 1984.

Ede, Lisa. "Audience: An Introduction to Research." *College Composition and Communication* 35 (1984): 140–54.

Elbow, Peter. *Writing without Teachers*. New York: Oxford, 1975.

———. *Writing with Power*. New York: Oxford, 1981.

Emig, Janet. *The Composing Processes of Twelfth Graders*. Urbana: NCTE, 1971.

———. *The Web of Meaning: Essays on Writing, Teaching, Learning, and Thinking*. Ed. Dixie Goswami and Maureen Butler. Upper Montclair: Boynton, 1983.

———. "Writing as a Mode of Learning." *College Composition and Communication* 28 (1977): 122–28.

Enke, C. G. "Scientific Writing: One Scientist's Perspective." *English Journal* 67.4 (1978): 40–43.

Faigley, Lester. "Names in Search of a Concept: Maturity, Fluency, Complexity, and Growth in Written Syntax." *College Composition and Communication* 31 (1980): 291–300.

Faigley, Lester, and Thomas P. Miller. "What We Learn from Writing on the Job." *College English* 44 (1982): 557–69.

Faigley, Lester, and Stephen Witte. "Analyzing Revision." *College Composition and Communication* 32 (1981): 400–07.

Flower, Linda S. *Problem-Solving Strategies for Writing*. 2nd ed. San Diego: Harcourt, 1985.

———. "Writer-Based Prose: A Cognitive Basis for Problems in Writing." *College English* 41 (1979): 19–37. Rpt. in Tate and Corbett 268–92.

Flower, Linda S., and John R. Hayes. "The Cognition of Discovery: Defining a Rhetorical Problem." *College Composition and Communication* 31 (1980): 21–32.

Flower, Linda S., et al. "Detection, Diagnosis, and the Strategies of Revision." *College Composition and Communication* 37 (1986): 16–55.

Frederiksen, Carl. H., and Joseph F. Dominic, eds. *Writing: Process, Development, and Communication*. Vol. 2 of *Writing: The Nature, Development, and Teaching of Written Communication*. 2 vols. Hillsdale: Erlbaum, 1982.

Fulwiler, Toby. "The Personal Connection: Journal Writing across the Curriculum." *Language Connections: Writing and Reading across the Curriculum*. Ed. Fulwiler and Art Young. Urbana: NCTE, 1982. 15–32.

Gagne, Robert, and Ernest Smith. "A Study of the Effects of Verbalization on Problem-Solving." *Readings in the Psychology of Cognition*. Ed. Richard C. Anderson and David P. Ansubel. New York: Holt, 1965. 380–94.

Gendron, Dennis. "Educational Software for Computers: Very Pretty, But Can I Teach It?" *WPA: Writing Program Administration* 6 (1983): 465–74.

Giannasi, Jenefer M. "Dialects and Composition." *Teaching Composition: Ten Bibliographical Essays*. Ed. Gary Tate. Fort Worth: Texas Christian UP, 1976. 275–304.

Goldfarb, Ronald, and James Raymond. *Clear Understanding: A Guide to Legal Writing*. New York: Random, 1983.

Goswami, Dixie. "Teachers as Researchers." Graves 347–58.

Graves, Richard L., ed. *Rhetoric and Composition: A Sourcebook for Teachers and Writers*. New ed. Upper Montclair: Boynton, 1984.

Gregg, Lee W., and Erwin R. Steinberg, eds. *Cognitive Processes in Writing*. Hillside, Erlbaum, 1980.

Griffin, C. Williams, ed. *Teaching Writing in All Disciplines*. San Francisco: Jossey, 1981.

Hamilton, David. "Reading the Wind." *Courses for Change in Writing: A Selection from the NEH Iowa Institute*. Ed. Carl H. Klaus and Nancy Jones. Upper Montclair: Boynton; Iowa City: U of Iowa P, 1984. 274–78.

Hayes, John R., et al. "Cognitive Process in Revision." Technical Report to the National Science Foundation. Carnegie-Mellon U, 1984. To appear in *Reading, Writing, and Language Processing*. Vol. 2 of *Advances in Applied Psycholinguistics*. Ed. Sheldon Rosenberg. Cambridge: Cambridge UP, forthcoming.

Haynes, Elizabeth F. "Using Research in Preparing to Teach Writing." *English Journal* 67.1 (1978): 82–88.

Hays, Janice N., et al., eds. *The Writer's Mind: Writing as a Mode of Thinking*. Urbana: NCTE, 1983.

Healy, Mary Kay. *Using Student Response Groups in the Classroom*. Berkeley: Bay Area Writing Project, 1979.

Herrington, Anne. *Writing in an Academic Setting: A Study of the Rhetorical Contexts for Writing in Two College Chemical Engineering Courses*. Diss. Rensselaer Polytechnic Inst., 1983. Ann Arbor: UMI, 1984. 840–9508.

Kasden, Lawrence, and Daniel Hoeber, eds. *Basic Writing: Essays for Teachers, Researchers, and Administrators*. Urbana: NCTE, 1980.

Kesling, Robert V. "Crimes in Scientific Writing." *Turtox News* 36 (1958): 276.

Kiniry, Malcolm, and Ellen Strenski. "Sequencing Expository Writing: A Recursive Approach." *College Composition and Communication* 36 (1985): 191–202.

Knoblauch, C. H., and Lil Brannon. "Writing as Learning through the Curriculum." *College English* 45 (1983): 465–74.

Kolln, Martha. "Closing the Books on Alchemy." *College Composition and Communication* 32 (1981): 139–51.

Kroll, Barry, and Roberta Vann, eds. *Exploring Speaking-Writing Relationships*. Urbana: NCTE, 1981.

Langacker, Ronald W. "An Initial Look at Language." *Language and Cultural Diversity in American Education*. Ed. Roger Abrahams and Rudolph C. Troike. Englewood Cliffs: Prentice, 1972. 95–100.

Langer, Susanne K. *Philosophy in a New Key*. 3rd ed. Cambridge: Harvard UP, 1960.

Lanham, Richard A. *Revising Prose*. New York: Scribner's, 1979.

Larson, Richard. "Bibliography of Research and Writing about the Teaching of Composition." Published each May in *College Composition and Communication*, 1975–79.

———. "Problem-Solving, Composing, and the Liberal Education." *College English* 33 (1972): 628–35.

————. *Writing in the Academic and Professional Disciplines: A Manual for Faculty.* New York: Lehman C, City U of New York, 1983.

Lauerman, David, Melvin W. Schroeder, Kenneth Sroka, and Roger Stephenson. "Workplace and Classroom: Principles for Designing Writing Courses." Odell and Goswami, *Writing* 427–50.

Lawrence, John. *The Electronic Scholar: A Guide to Academic Microcomputing.* Norwood: Ablex, 1984.

Lehr, F. "ERIC/RCS Report: Writing as Learning in the Content Areas." *English Journal* 69.8 (1980): 23–25.

Lloyd-Jones, Richard. "Primary Trait Scoring." Cooper and Odell, *Evaluating* 33–66.

Lunsford, Andrea A. "Cognitive Development and the Basic Writer." *College English* 41 (1979): 38–46.

Macrorie, Kenneth. *Searching Writing.* Rochelle Park: Haydon, 1980.

————. *Twenty Teachers.* Upper Montclair: Boynton, 1984.

Maimon, Elaine P. "Talking to Strangers." *College Composition and Communication* 30 (1979): 364–69.

Maimon, Elaine P., et al, eds. *Readings in the Arts and Sciences.* Boston: Little, 1984.

————. *Writing in the Arts and Sciences.* Cambridge: Winthrop, 1981.

Martin, Nancy. *Mostly about Writing: Selected Essays.* Upper Montclair: Boynton, 1983.

————, ed. *Writing across the Curriculum: Pamphlets from the School Council/London Institute of Education W.A.C. Project.* Upper Montclair: Boynton, 1984. [pamphlets first published separately, 1973–75].

Martin, Nancy, et al. *Writing and Learning across the Curriculum 11–16.* Schools Council Publications. London: Ward Lock, 1976.

McCarthy, Lucille P. "A Stranger in Strange Lands: A College Student Writing across the Curriculum." Diss. U of Pennsylvania, 1985.

Moffett, James. *Active Voice: A Writing Program across the Curriculum.* Upper Montclair: Boynton, 1981.

Monroe, James, Carole Meredith, and Kathleen Fisher. *The Science of Scientific Writing.* Dubuque: Kendall, 1977.

Murray, Donald. "The Listening Eye: Reflections on the Writing Conference." *College English* 41 (1979): 13–18.

————. *A Writer Teaches Writing.* Boston: Houghton, 1968.

Newcomb, Theodore M., and Everett K. Wilson, eds. *College Peer Groups.* Chicago: Aldine, 1966.

Nystrand, Martin, ed. *What Writers Know: The Language, Process, and Structure of Written Discourse.* New York: Academic, 1982.

Odell, Lee. "The Process of Writing and the Process of Learning." *College Composition and Communication* 31 (1980): 42–50.

Odell, Lee, Dixie Goswami, and Anne Herrington. "The Discourse-Based Interview." *Research on Writing Principles and Methods.* Ed Peter Mosenthal, Lynne Tamor, and Sean A. Walmsley. New York: Longman, 1983. 220–35.

O'Hare, Frank. *Sentence-Combining: Improving Student Writing without Formal Grammar Instruction.* Urbana: NCTE, 1973.

Perl, Sondra. "Understanding Composing." *College Composition and Communication* 31 (1980): 363–69.

Peterson, Bruce. "Additional Resources in the Practice of Writing across Disciplines." Griffin 75–82.

Piaget, Jean. *Six Psychological Studies.* New York: Random, 1967.

Progoff, Ira. *At a Journal Workshop.* New York: Dialogue, 1975.

Pufahl, John. "Response to Richard M. Collier." *College Composition and Communication* 35 (1984): 91–93.

Research in the Teaching of English. Semiannual bibliographies of research, May and Dec. issues.

Roundy, Nancy. "Heuristics in Student and Professional Composition." *English Record* 33.1 (1982): 13.

Selzer, Jack. "The Composing Processes of an Engineer." *College Composition and Communication* 34 (1983): 178–87.

Shaughnessy, Mina P. *Errors and Expectations: A Guide for the Teacher of Basic Writing.* New York: Oxford, 1977.

Siegel, Muffy, and Toby Olson. *Writing Talks.* Upper Montclair: Boynton, 1983.

Singer, Daniel, and Barbara Walvoord. "Process-Oriented Writing Instruction in a Case Method Class." *Proceedings of the Academy of Management.* Ed. John A. Pearce ii and Richard B. Robinson, Jr. Boston: Acad. of Management, 1984. 121–25. ERIC ED 249 500.

"Solving Business Problems with Mathematical Models." *Forum for Liberal Education* 8.3 (1983): 16.

Sommers, Nancy. "Responding to Student Writing." *College Composition and Communication* 33 (1982): 148–56.

———. "Revision Strategies of Student Writers and Experienced Adult Writers." *College Composition and Communication* 31 (1980): 378–88.

Stallard, Charles K. "An Analysis of the Writing Behavior of Good Student Writers." *Research in the Teaching of English* 8 (1974): 211–17.

Stock, Patricia L. *Forum: Essays on Theory and Practice in the Teaching of Writing.* Upper Montclair: Boynton, 1983.

Strunk, William, Jr., and E. B. White. *The Elements of Style.* 3rd ed. New York: Macmillan, 1979.

Tate, Gary, and Edward P. J. Corbett, eds. *The Writing Teacher's Sourcebook.* New York: Oxford, 1981.

Thaiss, Christopher, ed. *Writing to Learn: Essays and Reflections on Writing across the Curriculum.* Dubuque: Kendall, 1983.

"TSU Math Students Helping Industry." *Baltimore Sun* 7–8 Aug. 1985, education sec.: 13, 15.

Vygotsky, Lev S. *Thought and Language.* Cambridge: MIT P, 1962.

Walvoord, Barbara. *Four Steps to Revising Your Writing for Style, Grammar, Punctuation, and Spelling.* Glenview: Scott, forthcoming.

———. *Writing: Strategies for All Disciplines.* Englewood Cliffs: Prentice, 1985.

Walzer, Arthur E. "Articles from the 'California Divorce Project': A Case Study of the Concept of Audience." *College Composition and Communication* 36 (1985): 150–59.

Weddington, Doris C. "Taped Feedback—Have You Tried It?" *Journal of Developmental and Remedial Education* 1 (1978): 10–11, 18.

Whiteman, Marcia Farr, ed. *Variation in Writing: Functional and Linguistic-Cultural Differences.* Vol. 1 of *Writing: The Nature, Development, and Teaching of Written Communication.* 2 vols. Hillsdale: Erlbaum, 1982.

Williams, Joseph M. *Style: Ten Lessons in Clarity and Grace.* Glenview: Scott, 1981.

Winterowd, W. Ross. *Contemporary Rhetoric: A Conceptual Background with Readings.* New York: Harcourt, 1975.

———. *The Contemporary Writer: A Practical Rhetoric.* New York: Harcourt, 1975.

Woodford, Peter F. "Sounder Thinking through Clearer Writing." *Science* 156 (1967): 743–45.

Woolf, Virginia. *A Writer's Diary.* Ed. Leonard Woolf. New York: Harcourt, 1954.

Young, Richard, Alton Becker, and Kenneth Pike. *Rhetoric: Discovery and Change.* New York: Harcourt, 1970.

Index

abstract 8, 40, 41, 70 *See also* summary
accuracy *See* precision
acknowledgment 92 *See also* documentation
active voice 209 *See also* passive voice; verbs
adjectives 216 *See also* grammar; modifiers
adverbs *See* grammar; modifiers
agree/disagree (as assignment) 12
agreement *See* pronouns, agreement with
    antecedents; verbs, agreement with
    subjects
Allison, Graham 188, 193
ambiguity 214, 219
analogy 60–61
analysis 8
Anglin, Jeremy M. 4
antecedents *See* pronouns, agreement with
    antecedents
APA (American Psychological Association)
    129
    citation format of 72
apostrophe 95, 97, 148, 149, 234, 236
appointments, student *See* conferences
Ardrey, Robert 194
argumentation 51, 56, 58, 123, 124, 126
    See also topoi
Aristotle 60
assignment *See also* genre
    analyzing an 36–49
    book report as, writing 62–63
    checking an 37
    diagnostic evaluation as 43–47
    group discussion of 113–114
    information as, evaluating 74–75
    lab report as, writing a 39–43
    sociology journal as, keeping a 38–39
    term paper as, peer evaluation of 47–49
audience 7, 18, 33, 36, 38, 72, 107, 113, 120,
    146, 172, 175, 176, 207
    analysis of 52, 53
    appropriate 41
    for book review 62
    characteristics of 19
    defining 31, 54
    hypothetical 19, 52, 147
    instructor as 19, 20, 39, 207
    intended 31, 48

audience (*cont.*)
    purposes of 52
    qualities of 53
    real 19, 52
    secondary reader 52
    transparent reader 146–47
audiovisual programs 98 *See also* learning
    center; writing center; self-instruction
    programs
awkwardness 150, 152, 155, 172, 206, 207,
    211, 220, 224 *See also* syntax;
    word choice

Bartholomae, David 100
basic writer 90, 99, 100, 238 *See also* error;
    learning center; mechanics;
    Shaughnessy, Mina
Beach, Richard 108
Bean, John C. 87
Becker, Alton 61
bibliography 70, 135 *See also* citations;
    documentation; quotations; references
    as assignment 8
biology courses, case histories of 130–33
biology laboratory, writing in the 130–31
Bisconti, Ann S. 3
Black American English 90 *See also* dialect
block, writer's 32, 59, 85
Bloom, Benjamin S. 22
Bloom, Lynn Z. 85
boilerplate 142, 238
book report 8
    analysis of a 62–63
    audience for a 62
    characters, questions about 62–63
    comparing books, questions for 63
    content, questions about 63
    plot, questions about 63
    purpose of a 62
    short stories, questions for 63
    writing a (as assignment) 62–63
Book Review Digest 72
Bouton, Clark 122
brainstorming 9, 67, 70, 126
    on tape 59
Breihan, John R. 71, 123, 124–25, 133

Bridwell, Lillian S. 108
brief 8, 176
Britton, James 9, 21
Bruffee, Kenneth A. 121
Bruner, Jerome 4
buddy system 33, 35 *See also* peer response
bureaucratic language 208, 209
Burton, Michael 38, 133–34
business and writing 3

Cannon, Walter 18
capitalization 148
card catalog *See* library research
case histories 123–137
    biology courses 130–33
    history course, core 123–25
    history course, introductory 135–36
    literature course, core 125–28
    marketing research, graduate course in
        134–35
    psychology course, introductory 128–30
    sociology class, introductory 133–34
case studies 8, 20, 33, 35, 176
cause-effect 60, 61,
character 126
charts 89 *See also* diagrams; figures;
    graphs; scientific writing; tables
Christensen, Francis 98
Ciofalo, Andrew 118
citations 48, 72, 73, 74, 78, 96, 235 *See also*
    bibliography; documentation; quota-
    tions; references
clarity 168, 209, 215
classification 60
clauses 211, 216, 222, 226 *See also* punctu-
    ation; sentence combining; sentence
    composing; syntax
clinical report 176
clumsiness *See* awkwardness
coaching writing 29
    questions to guide 32–33
Coe, Richard M. 65
College Composition and Communication
    137
Collier, Richard M. 87
colon 96
comma 96, 146, 234 *See also* mechanics
comma splice 90, 238 *See also* punctuation
compare/contrast 12, 13 *See also* topoi
comparison 60
computer data base *See* data bases
computer editors 236
computer programs 119

computer programs (*cont.*)
    for the writing process 34
computer search 70 *See also* library research
computer simulation 134
computer spellers 236
computerized instruction 34, 98 *See also*
    data bases; self-instruction programs
computerized proofreading 236 *See also*
    editing; proofreading; revision
computers 87, 97
conclusion (as section of paper) 48 *See also*
    scientific writing
concreteness 225, 230–33
conferences 13, 36, 67, 76, 82, 87, 88, 103,
    108, 114, 124, 127, 141, 143–46, 151,
    157–58, 172, 180, 186, 209
    response group 113–15
    task group 121
content 146
    assessing 52–53
    in book reports, questions about 63
context 18, 120
contradiction 65–66
contrast 60 *See also* compare/contrast
Cook, Claire K. 207, 209
copying *See* plagiarism; quotations
Corbett, Edward 96–97
correcting papers *See* grading
Corson, William R. 193
Crystal, Daisy 103
Cunningham, Frank J. 160
Curchack, Mark P. 47, 114
Current Index to Journals in Education 137

Daiker, Donald 98
data bases
    DIALOG 137
    ERIC 33, 137
data collection 39
data in lab report 40
Dawe, Charles 97
debate 124
definition 12 *See also* topoi
dependent clauses 216 *See also* clauses
description 60
developmental psychology 129
diagnostic evaluation 94
    writing a (as assignment) 43–47
diagrams 82 *See also* charts; figures; graphs;
    photographs; scientific writing; tables
dialect 90, 100, 101–05 *See also* English as
    a Second Language
DIALOG 137 *See also* data bases

diction 223 *See also* word choice
disability, learning 236–37
discussion groups 128 *See also* peer response
   teacherless 59
documentation 51, 146 *See also* bibliography;
   citations; quotations; references
   in lab report 43
Doheny-Farina, Stephen 108
Doran, Edward 97
Dostoevsky, Fyodor 167, 168
drafts 16, 31, 33, 46, 55, 82, 84–88, 107, 108,
   109, 115, 123, 131, 135, 151, 158, 162,
   178, 206, 234 *See also* editing; revision
   essays, group discussion of (as assignment)
   113–14
   introductory section 48
   of lab reports 43
   peer groups check of 17
   polishing 87
   zero 85
dyslexia 236

EAE *See* Edited American English
economy (as characteristic of good writing)
   224–29
Ede, Lisa 53
Edited American English (EAE) 90, 93, 101,
   103, 104, 105, 235
editing 17, 33, 90, 91, 92, 206, 207, 234, 236,
   237 *See also* drafts; error; mechanics;
   proofreading; revision
editors, computer 236
Education Index 137
Elbow, Peter 59
Emig, Janet 4, 30
emphasis 210–12, 223
English as a Second Language (ESL) 90,
   101–05, 210
English handbooks *See* handbooks of English;
   self-instruction programs
Enke, C. G. 3
enumeration 60–61
equations 43
ERIC 33, 137 *See also* data bases
error *See also* grammar; mechanics; punctuation; spelling; usage
   knowledge-based 235, 237
   performance-based 235, 237, 239
ESL *See* English as a Second Language
essay tests 8, 9, 124 *See also* in-class writing
   student guide to taking 10–13
essays 8

essays (*cont.*)
   class discussion of 13, 113–14
ethnography 108 *See also* dialect
evaluation 144 *See also* grading; response
   to writing
   diagnostic *See* diagnostic evaluation
   of revision 86
   of task groups 120, 121
   written 141–42, 145, 179
evidence 7, 11, 33, 68, 79–84, 123, 124, 158,
   234
experimental method 27
experimentation 31, 33, 78–79
expository writing 30
expressive writing 9

Faigley, Lester 85, 98, 118
field notebook 8, 76, 79
figures 48, 89 *See also* diagrams; graphs;
   scientific writing; tables
   labeling 43
filmstrips 97, 98 *See also* learning center;
   self-instruction programs
five W's of journalism 31, 62
Flower, Linda S. 18, 31, 85, 86, 87, 210
focus 7, 11, 16, 30, 32, 33, 51, 53–68, 113, 162,
   164, 165, 167, 168, 171, 175, 176, 177,
   178, 179, 182, 188, 223, 225, 234 *See also*
   organization; thesis sentence; topic
footnotes 43 *See also* documentation
format 7, 18, 53
fragment, sentence 90, 97, 149, 234, 236, 238
free writing 8, 33, 58, 59, 80, 82, 85
   definition of 9
Fulwiler, Toby 133
fused sentences *See* run-on sentences
future tense *See* verbs, tenses of

Gagne, Robert 4
GANTT, 120
Garth, Russell Y. 122
Gazzam, Virginia J. 78, 130–33, 176
generality 11, 57
genre 18, 34, 160, 176–80, 188 *See also*
   assignment
Giannasi, Jenefer M. 104
Gilroy, Faith 60
Goldfarb, Ronald 210
Goswami, Dixie 18, 31, 108, 109
grading 7, 35, 36, 39, 50, 87, 88, 121, 126, 127,
   149, 151–53, 235, 237 *See also* re-
   sponse to writing

grading *(cont.)*
    minimal 124
grammar 7, 30, 43, 49, 51, 96, 98, 148, 149,
    152, 158, 216–24, 233, 234, 235, 238 *See*
    also mechanics
graphs 76, 89, 121 *See also* diagrams; figures;
    scientific writing; tables
    in lab report 42
    labeling 43
Gray, Geraldine 70
Greenfield, P. M. 4
Griffin, C. Williams 137
groups *See also* peer response
    feedback to 114
    response 210
    task 111, 118–22

Hamilton, David 123
handbooks of English 95, 148, 238 *See also*
    self-instruction programs
Hayes, John R. 18, 31, 85, 86, 87
Haynes, Elizabeth F. 29
Healy, Mary K. 114
heuristics 61, 64
history course
    core, case history of 123–25
    introductory, case history of 135–36
hypothesis 35, 39, 60, 66, 68, 78, 80, 108, 121,
    135, 161, 178 *See also* scientific writing
hypothetical audience 19, 52, 147 *See also*
    audience

"I-Search" 8
    definition of 9
identification (as assignment) 12 *See also*
    assignment
illustrations (in a paper) *See* charts; diagrams;
    figures; graphs; photographs; tables
in-class writing 7, 9–17, 127, 141, 158–59
    See also essay tests; writing
indexes, on-line computerized 69 *See also*
    library research
inflation 225–26, 228 *See also* economy
information
    evaluating (as assignment) 74–75
    gathering 31, 33
interviews 31, 33, 51, 76–78, 108, 109, 130, 131
    preparing questions for 77
    role-play in 78
    tapes of 76
irrelevance 180

Janeway, Elizabeth 33

jargon 172, 208 *See also* word choice
journalism, five W's of 31, 62
journals 8, 9, 33, 80, 133–34, 141, 159–61
    definition of 8
    professional 69
    sociology, keeping 38–39

Kerek, Andrew 98
Kesling, Robert V. 94, 209
Kiniry, Malcolm 22
Kolln, Martha 90, 98

lab
    biology, writing in the 130–31
    writing *See* writing center
lab notebook 8, 76, 79
lab report 7, 39–43, 176 *See also* scientific
    writing
    writing a (as assignment) 39–43
Lammers, Alice 136
Langacker, Ronald W. 102
Langer, Susanne K. 4
language *See also* dialect; English as a Second
    Language; jargon
    bureaucratic 208, 209
    jargon 208
    technical 19, 209
    thought and 4
Lanham, Richard A. 95, 207, 209, 210
Larson, Richard L. 56, 64
Lauerman, David 109
Lawrence, D. H. 11
Lawrence, John 70
learning
    and verbalization 4
    and writing 3, 4, 5, 6, 14, 34, 106, 107, 123,
    129, 240
learning center 17, 93, 94, 97, 100, 158 *See*
    also self-instruction programs; tutors;
    writing center
learning disability 236–37
legal briefs 8, 176
length of writing assignments 37
Lester, James 67
letters
    as assignment 8
    structure of 40
library 60
Library of Congress Subject Headings 69
library research 68–71 *See also* research paper;
    sources
    by computer 70
library sources 33 *See also* sources

literary analysis 7, 165–68, 223–24
literary-critical papers 127–28
literary review 8
literature course, case history of core 125–28
literature search 39 *See also* library research
Lloyd-Jones, Richard 22
logs 22, 30, 70, 80, 106, 107, 108, 109, 131
Lowe, Larry S. 134, 135
Lunsford, Andrea A. 5

Macrorie, Ken 9
Maimon, Elaine P. 33
management and writing 3
manuals *See* handbooks of English
marketing research, case history of graduate
    course in 134–35
marking *See* grading
Martin, Rubin 70
McCarthy, Lucille 34
mechanics 33, 37, 39, 43, 51, 89–105, 125, 148,
    152, 234, 235 *See also* grammar; punc-
    tuation; spelling; usage
microtheme 8 *See also* theme
    definition of 9
Miller, John 10
Miller, Thomas P. 118
MLA (Modern Language Association), ci-
    tation forms of 72, 73, 74
modifiers 212, 218 *See also* grammar; syntax
Morenberg, Max 98
mottoes 65
Murray, Donald 33, 143, 145, 146

narration 60
National Assessment of Educational Progress
    22
National Science Foundation 118
network, writer's 50, 92 *See also* peer response
never-again notebook 95–96, 97, 101, 237, 239
Newcomb, Theodore M. 122
news story (as assignment) 8
note cards 9, 76
note taking 10, 13, 15–16, 75–76 *See also*
    research paper
    as planning technique 31
notebook
    field 8, 76, 79
    lab 8, 76, 79
    never-again 95–96, 97, 101, 237, 239
notes 68, 70, 107, 108, 109, 131, 177
nouns, proper 148

observation 31, 33, 39, 78–79, 106, 107, 108

Odell, Lee 18, 31, 76, 108, 109
O'Hare, Frank 98
Oliver, R. P. 4
organization 7, 11, 16, 30, 33, 37, 47, 48, 51,
    79–84, 146, 148, 152, 154, 155, 184, 188,
    198, 199, 202, 224 *See also* focus; outline;
    thesis sentence
originality 27
outline 8, 11, 12, 13, 17, 30, 31, 33, 65, 66, 72,
    80, 81, 82, 84, 104, 121, 186, 193, 199 *See*
    also focus; organization

paragraphs 49, 145, 148, 152
    concluding 183–84
    opening 180–83
parallelism 216, 217–18, 220, 223
paraphrase 72, 73, 168, 206 *See also*
    quotations
partition 60, 61
passive voice 209, 225, 226, 227, 228, 236
past tense *See* verbs, tenses of
peer response 34, 36, 43, 49, 50, 53, 58, 59, 65,
    80, 90, 92, 107, 111–23, 126, 133, 147,
    161, 210
    buddy system 33, 35
    checking first drafts 17
    evaluating first draft of term paper (as
      assignment) 47–49
    self-evaluation 112
    writer's network 50, 92
perfect tense *See* verbs, tenses of
periodical index *See* library research
personal pronouns *See* pronouns
persuasion *See* argumentation
PERT 120
Peterson, Bruce 137
photographs 89 *See also* diagrams; figures;
    graphs; scientific writing; tables
phrases 211, 212, 214, 215, 216 *See also*
    subordination; syntax
    colloquial 46
Piaget, Jean 5
Pike, Kenneth 61
plagiarism 71, 75, 134, 135
    in-class writing and 13–14
planning writing 31, 32, 66, 72, 79, 81, 82, 84,
    85, 88, 120, 121, 161, 177 *See also* focus;
    free writing; hypothesis; outline; thesis
    sentence; writing
Plath, Sylvia 223
plays (as assignment) 8
plot 7, 126 *See also* literary analysis
    questions about, in book reviews 63

poetic writing 9
point of view 11, 72
polish 7, 17, 37, 87, 90, 160 *See also* editing;
    revision
precision (of diction) 43, 209, 225, 230–33
present tense *See* verbs, tenses of
Primary Trait Scoring 22
problem solving 64, 93, 106, 239
process strategies 37 *See also* writing;
    writing process
programmed texts 97 *See also* computerized
    instruction; self-instruction programs
pronouns 97, 172, 236, 238
    agreement with antecedents 238
proofreading 13, 92, 236, 237 *See also* editing;
    revision
    computerized 236
proper nouns 148
proposal 8
prospectus 66–67, 161
psychology
    developmental 129
    social 128–29
psychology course, case history of
    introductory 128–30
psychology lab 129–30
publication of student writing 135–36, 236
Pufahl, John 87
punctuation 7, 30, 43, 49, 51, 96, 97, 148, 152,
    158, 160, 233, 234, 236, 238 *See also*
    editing; error; mechanics
purpose in writing 7, 36, 38, 53, 72, 113, 120,
    172, 175, 176
    assessing 52–53
    of a book report 62

questionnaires for research 108
questions
    for book report 62–63
    as writing strategy 62
quotations 43, 72, 73, 95, 97, 148 *See also*
    bibliography; citations; documentation;
    references

Raymond, James 210
reader *See* audience
Reader's Guide to Periodical Literature 69, 70
    See also library research
reading 124
reading comprehension 27
reading notes 68
real audience 19, 52 *See also* audience

reasoning 7, 79–84
redundancy *See* economy; repetition
references 71, 75 *See also* bibliography;
    citations; documentation; quotations
    in lab report 41, 43
relations among ideas 60, 212, 223
relevance 180
repetition 198, 225, 226, 228
reports
    clinical 176
    lab *See* lab report
    scientific 176 *See also* scientific writing;
        technical report
    technical *See* technical report
research 37, 60, 78, 84, 106
    collaborative 108–09
research paper 3, 8, 39–43, 129, 134
    focus in 168
    prospectus for a 66–67
    scientific *See* scientific writing
researchers, students as 109
Resources in Education, 137
response groups 111–18, 210 *See also* peer
    response; task groups
    constructing 111
    guiding 111–13
    self-evaluation of 112
    teacher presence in 116
response to writing 141–61 *See also* coaching
    writing; conferences; grading; writing
    oral 179
    by tape 141, 142–43, 179
    written comments 141–42, 145, 179
résumé 8
revision 30, 31, 33, 84–88, 107, 124, 125, 127,
    130, 143, 152, 160, 172, 203, 210, 234 *See
    also* drafts; editing; mechanics;
    proofreading
    defining problems 86, 88
    evaluation of 86
    problem-solving strategy 86
    strategies for 88
    task definition 86
    teacher response 88 *See also* response to
        writing
Robison, Susan M. 78, 82, 128–30, 133
role-playing 129
Roundy, Nancy 53
run-on sentences 90, 149, 220, 238, 239 *See
    also* sentences

"Sciensch" 94
scientific method 39, 129

scientific writing 5, 8, 24, 27, 40, 95, 129, 131, 176–77, 227, 231 *See also* hypothesis; lab report; technical report

secondary reader 52 *See also* audience

self-evaluation, group 112

self-instruction programs 97, 98, 100, 210 *See also* computerized instruction; handbooks of English; learning center; writing center

Selzer, Jack 33, 81

sentence combining 98, 210, 238

sentence composing 98, 210, 238

sentence fragment 90, 97, 149, 234, 236, 238

sentences 27, 49, 98, 101, 152, 181, 211, 212, 224, 234 *See also* clauses; phrases; punctuation

  run-on 90, 149, 220, 239

Shaughnessy, Mina 100

shirkers 119–120, 127, 135

short stories, questions for book report on 63

Singer, Daniel 29, 35

slides 95, 97, 98 *See also* learning center; self-instruction programs

Smith, Ernest 4

social psychology 128–29

sociology class, case history of introductory 133–34

sociology journal, keeping a (as assignment) 38–39

Solomon, Lewis E. 3

Sommers, Nancy 32, 84

sources 33, 72, 74, 168, 172 *See also* library research; quotations; research paper

  citing 71–73

specificity 150, 182 *See also* precision; word choice

spellers, computerized 236

spelling 7, 43, 46, 49, 51, 92, 97, 98, 148, 149, 152, 164, 234, 235, 238–39 *See also* mechanics

Spencer, Linda 43, 94

Spiegel, Xavier 39

Stallard, Charles K. 32

Steele, Mildred 66, 67

Strenski, Ellen 22

Strunk, William, Jr. 207, 209

style 7, 33, 48, 51, 53, 63, 89–105, 182, 206–33, 235, 236 *See also* awkwardness; economy; precision; tone; word choice

  APA, 72, 129

  bureaucratic 209, 210

  MLA 72, 73, 74

  reading to improve 90

style manuals *See* handbooks of English; *See also* self-instruction programs; writing center

subject-verb agreement *See* verbs, agreement with subjects

subordination 97, 222 *See also* sentence combining; syntax

summary 7, 8, 14, 15, 24, 27, 31, 46, 54, 55, 78, 124, 126, 129, 155, 156, 176, 183, 184, 193 *See also* abstract

symbols 43

syntax 43, 154, 156, 160, 164 *See also* awkwardness; parallelism; subordination

Szanton, Peter 188, 193

tables (for data) 42, 48, 76, 82, 87, 121, 124, 135 *See also* charts; diagrams; figures; graphs; photographs; scientific writing

talking as a planning technique 31, 59, 84, 85, 112, 127, 129

Tanizaki, Junichiro 54

taping

  interviews as notes 76

  as a planning technique 31, 59, 85, 97, 108, 109, 114, 131, 132, 133, 178, 208, 209

  as a response to writing 141, 142–43

task groups 111, 118–22 *See also* peer response; response groups

  conferences of 121

  establishing 118, 119

  evaluation of 120, 121

  guiding 120–21

technical language 19, 209

technical report 7, 8, 39–43 *See also* lab report; research paper; scientific writing

tense, verb *See* verbs, tenses of

term paper 8 *See also* research paper

  peer evaluation of first draft (as assignment) 47–49

"test" reader 31

tests, essay *See* essay tests

Thaiss, Christopher 137

"that" 219 *See also* clauses

theme 7, 113, 126, 146 *See also* microtheme

thesaurus 70

thesis sentence 8, 11, 35, 37, 59, 66, 67–68, 123, 152, 158, 161, 162, 163, 171, 172, 193, 224 *See also* sentences

  definition of 9

thought

  language and 4

  writing and 6 *See also* learning and writing; reasoning

tone 19, 89, 206, 207
topic 12, 30, 35, 37, 51, 53–68, 79, 112, 113, 135, 149, 162, 164, 168, 181, 182, 183, 184, 186, 199, 202, 203 *See also* focus; thesis sentence
  developing through reading (as assignment) 56–58
topoi 60–61
tracings 69 *See also* library research
transactional writing 9
transitions 49, 149, 150, 198, 199–205
transparent reader 146–47 *See also* audience
tutors 3, 36, 49, 50, 93, 94, 95, 105, 237 *See also* learning center; response to writing

usage 149, 152

vagueness *See* ambiguity; generality
Van Hoeven, James 135–36
verbalization and learning 4
verbosity 94, 95, 148, 151, 152, 167, 228 *See also* economy
verbs
  active 209
  agreement with subject 97, 98, 101, 146, 221, 238
  passive 209, 225, 226, 227, 228, 236
  person 43
  tenses of 42, 97, 98, 172, 223, 238
visual aids 33, 89, 96 *See also* audiovisual programs; learning center; self-instruction programs
vividness 182, 228, 230–33 *See also* style
voice 206, 207 *See also* tone; verbs
  passive 209, 225, 226, 227, 228, 236
Vygotsky, Lev S. 4

Walvoord, Barbara 29, 35, 72, 107, 125
Walzer, Arthur 52
watchwords 65
web 8, 82, 83, 84
  definition of 9
Weddington, Doris 143
White, E. B. 207, 209
Williams, Joseph 207, 209, 210
Wilson, Everett K. 122
Winterowd, W. Ross 61

"WIRMI" strategy 210
Witte, Stephen 85
Woodford, Peter F. 5
Woolf, Virginia 31–32
word choice 89, 146 *See also* precision
word problem 8
word processors 87, 125, 142 *See also* editing; revision
wordiness 226 *See also* economy; verbosity
works cited 71 *See also* bibliography; citations; documentation; quotations; references
writing
  business and 3
  categories of student 21–22
  coaching 29, 32–33
  course 6–28
  difficulty of 22–28
  expository 30
  expressive 9
  importance of 3
  in-class 7, 9–17, 127, 141, 158–59
  learning and 3, 4, 5, 6, 14, 34, 106, 107, 123
  management and 3
  out-of-class 7, 9
  planning *See* planning writing
  poetic 9
  purposes in 7, 36, 38, 53, 72, 113, 120, 172, 175, 176
  scientific *See* scientific writing
  thought and 6
  transactional 9
  types of 8–9
writing across the curriculum 20, 134
writing block 32, 59, 85
writing center 49, 93, 210, 237 *See also* learning center; self-instruction programs; tutors
writing lab *See* writing center
writing networks 92 *See also* peer response
writing process 105–09 *See also* writing
  computer programs for the 34
  guiding the 132
  models of 33
  strategies for the 37

Young, Richard 61

zero draft 85